Hezbollah and Hamas

HEZBOLLAH and HAMAS

A Comparative Study | Joshua L. Gleis and Benedetta Berti

The Johns Hopkins University Press, *Baltimore*

© 2012 The Johns Hopkins University Press
All rights reserved. Published 2012
Printed in the United States of America on acid-free paper
9 8 7 6 5 4 3 2 1

The Johns Hopkins University Press
2715 North Charles Street
Baltimore, Maryland 21218-4363
www.press.jhu.edu

Library of Congress Cataloging-in-Publication Data

Gleis, Joshua L.
Hezbollah and Hamas : a comparative study / Joshua L. Gleis and Benedetta
Berti.
    p. cm.
Includes bibliographical references and index.

ISBN 978-1-4214-0614-5 (hdbk. : alk. paper)
ISBN 978-1-4214-0615-2 (pbk. : alk. paper)
ISBN 978-1-4214-0671-8 (electronic)
ISBN 1-4214-0614-4 (hdbk. : alk. paper)
ISBN 1-4214-0615-2 (pbk. : alk. paper)
ISBN 1-4214-0671-3 (electronic)
1. Hizballah (Lebanon) 2 Harakat al-Muqawamah al-Islamiyah.
3. Islam and politics. 4. Islamic fundamentalism. 5. Arab-Israeli
conflict. I. Berti, Benedetta. II. Title.
JQ1828.A98H6242 2012
322.4'2095692—dc23   2011048392

A catalog record for this book is available from the British Library.

*Special discounts are available for bulk purchases of this book. For more
information, please contact Special Sales at 410-516-6936 or specialsales@press
.jhu.edu.*

The Johns Hopkins University Press uses environmentally friendly book
materials, including recycled text paper that is composed of at least
30 percent post-consumer waste, whenever possible.

For Aden and Lily

Contents

Acknowledgments

First and foremost, I would like to acknowledge my family, who I thank God for literally every day. Without their love and support, I would have never been able to have completed this important, yet time-consuming undertaking. I am indebted to my wife in particular for allowing me to conduct research, write, and edit for so many hours over the years. Suzanne Flinchbaugh and the entire team at the Johns Hopkins University Press have been refreshingly professional and great to work with. I would like to recognize all of my colleagues, mentors, and friends from the Fletcher School of Law and Diplomacy, Tufts University, Columbia University's Saltzman Institute, and the Belfer Center at Harvard University. Last but not least, I would like to thank my dear friend and coauthor Benedetta Berti. Benni, you were a pleasure to work with, and it was great to collaborate with you on this important project. Writing such a serious book helps you appreciate even more all that you have in life.

Joshua Gleis

I am indebted to a number of people for the support, advice, and help they have given me through the different stages of this writing project. First, I would like to thank the International Security Studies Program at the Fletcher School and particularly Richard Shultz, who has been my academic mentor since I began graduate school, and to whom I recurrently turn to for professional and academic advice. William Martel, also at the Fletcher School, has offered invaluable insights and advice on this specific project, and I truly appreciate his contributions in making the work stronger. Second, I would like to thank the Institute for National Security Studies (INSS) at Tel Aviv University, its former director, Dr. Oded Eran, as well as its current director, Major General (ret.) Amos Yadlin, for the tremendous institutional support I have received since I first became associated with INSS in 2008. I am grateful to Brigadier General (ret.) Meir Elran at INSS and Mr. and Mrs. Joseph Neubauer, who, through the Neubauer Research Fellowships, first gave me the opportunity to join the INSS team. Among my esteemed colleagues at INSS, I would truly like to acknowledge Dr. Anat Kurz, who has been my mentor since I joined INSS in 2008, and whose advice and guidance has been tremendously enriching, both from a professional and a personal point of view. Third, I cannot thank enough the entire editorial team at the Johns Hopkins University Press and specifically Suzanne Flinchbaugh. Suzanne has been absolutely instrumental in each and every stage of this project, and I am truly grateful for her invaluable help, support, and guidance. Fourth, and most important, I want to thank my husband, Avi, for his support, help, and encouragement; for believing in me and in my research; and for his understanding of my sometimes-hectic professional life. Finally, I want to thank my coauthor, Josh: co-writing a book is not always easy, and you made this writing and research project smooth and fun.

Benedetta Berti

Abbreviations and Acronyms

Amal	Lebanese Resistance Detachments. Arabic acronym for Afwaj al-Muqawama al-Lubnaniya. *Amal* itself means "hope."
AMAN	Israeli Military Intelligence. Hebrew acronym for Agaf HaModiin.
CBR	chemical-biological-radiological. Usually used when referencing a weapons arsenal or mode of attack.
EFP	explosively formed penetrator
ESA	External Security Apparatus (Hezbollah)
ETA	Basque Homeland and Freedom. Spanish acronym for Euskadi Ta Askatasuna.
FARC	Revolutionary Armed Forces of Colombia. Spanish acronym for Fuerzas Armadas Revolucionarias de Colombia.
Hamas	Islamic Resistance Movement. Arabic acronym for Harakat al-Muqawama al-Islamiyya. *Hamas* itself means roughly "zeal."
HUMINT	human intelligence
IDF	Israel Defense Forces. Official name of the Israeli military.
IED	improvised explosive device
IMF	International Monetary Fund
IRGC	Iranian Revolutionary Guards Corps
LAF	Lebanese Armed Forces
MOIS	Iranian Ministry of Intelligence and Security
MP	member of parliament
NGO	nongovernmental organization
PA	Palestinian Authority
PFLP	Popular Front for the Liberation of Palestine
PIJ	Palestinian Islamic Jihad
PLO	Palestine Liberation Organization
PRC	Popular Resistance Committees
SDGT	specially designated global terrorist
SIGINT	signals intelligence
SLA	South Lebanon Army
UAV	unmanned aerial vehicles
UN	United Nations
UNIFIL	United Nations Interim Force in Lebanon
UNRWA	United Nations Relief and Works Agency. UN refugee agency exclusively for Palestinians.

Hezbollah and Hamas

Introduction

HEZBOLLAH AND HAMAS: Two groups that have come to symbolize the very essence of terrorism for so many in the West and the ideal "liberation fighters" for so many in the Arab world at large. The organizations became infamous in the 1980s and 1990s, when they conducted some of the most brazen and deadly terrorist attacks against civilian and military targets. With strikingly different beginnings, they increasingly came to share two common denominators: an adversary in Israel and a friend in Iran. As such, they have at times closely cooperated with each other. Both groups have also maintained a clear and separate identity, ideology, and organizational structure, contrary to many mainstream claims that all radical Islamist organizations are fundamentally alike. As a result of their multifaceted nature, the organizations are both hated and loved: ridiculed as cold-blooded terrorists and cherished as Islamist movements that seek to restore dignity and respect, not just to the Shiite Lebanese or Palestinian communities, respectively, but to the Arab and Muslim worlds as a whole.

Hezbollah—literally "Party of God"—is a Lebanese-based Islamist organization whose name comes from the Quranic passage, "The party of God shall be victorious." The phrase is written across the top of its yellow flag, while "The Islamic Revolution in Lebanon" is written on the bottom.[1] U.S. deputy secretary of state Richard Armitage once described Hezbollah as the "A-Team" of terrorist organizations, and al Qaeda as the "B-Team,"[2] an assessment with which former senior CIA officer Robert Baer agreed.[3] Unlike al Qaeda after 9/11, Hezbollah has not seen a loss of its state sponsorship or area of operations—both have grown significantly. The lingering effects of the "Arab Spring" and revolution in Syria, however, may change that in the future. In concert with its state supporters of Iran and Syria, Hezbollah backs organizations such as the Palestinian Islamic Jihad and Hamas, which seek among other things to counter U.S. influence in the Middle East and hijack any potential Israeli-Palestinian peace agreement. It continues to preach that nonviolence is ineffective and the destruction of Israel by force is an obligation of Islam.[4] Indeed, Hezbollah has gone so far as to recognize that it needs violence to survive as an organization and thus continues to find reasons for "resistance."[5] It is recognized and respected all over the world as a leader and innovator in all matters related to *jihad*.

Hezbollah's "resistance" comes in the form of low- and medium-intensity conflict, with a focus on irregular warfare tactics such as insurgency and terrorism. Hezbollah's main target has been, and remains, the Jewish State of Israel. Yet its reach has spread as far as South America and West Africa, and it has targeted Americans, French, Syrians, Palestinians, and even fellow Lebanese who stand in the way of achieving its very calculated objectives. However, Hezbollah is so much more than just a terrorist or insurgent organization. In 2011 the organization became part of the majority coalition in the Lebanese parliament, supporting the new prime minister, Najib Mikati, and asserting with increased strength its role within Lebanon. Hezbollah's power can be seen in the streets of Lebanon, Syria, Bahrain, the United Arab Emirates, Venezuela, and course, Iran. It maintains a fine balance between its Islamist principles and its recognition of more practical alliances to reach its more immediate goals.

The other group examined in this book is Hamas. Few organizations can claim the notoriety that is beholden to the Harakat al-Muqawama al-Islamiyya, or "Islamic Resistance Movement"—better known by its acronym HAMAS. The word *hamas* roughly translates from Arabic to mean "zeal" and is indicative of the manner in which it adheres to its radical interpretation of Islam. This interpretation intermingles more traditional pan-Islamist ideology with that of Palestinian nationalism, setting it apart from some of its roots in the Egyptian Muslim Brotherhood. Hamas was officially founded in 1988 largely as a result of the first Intifada, or uprising, against Israel. While it was born out of the violence of the Intifada, it has grown to become a terrorist organization, political party, and a socioreligious movement all in one. Ironically, it was Israel's occupation of Palestinian territories in 1967 that allowed Islamist organizations to operate more freely and which ultimately permitted Hamas to come into existence—but more on that later.

The rise of Islamism among Palestinian Arabs was gradual. A highly educated and traditionally secular people, the Palestinians differed from many of their fellow Arab brethren in many respects. Through a combination of factors, however, the Islamist political, religious, and military option became an increasingly attractive choice. What began as a marginal alternative to the secular Arab nationalism that was spearheaded by the Palestine Liberation Organization culminated in a schism so severe that there exists today two parallel and competing camps for the Palestinians. In the West Bank, Fatah party controls the governing Palestinian Authority, which is supported in one way or another by Israel, much of the West, and most of the Arab world. It is recognized as the moderate political party and is by and large viewed as the party most willing to reach a peace agreement with Israel. In the crowded Gaza Strip, however, Hamas is the ultimate ruler of the land. Sponsored chiefly by Iran and Syria, it enjoys the support of many in the Arab and Muslim worlds. While less corrupt and distinctly nationalist for an Islamist organization, it has in the past acted as spoiler of the peace process. In 2011 the Hamas and Fatah parties agreed to join a national unity government, but the results of the inter-Palestinian reconciliation process still remain to be seen.

When looking at the role and impact of Hezbollah and Hamas, it is obvious that the political, social, and military strength of these groups has broad significance not only within Lebanon and the Palestinian territories but also regionally and globally. In addition, these groups have been key actors in the context of the Arab-Israeli conflict, a conflict whose political repercussions extend far beyond its immediate confines to affect so many parts of the world.

The purpose of the book is to explore these two Islamist movements that are increasingly relevant not only to those interested in matters related to the Middle East and the Arab-Israeli conflict but also to those seeking a better understanding of international security and the fight against terrorism. Islamism is here to stay. As some of the world's most sophisticated and beloved terrorist and political organizations, Hezbollah and Hamas have come to embody the complexities of so many Shiite and Sunni Islamist groups.

Conceptualizing and understanding Hezbollah and Hamas in these terms, against a reductionist interpretation of both organizations as solely terrorist groups, has a series of important scholarly and, above all, political implications. First, identifying the multilayered and complex organizational, ideological, and operational structure of both Hezbollah and Hamas can inform the future scholarship on this topic, while encouraging similar descriptions of other armed groups. In turn, this can lead to new knowledge on the topic, while avoiding generalized or reductionist descriptions of hybrid armed and political organizations such as Hezbollah and Hamas. Second, tracking the organizational development of both groups, understanding their inherent dynamism and capacity to diversify, and grasping their ability to cope with shifting local and regional dynamics should also serve to shape the military and policy responses to these groups.

This book is a culmination of four years of research on Hezbollah and Hamas, including meetings and interviews with high-level players in the Middle East and the West. Its goal is to provide an in-depth view of two of the most popular and feared radical Islamist groups the world has ever known. In addition, through a focused and structured analysis of the historical origins, ideology, organization, and military and political evolution of these two groups, the book is also able to conduct a comparison of Hezbollah and Hamas. In turn, this allows us to counter a number of stereotypes regarding these organizations in order to uncover what truly lies behind the shadows.

Finally, the book also offers a more nuanced understanding of both Hezbollah and Hamas, while allowing the reader to grasp existing ideological and organizational commonalities between the two groups. This effort is valuable, as the existing literature on both Hezbollah and Hamas tends to focus on these groups separately, failing to provide a much-needed comparative perspective. Conceptualizing and understanding Hezbollah and Hamas in these terms has a series of important policy implications. By tracking the organizational development of both groups, understanding their inherent dynamism and capacity to diversify, and grasping their ability to cope with shifting local and regional dynamics, this book should contribute to making better-informed and effective military and policy responses to these groups.

PART I HEZBOLLAH

1 The Lebanese Players
A Background

SINCE IT LITERALLY EXPLODED onto the world scene in the mid-1980s, Hezbollah has been called many things by many people. To some it is a terrorist group, while to others it is a guerrilla organization. In much of the Arab world, it is considered a resistance and liberation movement. Many Lebanese, however, view it primarily as a mainstream political party or as a successful social movement with an extensive social welfare network. In truth, Hezbollah is all of these things and more.

To understand Hezbollah is to understand the difficult and complex nature that is both Lebanon and Lebanese history. The book of Genesis teaches that in the story of Creation, God created order out of chaos. Studying Lebanese history, however, one might imagine the Lord forgot about this little country along the way. Smaller than the state of Connecticut, Lebanon shares 79 kilometers of border with Israel to its south, 375 kilometers with Syria to its east and north, and the remaining 225 kilometers to its west with the Mediterranean Sea. Within these small confines of roughly 10,400 square kilometers, it has a population that in July 2011 totaled more than 4 million people, divided among eighteen different religious sects recognized by the Lebanese Constitution.[1] For political reasons, no census has been carried out in the country since 1932—years before Lebanon was even declared an independent state. Consequently, given the dated and unreliable nature of the country's demographic data, scholars and politicians alike often disagree as to the actual ethnic breakdown of the population. A generally agreed upon estimate asserts that the various Muslim sects make up roughly 60 percent of the population, and the Christians another 39 percent. The Shiites are estimated to constitute up to 38 percent of the Muslim population, and the Sunnis another 23–25 percent.[2] The remainder of the population is made up of Druze, Isma'ilite, and Alawite sects. Among the Christians, sects include the Maronite

Catholics, Greek Orthodox, Armenian Orthodox, Melkite Catholics, Syrian Catholics, Armenian Catholics, Syrian Orthodox, Roman Catholics, Chaldeans, Assyrians, Copts, and Protestants.[3]

When France wrested control of Lebanon from the Ottoman Empire during World War I, it envisioned that the area would become a safe haven for the small Christian population found in that corner of the Middle East. The Maronites, however, traditionally inhabited only the area around Mount Lebanon—a space considered too small to constitute an independent country in that part of the world. Consequently, the French decided to expand the territory of Lebanon at the expense of what had traditionally been considered "Greater Syria." It incorporated lands that included within them many different religious convictions, several of which had themselves been minorities within their respective religions.[4] The Shiites, Druze, Greek Orthodox, and Maronites—to name but a few—are all considered illegitimate or misguided by many of their more numerous coreligionists, thus making their own yearning for independence and recognition all the more pronounced.[5] It was this volatile reality that created a nation too weak and fractured to assert its autonomy in the eyes not only of its neighbors but of its own inhabitants as well.

The Shiites and Amal

The Shiites make up approximately 10 percent of the world's Muslim population.[6] Present in Lebanon since the ninth century, they settled in an area known as the Bekaa Valley on the southeast border of present-day Syria, as well as in Jabal Amin, which exists roughly in the area of south Lebanon today.[7] The Shiites chose these locations as they were on the periphery of any ruler's radar screen and thus practically out of reach of most administrative authorities.[8] Today, southern Lebanon and the Bekaa Valley remain two areas of considerable Shiite Arab density, as well as some of the country's poorest locations.

Though traditionally smaller and weaker than their Sunni brethren, the Shiites originally reached their peak of dominance in the tenth century when the Twelver Shiites ruled Iraq and Iran, and the Ismailis (or Seveners) ruled Egypt, North Africa, and Syria. These dynasties were relatively short-lived, as those areas were conquered and reconquered, until they eventually fell under the rule of the Sunni-led Ottoman Empire, which controlled much of the

Middle East until its defeat in World War I.[9] Under Ottoman control, the Lebanese Shiites were by and large persecuted, discriminated against, and excluded from nearly all forms of political power, in large part because the Sunni-Ottomans viewed their Shiite subjects as heretics.[10] The gap between the Shiites and their neighbors grew larger in the nineteenth century, as Lebanon began to emerge from its isolation and experience a political, social, and intellectual revival.

The Shiites continued to receive the short end of the stick with regards to politics, economics, health care, and education. Their only gains against the Christians and Sunnis seemed to come in their rate of birth. As a rural people, the Lebanese Shiites accounted for approximately 19 percent of the total population in 1950, yet before long they outnumbered all other sects. This resulted in their migration to the poor slums of Beirut and other urban centers in search of work as well as a self-realization that their traditional *zuama* (lords) were not doing enough to help them. In time this would lead to a greater demand for political rights and a more equitable share of the national budget as well.[11]

Under the French Mandate in 1926, the Shiites finally achieved the right to practice their religion as freely as most other Lebanese.[12] Yet the Shiites remained second-class citizens, leading them to develop somewhat of an identity crisis, whereby they felt as though "they were despised stepchildren of a state governed by a Sunni-Maronite alliance."[13] These feelings of humiliation and subjugation would later be capitalized on by Hezbollah, when it first hit the Lebanese stage in the early 1980s.

In the early 1970s, many influential ayatollahs happened to converge in the Shiite holy city of Najaf in Iraq. They included Iraqi ayatollahs Muhammad Baqir al-Sadr and Muhsin al-Hakim, as well as the Iranian ayatollah, Ruhollah Khomeini, who had earlier been expelled by the shah of Iran and later by Iraq's Saddam Hussein. Additional future Hezbollah leaders and mentors would also come to study in Najaf. These included Imam Musa al-Sadr, Sheikh Sayyid Muhammad Hussein Fadlallah, Sheikh Naim Qassem, Hezbollah founder Sayyid Abbas al-Musawi, and its longest-serving secretary-general, Sayyid Hassan Nasrallah.[14] It was during this period, when lectures were given and ideas exchanged, that an important ideological network was established that helped elevate the political role of religious Shiite figures to previously unseen levels. This change would have a profound impact on the Muslim world in general, and Hezbollah in particular.

In traditional Shiite Islam, religious leaders such as ayatollahs intention-ally steered clear of politics and political rule. This began to change during Khomeini's thirteen years in exile from Iran. Under his careful guidance, the role of religion in politics was transformed into one of prime importance.[15] Contrary to other Lebanese Shiite groups, for Hezbollah, Ayatollah Khomeini became the ultimate decision maker. This was a sharp departure from the previous leaders of Lebanon's Shiite community, known as the zuama. This small, wealthy group of Shiite families had considered themselves the repre-sentatives and leaders of their community going back to 1858, when Ottoman land reforms were put into play. In actuality, however, the zuama did little to improve the lot of the Shiites in Lebanon.[16]

Besides Hezbollah and the zuama, Amal is another central player in Leba-nese Shiite politics. It is a Shiite organization that predates Hezbollah and is still very much in existence today. Although it has been overshadowed by Hezbollah both domestically and internationally, it continues to play an im-portant role in the lives of Lebanon's Shiite population. Amal was originally founded by Musa al-Sadr, an Iranian-born imam who was invited by the Shiite community in 1957 to become the religious leader of the city of Tyre. Born in the holy city of Qom in Iran and educated in Najaf in Iraq, Sadr was thus as-sociated with two of the Shiite religion's most important cities. As a charis-matic leader, Sadr was friendly with both the Iranian Ayatollah Khomeini and the Syrian president Hafaz al-Assad. In order to secure Syrian support for his community, Sadr declared that the Alawite religion—an offshoot sect of Islam of which Assad and his clan adhered—was in fact a part of Shiite Islam.

Alawites had traditionally been viewed by Muslims as a heretical sect, and this declaration provided Assad with the political and religious cover and le-gitimacy he had been seeking. Consequently, Sadr gained badly needed sup-port from the Syrian leadership. He also created the Lebanese Shiite Islamic Higher Council and the Movement of the Deprived, two groups that helped Shiites gain greater political representation and attention from the Lebanese government. Throughout his lifetime, Sadr continued to develop ties with religious sects and party factions across the Lebanese spectrum, often to the chagrin of traditional Shiite religious leaders, who shied away from such ac-tivities.[17] These were but a few examples of the shrewd political maneuvering that Sadr used to help improve the state of Lebanon's Shiite community.

As the situation in Lebanon continued to deteriorate in the 1970s, Pales-tinian fighters added to the explosive mix operating in Lebanon. Sadr reacted by creating his own Shiite militia, called the Lebanese Resistance Detachments, but better known by its Arabic acronym AMAL, which means "hope" in Arabic. Before Iran's Islamic Revolution in 1979, as many ayatollahs began flexing their political muscle, Sadr's politicization of the Shiite community in Lebanon received considerable attention and admiration from many of them. The relationships and the political exchanges between Shiites in Lebanon and Iran would later help create Hezbollah.[18] On August 31, 1978, soon after he met with former Libyan leader Muammar Qaddafi during an official visit to that country, Sadr disappeared. While the Libyan officials insisted that Sadr left their country on a flight bound for Rome, no record of his presence on that flight was ever found.[19] Needless to say, Sadr was never heard from again. His disappearance echoed that of the Twelfth Imam—a leading Shiite Islamic leader. "Twelver Shiites," who are prominent in Lebanon, Iran, and Iraq, believe the Twelfth Imam to be the Mahdi, a Messiah-like figure who will appear before the Day of Judgment. Long considered a savior of the Lebanese Shiites, Sadr's disappearance elevated his status to that of a martyr. He is celebrated as such to this day by the Shiites in Lebanon.[20]

After Sadr's suspected murder, Sheikh Sayyid Muhammad Hussein Fadlallah took over as the Shiite Lebanese spiritual leader. Sheikh Fadlallah's relationship to Hezbollah is clouded in debate. To define him as the spiritual leader of Hezbollah would not do justice to his following. Additionally, while there is a clear level of respect bestowed upon Fadlallah by Hezbollah, theological views of the two do not always match up. More generally, however, Sadr and Fadlallah together represented the emerging breed of Shiite revivalists in Lebanon. Sadr provided the necessary ingredient of a Lebanese component of Shiite political Islam, while Fadlallah offered the transnational connection to Iran. Both elements would play an important role in Lebanon for the empowerment of the Shiite community.

Unlike many of its contemporary militias in Lebanon, Amal was as much a movement as it was a loosely arranged and run organization. With its fighters poorly paid, Amal members were more easily susceptible to opportunistic agents from competing militias and organizations. Its fighters often clashed with these competing militias, especially those of the Lebanese Communist Party, which vied for supporters.[21] Amal was active in three areas: southern Lebanon, Beirut, and the Bekaa Valley. Like many of the militias and organizations in those areas, including the Iranian Revolutionary Guards, Amal initially received both training and arms from the Palestine Liberation Organization

(PLO).[22] However, as time passed, the relationship between the two groups began to fray. Palestinians were increasingly reported as treating their Lebanese kinsmen "arrogantly and obnoxiously."[23]

It was this rising animosity between the PLO and the local Shiite community that was the major reason for the Shiites' initially favorable reaction to the Israeli invasion of Lebanon in 1982. Many Lebanese Shiites had expressed gratitude toward Israel at the time for freeing them from their Palestinian "tormentors."[24] They had been fearful of the PLO attempting to create a Palestinian state in southern Lebanon to supplant the land they had lost in 1948, and were pleased that the Israelis had initially taken proper care to ensure relatively little loss of life or physical damage to the Shiite communities during the invasion in 1982.[25] As it became increasingly clear that the Israelis were not planning on leaving the country, the attitude of the Shiites began to change.

During the civil war, the Shiites became cannon fodder for the Palestinians and suffered more deaths than any other sect.[26] As those who suffered most from the Palestinians' activities, Shiites living in southern Lebanon viewed the Israeli invasion differently from their counterparts in Beirut and Bekaa, who were more suspicious of the Jewish state. While many forces from Amal also welcomed the Israeli invasion, Amal fighters around Beirut put up some of the stiffest resistance.[27] Although Amal's leadership did not openly cooperate with either the Israel Defense Forces (IDF) or its proxy Lebanese leader, Major Saad Haddad, its role in combating the PLO was viewed positively by the Israelis. Eventually, Amal's lack of organizational unity and its confrontational stance with regard to the PLO led to increasing fissures within the organization. For Amal's leadership, some saw a natural alliance with the Israelis who shared a mutual adversary in the Palestinians.[28] However, some of the more religious members of the organization, and particularly those who were more strongly connected to Iran, were unhappy with the direction of the movement and the relationships it was developing. One of these leaders, Husain Mussawi, accused other Amal leaders of collaborating with Israel and attempted, with Iranian support, to steer the group toward a more Islamist orientation.[29] When Mussawi failed to reach this goal, he broke with the movement and created his own group instead, known as the Islamic Amal. Mussawi led the Islamic Amal from the Baʿalbek area in the Bekaa Valley.[30] Soon after this break, Nabih Berri was reelected as head of the main Amal movement—a group he still heads. His party remains involved in government life, and as of April 2012 he still held the title of speaker of the Lebanese Parliament.

Berri played an interesting role in the creation of Hezbollah. Earlier in his career he had participated in efforts to reach agreements with Israel and the United States.[31] In fact, a short-lived window of opportunity was opened for a potential alliance with Israel, when Berri tried to convince the Israelis to withdraw completely from Lebanon in the early 1980s. These efforts failed in part because the Israelis did not show their seriousness to assist and ally themselves with the Shiites at the expense of the Christians, and in part because Berri boycotted direct negotiations with Israel for fear of reprisals from Syria and Iran. As a result, nothing ever came of the negotiations, and Israel moved ever closer to the pro-Christian camp.[32] However, these back door activities were seen by more radical elements within Amal as sacrilegious and contrary to Shiite sensibilities and interests. Berri had also made statements that called attacks against Israel within its own borders acts of terrorism— a stance few Arab leaders took. And though he stated his admiration for Khomeini, he also made it clear that he was "above all else a Lebanese."[33] This resulted in disapproval not just from the Islamist elements of Amal but from the Iranians and Syrians as well. It also undoubtedly led the Syrians to support Hezbollah during its nascent stages, in order to serve as a counterbalance to Amal's apparent tilt westward.[34]

Although Amal remains a more secular and moderate competitor of Hezbollah, its existence was a direct factor in Hezbollah's creation. Most of Hezbollah's leadership, including Hezbollah secretary-general Hassan Nasrallah, was involved in Amal before leaving the group for the burgeoning Hezbollah. The relationship between these two organizations was the outset been characterized by open rivalry. Even after twenty-five years of existence, Hezbollah continues to compete with Amal for Shiite affection, with no one party maintaining a complete majority of Shiite Lebanese support—this despite Amal's significantly lackluster political and military organizations when compared to Hezbollah's.[35] Clashes between Amal and Hezbollah reached their peak between 1988 and 1989, when the two groups engaged in repeated armed confrontations to assert their control over the Shiite population in southern Lebanon and the suburbs of Beirut. Although Amal won the first round of fighting, it ultimately collapsed in the second, under the weight of the more organized, professional, and ideologically driven Hezbollah forces. From that point on, Hezbollah asserted armed might over all other militias.

The defeat of Amal also resulted in it losing most of its political presence in the Shiite suburb of Beirut known as Dahiyeh, where Hezbollah's main offices are located today.[36] The internecine violence was also indicative of Berri's and other more secular Shiites' inability to stop the spread of Islamist ideology that increasingly swept through their population after the 1979 Islamic Revolution and Israel's 1982 invasion of Lebanon.

The stage of open armed confrontation between Amal and Hezbollah ended on November 9, 1990, when an agreement was reached that formally ended hostilities between the two sides.[37] Syrian intervention was key in imposing this agreement and forcing the two parties to cease their military conflict. Later, Syrian pressure would co-opt Hezbollah and Amal into forming a political alliance—an electoral partnership that survives to this day.

Before Hezbollah's founding, Iranian leadership and Lebanese Shiite religious figures such as Sheikh Fadlallah encouraged Shiites returning from their religious studies in Iraq to abandon the religious Hizb al-Da'wa party they had associated with there and brought to Lebanon. Instead, the sheikhs argued, it was better to infiltrate Amal and transform it from the inside out.[38] It was only when this endeavor proved unsuccessful that Hezbollah gained the support necessary for its founding. Today, Hezbollah leadership calls its relationship with Amal part of "one family."[39] The two parties generally work in conjunction with one another to represent the interests of the Shiite population in the Lebanese government, usually forming a coalition to improve their credibility and numbers. While Amal remains an important party in the lives of Lebanese Shiites, it is overshadowed by its better-organized, better-armed Islamist competitor, Hezbollah.

The Maronites

The Maronites are the largest group of Christians in Lebanon.[40] Since the creation of the modern Lebanese state, they have been considered the most "pro-Western" sectarian group and make up the bulk of the country's political elite. When France seized control of modern-day Syria and Lebanon from the dying Ottoman Empire during World War I, it set about the task of creating a safe haven for the Maronite Christian community. In an effort to secure support for their plan to break off from Syria, the Maronites turned to the Shiites, who had been, as previously noted, the most neglected of the major Lebanese groups at the time. The Shiites were quick to see an opportunity available to them and consequently supported the Maronites' quest for independence from Sunni-dominated Syria. It was this move that drove the French to grant the Shiites religious freedoms for the first time. As France permitted the Shiites to establish religious courts and practice their religion freely, it also provided them the opportunity to develop their own unique identity in Lebanon.[41] These activities, of course, all served the purposes of France at the time as well. Acting in typical colonialist fashion, the French had managed to play off the traditional divisions already present among the locals in order to achieve a form of divide-and-rule policy that weakened the more powerful Sunnis right in their own backyard. This activity was not much different from what the Ottomans had done for so long, except that the French favored the minorities, thus turning the traditional system on its head.

When Lebanon received independence in 1943, a system was set up to ensure that power would remain first in the hands of the Christians and second in the hands of the Sunnis. This objective was formalized in the 1943 National Pact, which was based on the 1932 National Census that recognized the Christian population as the majority, representing 54 percent of the population at the time. Because of political considerations—namely, Christian refusal—no additional census was ever taken, and hence the government formed in 1943 was based on the demographics of 1932. As a result, a 6:5 ratio was created that allotted six Christian deputies for every five Muslim deputies, with each confession represented according to what was by that time an outdated census, whose statistics were questionable even when first recorded.[42] The National Pact became Lebanon's "unwritten constitution" and remained the way power was allocated until the National Reconciliation Accord, better known as the Taif Accord, of 1989. This newer accord better apportioned the ratio of seats allocated to Muslim and Christian representatives.

From the outset, the confessional system implemented by the French proved itself to be an ineffective solution to balance Lebanon's delicate ethnic composition, as it encouraged fractious behavior among the various confessions. Specifically, it heightened the existing divisions already present among the different sects, encouraging them to create their own political parties and militias. Ultimately, the arrangement reached by the National Pact was a disaster for Lebanon that would contribute to the country being dragged into a long and bloody civil war.

The first spark for that civil war came in 1958, when Christian president Camille Chamoun attempted to alter the delicate balance of power by seeking a second six-year term, in contradiction to past agreements. Though he eventually backed down, the act ultimately led to war.[43] As Hala Jaber explained, "The pro-Western orientation of the Christians ultimately came into conflict with the pan-Arab ideology of the Muslims."[44] Egypt's Gamal Abdel Nasser was increasingly influencing the Arab population, much to the chagrin of many Maronites. With the Cold War in full swing, Chamoun called Nasser a communist and requested U.S. intervention under the premise of the Eisenhower Doctrine, which promised economic and military assistance to states under threat of communism. Consequently, U.S. Marines landed in Lebanon in 1958 and helped put an end to the fighting, while also restoring the status quo balance of power. However, even in the aftermath of the U.S. intervention and the restoration of the preexisting balance of power in favor of the Maronite Christians, Lebanon was far from pacified. In 1975, a second civil war exploded. This time the hostilities would last more than fifteen years, involve all major sectarian groups in the country, and lead to widespread human, social, and economic destruction.

The Maronite Christians once again fought the war by relying on their pro-Western allies. It was during these early years of the second civil war that the Maronite community in Lebanon and the Jewish State of Israel grew increasingly close. By 1976, the two sides were holding high-level meetings.[45] Israel later established a "Good Fence" policy, according to which Lebanese that were friendly to Israel were allowed access into the country to receive medical care, supplies, and sometimes even employment. This relationship would later spread to the Maronite militias as well, who, in return for training and supplies, provided Israel with intelligence on Palestinian and other groups. Maronite militias received upward of $50 million annually from Israel in the years leading up to the 1982 invasion, the bulk of which went to militias associated with Bashir Gemayel, the charismatic and ruthless commander of the Phalange (Kataib) militia and son of the group's founder, Pierre Amin Gemayel. Israel also lent support to other Christian powerhouse families in Lebanon, such as the Chamouns.[46] Under the governments of Israeli prime ministers Yitzhak Rabin and Menachem Begin, aid to Christian militias grew even further, as they began to receive military training in Israel. Prime Minister Begin did not just see the relationship with the Maronites as strategically sound but believed assistance was due to moral obligation as well.[47]

Although somewhat hesitant at first, Bashir Gemayel turned to the Israelis for support largely as a result of the Syrian invasion of Lebanon in 1975. While the Maronites had warily given their blessing to the invasion in its earliest stages, they soon began to suffer under Syrian occupation as they were subjected to arrests, confiscations, rape, and overall destruction.[48] These actions helped convince Gemayel to turn on Syria and its Christian ally Tony Frangieh, thus opening up a Pandora's box of trouble and forcing the Gemayels' Phalange militia further into the hands of the Israelis, whom they relied on for arms, training, funding, and protection.[49] As the Christian-Israeli alliance grew, so did demands by Gemayel for Israel to intervene militarily on the Christians' behalf. Israel eventually acquiesced, first in the more limited campaign known as Operation Litani in 1978, and later in what Israel dubbed Operation Peace for Galilee, better known as the 1982 Lebanon War. Until 1982, however, Israel tended to stick to the policy articulated under Prime Minister Yitzhak Rabin during his first term in office: Israel would help the Lebanese Christians only to help themselves and would not intervene militarily on their behalf.[50]

Accordingly, in addition to dealing and arming the Gemayels, Israel also set its sights on a south Lebanese major in the Lebanese Armed Forces (LAF) named Saad Haddad. As a Greek Catholic, Haddad was a relative outsider among his Maronite neighbors, but he quickly asserted himself in 1977 when a battalion under his command broke off from the Lebanese military and he created his own militia, known as the Free Lebanon Army. Haddad would become the "linchpin for Israel's policy in the south," despite his emotional outbreaks and his failure to be seen as much of a military leader.[51] By 1978 the Lebanese government had withdrawn its support for the major. However, thanks to Operation Litani, Haddad and his forces grew powerful enough to declare a portion of south Lebanon the "Independent Free Lebanon," or the "Free Republic of Lebanon." This area would later become part of Israel's self-styled Security Zone.

When Haddad died in 1984, Major General Antoine Lahad of the LAF took over as commander of the militia and officially renamed it the South Lebanon Army (SLA). Established first to combat PLO forces operating in the south of the country along Israel's northern border, the SLA would later combat Hezbollah as well. Within Lebanon, many came to see the SLA as an "army of collaborators." It would become Israel's main proxy force during its occupation of southern Lebanon from 1982 to 2000.

The SLA was divided into a Western Brigade, Eastern Brigade, intelligence service (known as MABAT), and central command. Though its leadership was made up of Maronite Christians, the force was composed of Muslims as well. In fact, for much of its history a sizable portion—at times nearing 30 percent—of the SLA's force was actually Shiite. Those Shiites were consistently targeted and pressured to cooperate with Hezbollah.[52] While highly reliant on the IDF for its ultimate survival, the SLA played an important role as it could provide an insider's perspective on matters of intelligence, operations, and overall understanding of the Lebanese mindset. Although the SLA and its effectiveness were less than stellar, the difficulty a counterinsurgency force has in creating a reliable local proxy force is somewhat like "eating soup with a knife," as John Nagl once famously wrote.[53] It was for this reason that Israel invested so much time and effort into the SLA. When Israel finally withdrew from Lebanon in the spring of 2000, the SLA disintegrated almost immediately. Although most of its supporters were able to return to civilian life in Lebanon, the core leadership of the SLA was prosecuted for treason. In total, many thousands of members would flee from prosecution and seek refuge in Israel.

Through whatever lens one observes the Israeli-Maronite relationship, two things come across loud and clear. The first is that Israel's ties to the Lebanese Christian community further alienated the Jewish state from its Muslim neighbors at a time when the Christians were diminishing in numbers. Second, by siding so heavily with the Maronites, the Israelis in essence abandoned any opportunity they may have had to develop a more strategic relationship with Lebanon's largest and most disenfranchised sect, the Shiites. In the course of fieldwork for this book, this sentiment was expressed numerous times by Lebanese, UNIFIL officials, and Israeli military commanders.

Maronite Christian Parties Today

The seeds of Lebanon's modern Christian parties can be found in the largest Maronite groups that had fought in the civil war. Like their Sunni and Shiite counterparts, from the outset Christian Lebanese political organizations were established on the basis of sectarian and communal principles, often conceived as hybrid politico-military organizations. Through their formative stage, these parties developed and maintained a community-based, rather than a nation-based, political platform. This reality, in turn, lowered their potential to promote and achieve national integration and cooperation.[54]

The most important Christian paramilitary group during the civil war was Pierre Gemayel's Phalange. The organization was founded in 1936 as a youth movement, modeled after European fascist organizations. It emphasized internal discipline, paramilitary organization, and ultranationalist ideals.[55] By the 1950s, the Phalange had grown in terms of both power and supporters. It had become a parliamentary party and began to actively recruit and arm its own militia.[56] During the second civil war, in the 1970s, under the military leadership of Pierre's son Bashir, the group also became one of the leading organizations of the Christian-dominated Lebanese Front—fighting to preserve the political status quo and the Maronite's political privileges, while opposing the Sunnis' requests for political parity within government.[57] The Phalange would later become infamous for its massacres of Palestinians at the Sabra and Shatilla refugee camps during Israel's invasion of Lebanon in 1982, following the assassination of its leader, Bashir Gemayel. In the midst of the civil war, Bashir Gemayel had also created another subsidiary military group of the Phalange, known as the Lebanese Forces. This latter group would later become completely autonomous from the Phalange after Bashir's death in 1982.[58]

The Phalange's political decline began in the years after Bashir Gemyael's passing and continued during the post–civil war era, when the party's militia was dismantled and the group—under the leadership of George Saade— assumed a pro-Syrian position.[59] The party remained politically marginalized during the years of Syrian presence in Lebanon. That role started to change in early 2000, when its historic leader, Pierre Gemayel—who had voluntarily gone into exile in 1988—returned to Lebanon and became one of the key leaders of the rising anti-Syrian political movement.[60] As a result, the party temporarily split between the "unofficial" Phalange Party—led by Gemayel and active in the anti-Syrian reformist movement—and the "loyalist-official" Phalange Party, supported by the Syrians.[61] Following the Syrian withdrawal from Lebanon in 2005, the "official" and "unofficial" Phalange factions reunited, and the group is currently a member of the "pro-Western" March 14 coalition. In the 2009 elections, the party was awarded five parliamentary seats.[62] The Phalange Party continues to maintain its Christian and right-wing orientation.

Apart from the Phalange Party, the other main Christian party that originated in the midst of the civil war was Bashir Gemayel's Lebanese Forces.

This group gained full independence and political status under the leadership of Samir Geagea in 1986. As the Lebanese Forces' chief of staff, Geagea was able to gain control of the organization and oust its previous leader, Elie Hobeiqa, after he had attempted to broker a deal with the Syrians.[63] Like the Phalange, the Lebanese Forces agreed to transform its militia into a full-fledged political party during the reconciliation process established by the Taif Accord after the civil war. However, unlike the Phalange, the Lebanese Forces never fully accepted the role of Syria within Lebanese political affairs. As a result, the party was outlawed, and Samir Geagea arrested in 1994.[64] During the years of Syrian occupation, the party continued to work outside the realm of institutional politics, and in 2001 it converged into the main Christian anti-Syrian coalition, known as the Qornet Shehwan Gathering (QSG), which included the National Liberal Party, the "unofficial" Phalange Party, and the National Bloc.[65] The Lebanese Forces was a key actor in the anti-Syrian political movement, and it would later rejoin the political system for the first parliamentary elections held in the aftermath of the Syrian withdrawal in 2005, when Samir Geagea was released from prison. Since that time, the Lebanese Forces has been a member of the March 14 coalition, together with the Phalange Party, and in the 2009 parliamentary elections, it won five seats.[66]

The third main Christian party in Lebanon, the Free Patriotic Movement (FPM), was created after Lebanon's second civil war, although its leader, General Michel Aoun, was chief of staff of the Lebanese Armed Forces during the war and was also the one of the Christian leaders opposed to the Taif Accord. Aoun had demanded a complete Syrian withdrawal as a precondition to sitting down at the negotiating table, and unlike the Phalange and Lebanese Forces' leadership, he refused to recognize the post-civil-war government.[67] This led to a bloody internal confrontation among the former Christian allies turned foes, which ended with the defeat of General Aoun and his exile to France.[68] That exile would end fifteen years later, following the Syrian withdrawal from Lebanon. After Aoun's return to Lebanon in 2005, he and his Free Patriotic Movement ran in the 2005 elections independent from other Christian parties. On this occasion, the FPM obtained twenty-one parliamentary seats, confirming Aoun's personal popularity among Lebanon's Christians.[69] After the elections, the FPM did not join the March 14 coalition as had the other main Christian parties. Rather, after clashing with the elected government on several points—including Aoun's request to obtain five cabinet seats for his party—the FPM started to drift toward the opposition camp. In 2006 the Free Patriotic Movement took the monumental step of signing a memorandum of understanding with Hezbollah, marking the beginning of a highly improbable political alliance between two parties with widely different political agendas and constituencies.[70] Currently, the group is still a key member of the March 8 coalition together with Amal, Hezbollah, and Lebanon's pro-Syrian parties.

Understanding the current political alignment of the Christian parties, which are divided, respectively, between the "pro-Western" March 14 forces (the Phalange Party and the Lebanese Forces) and the Hezbollah-led March 8 group (the Free Patriotic Movement), is crucial to grasping Lebanese politics today. With the Sunni and Shiite votes going to the March 14 and March 8 coalitions, respectively, the Christian community represents the only "wild card" in Lebanese elections and, as such, determines the final electoral outcome.

The Palestinians

Palestinian Arabs have been living in Lebanon ever since the 1948 Arab-Israeli War, which resulted both in Israel's independence and in the creation of a Palestinian refugee population scattered throughout much of the Middle East, including (and especially) in the immediate areas surrounding the Jewish state. After the 1967 Six-Day War, a new wave of Palestinians entered Lebanon, swelling the number of refugees living there to 350,000.[71] As was the policy throughout most of the Arab world, Palestinians who entered Lebanon were not granted citizenship. Most of the Palestinians were Sunni, and their incorporation into the Lebanese political landscape would have altered the fragile balance of power that already existed. The Palestinian refugees lived throughout southern Lebanon, with about half settling in seventeen refugee camps administered by their own UN refugee agency, known as the United Nations Relief and Works Agency (UNRWA). The camps were spread out from Tyre to Tripoli to Ba'albek, with the largest one, Ein al-Hilweh, existing right outside the city of Sidon. The Palestinian militants and their militias generally operated out of these camps.[72]

The year 1968 saw the beginning of PLO raids into Israel from Lebanon, including terrorist attacks such as hijackings against Israel's civilian population. By 1969 the PLO and the Lebanese government had reached an understanding known as the Cairo Agreement, under the mediation efforts of Egyptian president Gamal Abdel Nasser. The agreement allowed for the Palestinians to arm, recruit, and acquire military training, in addition to a few political privileges. One of the main objectives the Lebanese had in mind when entering into the Cairo Agreement was to control the Palestinians' activities and contain them within their refugee camps. But, in reality, the accord did little to regulate their activities and indirectly helped spur on Lebanon's second civil war. In essence, the agreement granted the PLO unhindered access to launch attacks from Lebanon into Israel, with the Lebanese Army actually charged with protecting Palestinian bases and supply lines.[73] Partly as a result of the agreement, in 1969 Palestinian militants carried out approximately 3,900 attacks from Lebanon and Jordan against Israel. By 1970 that number had reached 6,000.[74] In Lebanon, the Palestinians were organized as a guerrilla force. They had thousands of light weapons, rocket-propelled grenades, anti-tank guns, and tanks, as well as mortars, artillery pieces, and katyusha rockets, which they fired at civilian targets in Israel.[75]

Palestinian militants in Lebanon were further strengthened as a result of a civil war in Jordan from 1970 to 1971 that threatened the leader of that country, King Hussein. Jordan is the only Arab country that granted Palestinians citizenship en masse, and as a result the Palestinian population makes up more than half of the population of Jordan today.[76] Three factors resulted in the explosion of what was essentially the Kingdom of Jordan's civil war. The first was the Palestinian launching of attacks against Israel from Jordanian territory, which resulted in Israeli reprisals. The second was the Jordanian attempt to lay claim to being the chief representatives of the Palestinian people, in direct opposition to the PLO.[77] The third was that Palestinian organizations were ignoring Jordanian rule of law and essentially acting as a state-within-a-state.[78] Eventually, violence erupted between the two sides, and King Hussein's forces moved against the Palestinians. What ensued was a bloody fight, with PLO chairman Yasser Arafat vying for control of the country. In what has become one of the most controversial episodes in Arab history, heavy fighting resulted in the expulsion of Palestinian armed fighters from Jordan after approximately three thousand were killed.[79] Dejected, the Palestinian militias moved to Syria and Lebanon. Once in Lebanon, they created for themselves a state-within-a-state, where the PLO was quick to make itself at home along western Lebanon, from Beirut and down south to the Israeli border.[80] This area became known as Fatahland, after the largest group within the PLO, Fatah, which was also led by PLO chairman Yasser Arafat.

In the years leading up to the 1982 invasion, Palestinian militants in Lebanon received plenty of help from outside actors, including Arab states and the Soviet Union, which supplied it with weaponry and $300 million in aid per year.[81] Israel did not sit idly by while it was attacked either; it carried out numerous counterinsurgency and counterterrorism operations against PLO forces in and around Lebanon.[82] These attacks caused destruction not only of Palestinian enclaves but of Christian and especially Shiite ones as well. Israeli reprisals eventually led Shiite Musa al-Sadr to demand protection. Sadr worked to establish training camps for Shiites, under the slogan "Arms are an ornament to men." The Shiites had always sensed a kinship with the Palestinians as they felt that both their peoples had suffered, and as a result Sadr made efforts to establish good relations with the Palestinians. However, when Palestinians continued to attack Israel and the reprisals continued to cause Shiite suffering, relations between the two groups soured.[83] As Palestinian attacks and Israeli counterattacks flared, the confessional system began to fall apart, and the various sects started to more rigorously build up their militias, which led Sadr to found Amal.[84]

The Palestinians' biggest blunder was forgetting the golden rule of guerrilla warfare: keep the support of the local population. Outside of its strongholds in refugee camps and the poor suburbs of Beirut, the PLO managed to alienate most other Lebanese, including the Shiites, resulting in an easy routing by the IDF in later years.[85] As Sandra Mackey put it,

> The Palestinians were both victims and villains in Lebanon. Cast out of the society and deprived of a political voice and economic opportunity, the Palestinians, particularly those of the camps and lower socioeconomic groups, epitomized the downtrodden. But the Palestinians could be as arrogant and contemptuous of Lebanon and the Lebanese as the Lebanese were of them.[86]

Without any government control during its second civil war, southern Lebanon became a "magnet for regional powers intent on engaging Israel without jeopardizing their own borders."[87]

The Sunnis

Representing more than one quarter of the Lebanese population, the Lebanese Sunnis have historically been concentrated in the country's urban centers—especially the areas surrounding Tripoli in the north of the country, the capital Beirut, and Sidon in the south.[88] The Lebanese Sunnis represented the country's social and political elite during the Ottoman Empire. Because they suffered greatly from both the fall of the Ottomans and the rise of French influence in the area, they initially opposed the creation of a Greater Lebanon in 1920.[89] Over time, Sunni political elites reached an amenable agreement with the Maronite Christian leadership and supported the 1943 National Pact, creating a Sunni-Christian (and, to a lesser degree, Druze) alliance that would control Lebanon until the 1975 civil war.[90]

Although the Sunni urban upper-class elites were completely integrated into Lebanon's political machine, as early as the 1960s Sunni leaders found themselves in a complex political position. On the one hand, they had an interest in preserving the status quo and their privileges, thus continuing their alliance with the Maronite Christians. On the other hand, they felt increasing pressures from within their own constituency to push the cause of pan-Arabism and achieve political parity with the Christians. Sunni leaders attempted to balance these conflicting needs, but part of the Sunni population still felt unrepresented by its traditional leaders. This situation eventually led to an internal split within the Sunni community, and the rise of alternative power centers, from Islamist parties to pro-Nasser, pan-Arab political organizations.[91] With the beginning of the civil war, this reality led to the creation of multiple Sunni militias, engaged mostly against Maronite Christian groups under various political leaders and warlords.

With the end of the civil war and the en masse demobilization of armed militias that followed the Taif Accord, the Sunni community found itself more united, and a key part of the post-civil-war Lebanon that was now under Syrian control. The end of the war also saw the rise of a new Sunni politician who would become prime minister in 1992 and hold that post, on and off, for over a decade: Rafik Hariri.[92] Hariri was very different from the traditional Sunni leadership. He did not belong to a political family and he had not been a military leader during the civil war. Rather, Hariri was a self-made billionaire who had found his fortune in Saudi Arabia and was committed to both economic liberalism and political reform. During the 1990s, Hariri emerged as the main leader of the Sunni community, building a widespread consensus and uniting the Sunnis under the banner of his political movement, Tayyar al-Mustaqbal (Future Movement).

In the 1990s Hariri's relationship with Syria was rather amicable, but as his political power and personal status rose, his relations with both Syrian

forces and Syria's domestic allies (including Hezbollah) grew more complicated. These relations would later deteriorate even further with the death of
Hafez al-Assad in 2000 and the rise of his son Bashar al-Assad to power.[93]
Hariri and the Sunni political leadership would grow increasingly uncom-
fortable with Syrian control of the country, gradually drifting more toward
the anti-Syrian camp. This trend was accelerated in 2004, when the Syrians
coerced Hariri into voting in favor of extending President Emile Lahoud's term
in office—a move that was followed by Hariri's resignation and the progressive affirmation of the former prime minister as an anti-Syrian, opposition
leader.[94]

In this context, Hariri's political assassination on February 14, 2005—intended to stall the efforts of the anti-Syrian opposition—completely backfired.
The assassination cemented a political alliance of Christian and Sunni political forces and brought the entire Sunni community together to stand behind
Hariri's Future Movement. In the months between February and April, rallies
and political protests of anti-Syrian political forces and civil society—named
the March 14 coalition after a massive anti-Syrian rally organized on that
date—obtained the final withdrawal of Syrian troops from Lebanon, achieving
a historic political change. The rallies also confirmed the widespread Sunni
backing of Hariri's Future Movement, which would obtain thirty-six seats
in the 2005 elections, becoming the largest political party in Parliament.[95] In
the 2009 elections, the Future Movement obtained similar results.[96]

Although the Future Movement represents politically the majority of Lebanon's Sunni community, it would be too simplistic to define its political and
religious orientation as entirely homogeneous. In this sense, another important component of the Sunni political arena is in fact represented by the political Islamist movements—political and social organizations that embrace
the notion of Islam as the ideal framework for both political and social development. These groups include political Islamist forces such as Al-Jamaa al-
Islamiyya (Islamic Group) as well as more radical Salafist groups.

Al-Jamaa al-Islamiyya was created in 1964 to serve as the local autonomous
branch of the Egyptian-originated Muslim Brotherhood. Since its founding,
it has embraced the notion of working within the political system to gradually make the society more Islamic, while opposing the state-funded official
religious establishment, Dar al-Fatwa.[97] Under the leadership of Fathi Yakan,
Al-Jamaa al-Islamiyya participated in the civil war on the side of the Palestinians, promoting the notion of "resistance against Israel." But its role later

became more subdued during the years of Syrian occupation.[98] In the aftermath of the Taif Accord, the group attempted integration into the political system, and it participated in the 1992 parliamentary election—winning three seats in Beirut and Tripoli.[99] Al-Jamaa al-Islamiyya's political relevance faded during the 1990s, but its level of activism and legitimacy gradually increased after the Syrian withdrawal in 2005.

In fact, during the Syrian occupation of Lebanon, Islamist groups were closely watched by Syrian intelligence and prevented from criticizing both the government and the occupation, thus reducing these groups' political status as well as their level of activity.[100]

Al-Jamaa al-Islamiyya obtained one seat in the 2009 Parliament—where it was formally allied with Hariri's Future Movement.[101] The group's historical leader, Fathi Yakan, left Al-Jamaa al-Islamiyya in 2006 to protest the group's alliance with the Future Movement. Yakan criticized this alliance because of the Future Movement's pro-Western orientation and "moderate" stance.[102] He has since founded Jabhat al-Amal al-Islami (Islamic Action Front), an umbrella organization, to better coordinate among Sunni Islamist groups.[103]

Another important splinter of Al-Jamaa al-Islamiyya is Harakat al-Tawhid al-Islam (Islamic Unification Movement), created in the early 1980s to fight both Israeli and Syrian troops under the leadership of Said Shaban.[104] In 1985 the revivalist movement, which later also broke down into a number of smaller groups, attempted to gain control of the areas surrounding Tripoli, in alliance with the PLO. On that occasion, Harakat al-Tawhid al-Islam was militarily crushed by the Syrians, which sent a powerful signal to all other Islamist movements that dissent would not be tolerated.[105] To this day, the movement is still active, and its political and social activities have also resurged in the aftermath of the Syrian withdrawal.

Finally, since 2006 Lebanon legalized another Islamist party with a strong Islamist agenda: Hizb al-Tahrir.[106] Licensing this previously outlawed party was part of the Future Movement's strategy to gradually placate and co-opt all local Islamists to ally with Hariri's political party, thereby boosting the unity of the Sunni community. Critics of this approach have questioned the desirability of encouraging and promoting Islamist parties, pointing to both the risk of radicalizing the Sunni community and the threat of upsetting Lebanon's delicate sectarian balance.

Lebanon has also seen a trend of increased presence and visibility of Salafist groups in social and political activism as well as through military-jihadist operations. Salafism is a revivalist movement within Sunni Islam, demanding a return of the religion to its early roots (*salaf* means ancestors) and preaching for the re-Islamization and "purification" of society. A particular current within Salafism, the jihadist stream, openly demands and employs violent means to pursue these political ends.

Within Lebanon, Salafist groups have been active since the 1980s. They are concentrated in areas around Tripoli and the Nahr al-Bared refugee camp in the north, and Sidon and the Ein al-Hilweh Palestinian camp in the south.[107] There are a few nonviolent, "mainstream" Salafist movements, including the *dawa*-based, Wahabbi-inspired, al-Harakat al-Salafiyya, and the more reformist Lebanese Islamic Forum for Dialogue and Dawa.[108] While the Future Movement does not publicly endorse these groups, it has in the past fostered links with them by relying on the common anti-Syrian and anti-Hezbollah agenda in an effort to unite the Sunni community and ensure the political dominance of the party.

Furthermore, in order to build a more powerful anti-Syrian and anti-Hezbollah coalition, Future Movement leaders have also been accused of turning a blind eye to the rising influence of violent Salafist groups, allowing them to prosper and receive assistance from Saudi Arabia. The extremist Salafist movement gained momentum in the aftermath of the 2005 Syrian withdrawal, as it became more independent and confrontational with other organizations, including Hezbollah. To date, the main Salafi-jihadist groups within Lebanon are Asbat al-Ansar, Jund al-Sham, and the more recent Fatah al-Islam.

Lebanese Salafi-Jihadist Groups

Asbat al-Ansar is a Salafi-jihadist movement classified by the United States as a foreign terrorist organization (FTO) and largely composed of Palestinians.[109] The organization is predominantly based in the Palestinian refugee camp of Ein al-Hilweh, located next to the town of Sidon, in southern Lebanon.[110] The group was founded by Palestinian cleric Sheikh Hisham Shreidi in the late 1980s, and its rise must be understood in the wider context of Islamization and radicalization of both Tripoli and Sidon during the 1990s. After Fatah members assassinated Sheikh Shreidi in 1991, the group split into three factions: Asbat al-Nour, Jamaat al-Nour, and Jund as-Sham. Currently, Asbat al-Nour has rejoined Asbat al-Ansar, while Jund al-Sham seems to have remained autonomous.[111]

Asbat al-Ansar is actively present in the Palestinian refugee camps in Lebanon, where it retains a degree of control and authority, and where it recruits most of its active and passive followers. The organization is rather small, and during the 1990s it was mostly involved in a local struggle against other Islamist groups.[112] Toward the end of the 1990s the group increased both its presence and the significance of its military targets. Additionally, after the September 11 attacks, Asbat al-Ansar focused more on striking foreign targets and embassies and increased its contacts with transnational terrorist networks, in part thanks to its relations with Afghani returnee and Salafist leader Bassam Kanj (aka Abu Aisha).[113] As early as 2001, Jordanian security sources revealed and foiled an Asbat al-Ansar plot to target Arab embassies of countries perceived as pro-Western and allied with the United States. [114]

In the following years, several terrorist operations marked the increased importance of the group and the transition from a local to a more global agenda. Among these actions, it is worth mentioning the killing of four Lebanese judges in 1999, numerous failed plots to assassinate the American ambassador in Lebanon, and in 2004 the attempt to attack the Italian Embassy, the Ukrainian Consulate General, and Lebanese government offices.[115] In 2003 Lebanese security forces arrested Ibn al-Shahid, allegedly affiliated with Asbat al-Ansar, and accused him of planning the bombing of three fast-food restaurants during the previous year and of masterminding the failed April 2003 bombing attack of a McDonald's restaurant in the suburbs of Beirut.[116] In September 2003 Lebanese forces also arrested Othman Kaaki and Khaled Mohammed al-Ali, both connected to Asbat al-Ansar and members of a transnational network affiliated with al Qaeda that linked Lebanon with Australia.[117] In May 2004 Lebanese forces arrested another Australian national, Saleh Jamal, who was accused of being both affiliated with al Qaeda and in contact with Asbat al-Ansar. They also accused Lebanese-Australian Haytham Melhem and Australian Zuhayr Mohammed Isa of assisting Jamal in the preparation of a terrorist attack.[118] Since the beginning of the U.S. war in Iraq, Asbat al-Ansar was actively involved with the Iraqi insurgency, while maintaining a degree of control and political power within the Palestinian Ein al-Hilweh camp.

Jund al-Sham, which means the Army of Greater Syria, is a splinter group of Asbat al-Ansar. The group's members are mostly Lebanese, although they include some Palestinians as well.[119] Like Asbat al-Ansar, Jund al-Sham's headquarters are located in the Ein al-Hilweh refugee camp, where its presence is estimated to be only around fifty men.[120] The camp was traditionally a foot-hold of Fatah and the former operating base of Yasser Arafat in the 1980s, but since the late 1990s it has increasingly come under the control of Salafists. The rising polarization and factionalism within the camps and the internal weakening of Fatah's authority provide fertile ground for Salafist organiza-tions to develop. This in turn has partially undermined the historic bargain between the PLO and the Lebanese government, according to which Beirut abstained from interfering in the Palestinian camps' administration and al-lowed Fatah to be in charge of running them in exchange for preventing "spill-overs" of internal violence into Lebanon.

In the aftermath of the Syrian withdrawal from Lebanon, this agreement is increasingly being undermined by the Salafists' activism outside of the camps. For example, in 2007 Jund al-Sham joined forces with Fatah al-Islam and directly confronted the Lebanese Armed Forces (LAF).[121] This episode marked the beginning of open hostilities between Salafi-jihadist groups and the state, spreading the internal violence of the camps to other areas of the country. Only a year later, in March 2008, following internal clashes between members of Fatah and Jund al-Sham fighters, the armed confrontation once again spread outside of camp, partly as a response to Jund al-Sham's attempts to expand its area of operations and attack the LAF. On May 31, a Jund al-Sham militant was shot to death by Lebanese forces at a checkpoint in Ein al-Hilweh.[122] Two weeks later, another clash took place at a checkpoint located at the western entrance of the camp, leading to the death of another Jund al-Sham gunman and the wounding of a second militant as well as a Lebanese soldier. Notably, Jund al-Sham has also conducted a series of operations against Hezbollah, including the killing of an official in July 2004 and an April 2006 foiled plot to assassinate Hezbollah leader Hassan Nasrallah.[123] These epi-sodes were not the first instance of clashes between Salafists and more tradi-tional Lebanese forces; in fact, a similar (isolated) confrontation between the army and Salafi-jihadist fighters occurred back in 1999.[124] The armed clashes in 2007 and 2008, however, would prove to be more widespread and violent than those in 1999.

Fatah al-Islam emerged as an autonomous group in 2006, claiming to be a splinter group of the Syrian Fatah al-Intifada—a link that seems to justify the claim that Syrian intelligence was at least partially involved in establishing the group in Tripoli.[125] Yet Fatah al-Islam is not merely a Syrian creation. The group is a fluid network of both Palestinian and Lebanese militants, as well as foreign fighters who mostly arrived into Lebanon from Iraq, creating a critical link to al Qaeda.[126] The organization also operates, namely, from the Nahr al-Bared refugee camp and began its attacks against Lebanese targets in early 2006, when it placed two bombs on a bus in the Christian town of Ein Alaq.[127] When the Lebanese military began to respond to the group's operations in 2007, Fatah al-Islam chose to retaliate by ambushing an army checkpoint patrol near Nahr al-Bared in May 2007. This episode led to a prolonged and bloody confrontation between Fatah al-Islam and the Lebanese Army, which claimed more than four hundred lives.[128]

Although in the end the Lebanese military clearly prevailed and Fatah al-Islam was dealt a severe blow, the May 2007 confrontations still represented a major source of concern within Lebanon, signaling both the rise in power of violent Salafist groups and the inability of the LAF to effectively combat them. In fact, even in the period following these hostilities, violent Salafists have not been entirely pacified. For example, after Hezbollah's armed take-over of West Beirut in May 2008, progovernment Sunni factions repeatedly clashed with the pro-Hezbollah Alawite community in northern Lebanon, leading to more than twenty people being killed during June and July 2008. The Sunni-Alawite confrontation, which also saw the involvement of groups such as Jund al-Sham, was finally resolved in September 2009 when the two parties signed a reconciliation agreement.[129] This agreement did not, however, put an end to the tensions between the militant Salafist groups and Hezbollah. In an effort to strengthen the LAF so that it would be willing and able to stand up to Shiite and Sunni Islamist groups alike, the United States boosted aid to that country's military since 2006, providing it with more than $700 million over five years. Now that Hezbollah is a major player in the ruling government, and there is no evidence that the LAF would ever confront Hezbollah, there is pressure within the U.S. government to cut military aid to the Lebanese military.[130]

The Lebanese Political System

As of early 2011, the Lebanese political system still stands upon the basis laid out in the Taif Accord, which was negotiated at the end of the second civil war.[131] The main goal of Taif was to stop the bloodshed and prepare the ground for a subsequent normalization of Lebanese political life. To do so, the agreement aimed at abolishing the sectarian system that had dragged the country into war in the first place.[132] However, prompted by the need to achieve a speedy end to hostilities, the Taif Accord failed to address the confessional basis of the political system, according to which each ethnoreligious community within Lebanon was assigned a number of fixed seats in Parliament. On the contrary, the agreement ratified the 1943 National Pact and the existing confessional distribution of power.[133] Yet, rather than reproduce the 1943 sectarian distribution of seats, it granted the Muslim community political parity by shifting the ratio of seats from 6:5 to 5:5 between Christians and Muslims.[134] These changes provided for greater equity among the different confessions but left unchanged the elections of political figures based on their religious background.[135] This means that country's president still must remain a Maronite Christian; the prime minister, a Sunni; and the role of speaker of Parliament, a Shiite politician.

In this sense, the Taif Accord had the unintended consequence of solidifying preexisting sectarian dynamics into the political system, which were then strengthened during the years of Syrian political and military occupation of the country. The Syrians were never interested in repealing the confessional system, and the main electoral reforms passed during the Syrian occupation addressed logistical issues, while further endorsing the confessional system. Moreover, in the aftermath of Taif and during the years of Syria's presence in Lebanon, it was the absence of a nation-building project that further weakened the national political system as well as the limits of confessional politics. As a result, in the post-Syrian-occupation phase starting in 2005 Lebanon has been struggling to move beyond these conceptual and institutional obstacles entrenched within its political system, with Lebanese confessional politics continuing to reproduce and enhance societal divisions and conflict dynamics.

In the aftermath of the Syrian withdrawal, the Lebanese government has undertaken a series of efforts to reform the political system and address these practical and logistical failures. The Parliament created the National Commission for a New Electoral Law, led by Fouad Boutros, and tasked the new organ to restructure the existing electoral laws. The Boutros Commission, which was created in August 2005, was designed to be composed of "all political forces including representatives of parties and movements unrepresented in government," including civil society members.[136] After a year of consultation, in May 2006 the commission presented the Lebanese Parliament with the Electoral Draft Law.[137] The law proposal slowly made its way through the political system, and on September 29, 2008, the Lebanese Parliament approved a new electoral law, based on the Boutros draft. This new law contained important improvements that addressed some of the previous problems in the Lebanese electoral system, but it failed to modify its core premises.

The 2009 electoral law revised the previous electoral architecture and repealed the Syrian-based demarcation of the electoral districts. This new electoral system, based on an amended version of the 1960 electoral law, allowed for more proportional results than the Syrian-based one, while preventing occurrences of one political group winning with a narrow majority all the seats in a large electoral district, which would leave the other groups underrepresented. Instead, the creation of more numerous and smaller districts made seat allocation more proportional, while promoting competition among parties. Yet the new electoral law failed to go the extra mile toward increasing the principle of "effective representation" of the political system. It failed to incorporate the most important recommendation of the Boutros Commission: the introduction of proportional representation into the Lebanese electoral system. The Boutros Commission had proposed to elect the 128 MPs according to a mixed system, with 77 deputies selected according to the current majoritarian system and 51 representatives chosen with a proportional system.[138]

Instead, the approved electoral law disregarded this recommendation and left in place the preexisting majoritarian block-vote system, which guaranteed each voter the right to cast as many votes as the number of seats allocated in his or her electoral districts. Each seat is then won by the candidate who is awarded the highest number of electoral preferences within his own confessional group.[139] This "new" system has several flaws, including the fact that it contributes to the entrenching of confessional dynamics within Lebanese politics.

The problem of corruption and vote buying is another important topic upon which the new electoral law touched and which is one that deeply characterizes the Lebanese political system. Lebanon's anticorruption record is particularly weak when it comes to preserving the integrity of elections, as virtually all political parties are engaged in buying votes, through either cash or in-kind payments.[140] This destructive voting pattern is widespread in all political parties and sectarian groups and builds upon the traditional clientelist relationship between political leaders and their constituencies. Aside from the historical roots of buying political support through political goods and bribes, another reason why vote buying is extremely widespread in Lebanon is the fact that the country does not rely on unified, preprinted ballots. Currently, each voter can in fact use any piece of paper to cast his or her vote, thus leaving parties the right to distribute their own preprinted ballots to "clients" and supporters, which makes it relatively easy to ensure that the money invested in buying votes does not go to waste.[141] This practice also allows for political intimidation, as party members can easily monitor the voting stations and recognize whether a given voter employs the premade ballot handed out to him.

To solve this problem, the Boutros Commission suggested introducing official uniform ballots to minimize the chances of vote buying, to guarantee the secrecy of voting, and to ease the tabulation process.[142] Unfortunately, the Lebanese Parliament rejected this proposal, but it nevertheless agreed to introduce transparent ballot boxes and the inking of fingers, which partially helped in lowering the chances of electoral fraud and corruption.[143]

In order to contain and regulate the vote buying, Lebanon enacted laws to render campaign financing more transparent, by requiring candidates to account for the money they receive and invest in their election campaigns and by setting caps for campaign-related expenditures.[144] The hope was that this provision would regulate corruption by monitoring parties' finances, but it is unclear whether in practice "unofficial" and "under-the-table" financing and bribes would be tracked down and regulated. The Lebanese Parliament also agreed to adopt another important recommendation of the Boutros Commission: scheduling elections to take place during the course of one day, thus reducing the chances for political and armed groups to assert pressure or disrupt the electoral process.[145] This change could also impact on the degree of fairness and transparency of the elections.

Yet, despite these changes, there were many other important reforms that the new electoral law failed to address, which would likely be needed to improve the state of the political system. These included the creation of an effective independent electoral commission, the introduction of stricter regulation of the media's role in political campaigning, and the establishment of electoral quotas for women.

In the years following the 2005 Syrian withdrawal from Lebanon, the country has been actively trying to improve the degree of openness and internal democracy of its political system. Lebanon has embarked on an important and positive process and has adopted a series of substantive electoral and political reforms to achieve such results. However, various procedural and structural obstacles, such as the confessional basis of the political system, should be effectively addressed before the country can truly normalize its political and intersectarian relations. Meanwhile, Lebanese politics remains highly sectarian and continues to strengthen the preexisting ethnic and religious divisions within the country, with the main political parties becoming de facto representatives of a specific ethnic community. This is especially true in the case of Hezbollah, which—together with Amal—holds a virtual monopoly over the Shiite votes and acts as representative of the Lebanese Shiites. However, the existing political system is not as favorable to Hezbollah as one might think: because the confessional distribution of seats is based upon an outdated census, the number of seats assigned to Shiite candidates does not correspond to the actual size of the Shiite constituency. In other words, the Shiites are systematically underrepresented in the Lebanese government, which is one reason why Hezbollah has been historically invested in abolishing the sectarian system and creating a proportional one.

2 Hezbollah

History and Development

INFORMATION ON HEZBOLLAH'S origin is murky. It is generally believed to have been founded sometime between 1982 and 1983, while becoming more fully operational—in terms of both structure and guerrilla warfare tactics—only in 1984. Initially, it began its operations out of the Bekaa Valley and later moved to southern Lebanon.[1] Hezbollah officially announced itself and the creation of its military wing, the Islamic Resistance Brigades (Muqawama al-Islamiyyah), on February 16, 1985, when it published in *Al-Safir* "An Open Letter: The Hezbollah Program," addressed to "all the oppressed/downtrodden in Lebanon and the world."[2] In that letter, referred to as either the "Open Letter" or the "Program," the group extols Ayatollah Khomeini; the suicide bombing attacks against the United States, France, and Israel; the conflicts that Muslims have been involved in throughout the world; and the Quran. The manifesto explains that "all the Western ideas concerning man's origin and nature cannot respond to man's aspirations or rescue him" and "only Islam can bring about man's renaissance." It lists three objectives: expelling the Americans, French, and their allies from Lebanon; bringing the Phalange to justice for its "crimes"; and setting up an "Islamic government," which it stresses is the only way to end "attempts at imperialistic infiltration into our country."[3] It further denounces the United States, capitalism, the Soviet Union, and UNIFIL; rejects all forms of imperialism; and explains the need for the government of Lebanon to change. Under the section "Our Fight," it calls the United States an "arrogant superpower" and "an abomination," whose "primary roots" Hezbollah will "tear out."[4]

The manifesto devotes an entire section to "the necessity for the destruction of Israel," in which it is explains that Israel is the "vanguard" and "agent" of the United States, is inherently aggressive, and usurps the rights of Muslims. As a result, Hezbollah condemns any negotiations with Israel, rejects any past agreements such as the Camp David Accords, and promises never to accept a cease-fire with Israel. "Only when this entity is obliterated" will its struggle with Israel end. "Let us put it truthfully; the sons of Hizballah know who are their major enemies in the Middle East—the Phalanges, Israel, France, and the United States."[5]

Hezbollah's anti-American and anti-Israeli sentiments have been echoed over the years and are still uttered today by Hezbollah's leadership and spokespersons in speeches, books, and newspapers, as well as on television and radio. Though its anti-Israeli sentiment is perhaps better known today, the group continues to evoke rabidly anti-American language. In a video confiscated from a captured Hezbollah cell operating in the suburbs of Charlotte, North Carolina, Hassan Nasrallah is seen yelling to an exultant crowd, "We are people whose slogan was, is, and will remain to be, 'Death to America!'"[6]

The Beginning

Various conditions coincided to help spawn the creation of Hezbollah. Timing, of course, was central to its rise, and Iran's Islamic Revolution in 1979 was particularly crucial. That revolution ushered in a new sense of political Islam around the world—particularly among the Shiite population—that caught both the West and the Sunni Arab world by surprise. Before the revolution, Shiite clerics had made a point of shunning politics, thus keeping a clearer separation between mosque and state in the Shiite world. With the fall of the shah, a major change took place as Shiite clerics suddenly became the ultimate authority for the Iranian regime. This newfound political strength led to a sense of empowerment, pride, and independence for the Shiite community worldwide, which had suffered so long under the yoke of the Sunnis.

More generally, the year 1979 corresponded with a rise of political Islam around the globe, a movement more militant and radical than had been experienced in the past. For the Sunnis, this radicalization manifested itself in Afghanistan, where it was nurtured not just by Pakistan and Arab states such as Saudi Arabia but by the United States and the rest of the Western world as well. The Iranian Revolution was markedly different in that the ayatollahs managed to alienate themselves from the Arab world, the West, and the Soviet Union—no small feat during the Cold War. The emerging Iranian regime made it a policy to export its revolution to other Muslim communities, an issue that has become particularly worrisome to the Sunni-dominated Arab world.

As one of the oldest Shiite communities, and one beset with conflict that involved the "Little Satan" of Israel and the "Great Satan" of the United States, the Lebanese Shiite population became the perfect battleground for this new Iranian agenda. In addition to the Lebanese theater, by the early 1980s the Iranians were already heavily involved in the Iran-Iraq War. Although the Iraqis had the clear technological advantage and support of Western powers, the Iranians fought them into a virtual stalemate using relatively low-level technology and warfare tactics that required an enormous loss of life, in which indoctrinated Shiite youths were more than willing to sacrifice themselves. Thus the Iran-Iraq War provided the first battleground for the Iranian Revolution to prove itself and, in the redoubling of its efforts, to spread the revolution outward. The rise of Hezbollah also coincided with the early stages of globalization and, more specifically, the expansion of the arms industry, which culminated in the world market being flooded with the kind of cheap weaponry that is perfect for irregular warfare. Globalization also saw improved media communications that allowed the ayatollahs to more effectively reach their target audiences in Lebanon and around the world.

As if these developments were not enough, in the late 1980s the Middle East was still smarting from the failure of pan-Arabism to improve the lives of the population in the Arab world. One of the responses to this breakdown came in the form of political Islam. Pan-Arabism was in fact a secular notion touted by famous Arab leaders such as Egypt's Gamal Abdel Nasser, who argued that only a united Arab world could resolve its past failures. Pan-Arabism took the Middle East by storm in the 1950s and 1960s, with Nasser and his cohorts encouraging revolutions against the monarchies that lined the Maghreb and Mashreq regions of the Middle East. The ideology was quite secular and helped spawn the Ba'ath political party and encourage socialist and communist movements. With Israel's trouncing of its Arab neighbors in the 1967 Six-Day War, pan-Arabism began its decline. Its downturn was only enhanced by the political inability of the leadership in the Arab world—both monarchist and pan-Arabist—to substantially improve the well-being of the Arab "street." As a result of this double political and military failure, as well as the fact that pan-Arabism stressed the socialist ideals of secularism that supported crackdowns on religious groups, a backlash arose in the form of political Islam.

In the Sunni community, this response came in growing support for the writings of Sayyid Qutb and the rise of the Muslim Brotherhood, led by Hassan al-Banna in Egypt. The backlash also resulted in Arab monarchies increasingly turning toward their religious establishments to help legitimize their positions of power, as is evidenced by the Saudi regime today. These developments helped produce the dramatic increase in Wahabi and Salafi-jihadist ideologies in the Sunni Muslim world. At approximately the same time, the Shiite Muslim world saw a rise in the role of Islam in both political and foreign affairs, but this trend was largely a result of the Iranian Revolution. What political Islam brought to the table was leadership and activity generally void of the rampant corruption so widespread throughout the Arab and Muslim worlds. It also brought about better social welfare networks and a strong ideology that provided a sense of unity, pride, and indoctrination.

Aside from these global and regional factors, events within Lebanon also resulted in Hezbollah's creation. Chief among these was the second-class treatment of the Shiites by the Christian and Sunni populations. Like the Israelis and Palestinians, the Christian Lebanese communities had failed to properly consider Shiite reactions to their own goals and aspirations.[7] After the rise of Fatahland in the late 1970s, Palestinians also contributed significantly to the Shiites' maltreatment. Lebanon's second civil war and Syria's subsequent invasion of Lebanon in 1975 further assisted the Shiite community in coming to the realization that it needed to defend itself or risk total submission and capitulation to other sects. Finally, Israel's 1982 invasion of Lebanon served as the ultimate accelerator for Hezbollah's formation.[8] When Israel invaded in June 1982, Lebanese religious authorities were coincidentally attending an annual Islamic conference in Tehran.[9] This made coordinating Iranian support for Hezbollah in its beginning stages nearly effortless.[10]

Although the Shiites had been generally welcoming of the Israelis at the outset of the invasion, they soon turned against them after the IDF engaged in multiple blunders. Although it is possible that the Iranians would have attempted to create a group such as Hezbollah even if Israel had withdrawn from Lebanon soon after it entered in 1982, we will never know. What is undeniable is that the Israeli occupation was a crucial factor in explaining the emergence of Hezbollah, as well as in understanding the rather rapid level of support that the newly formed group obtained from the Lebanese Shiite population.

Hezbollah was founded by a union of young, zealous leaders from multiple existing parties who broke off to create the new organization, under orders of Ayatollah Khomeini. They came from a variety of parties. From the group

Hizb al-Da'wa, members included Hezbollah's first and second secretaries-general, Subhi al-Tufayli and Sayyid Abbas al-Musawi. Husain Mussawi broke off from Amal to form the Islamic Amal, which was later wholly incorporated into Hezbollah.[11] From within Amal, members who left the party and joined Hezbollah included its third secretary-general, Hassan Nasrallah, and his deputy, Naim Qassem. The Lebanese Communist Party also contributed a number of leaders, as did the Islamist wing of an organization known as Harakat Fatah, from which the notorious Imad Mughniyah had come.[12]

Hizb al-Da'wa has been described as the essence of the newly formed Hezbollah, whereby the "al-Da'wa" of the name was dropped, and that party's ideology was given a more militant nature.[13] According to one explanation, Hezbollah was chosen as a name as it was free of past associations with other organizations and thus could help unite all Shiite Islamists drawn from competing groups.[14] Before 1985, when it declared the existence of its military wing, the Islamic Resistance, Hezbollah initially launched the majority of its attacks under the umbrella group called the Lebanese National Resistance (LNR), an organization described by author Hala Jaber as the "official resistance organization" of the Lebanese Shiites and one that had been dominated by Amal fighters.[15]

Hezbollah's early years have been described with longing and a touch of romanticism by its leaders past and present. Hezbollah's first secretary-general described it as following Khomeini's orders to "create a movement that springs from pure Islamic fundamentals, a movement that shakes the current situation."[16] The charismatic Nasrallah added nostalgically that Hezbollah was just "a resistance movement and nothing else. We were a young movement wanting to resist a legendary army [the IDF]. . . . The need was for men with the spirit of jihad, self-sacrifice, and endless giving. The only name that befits a group born with such motivations and spirit . . . is the name *Hezbollah*."[17]

Soon after Israel's invasion in 1982, Iran sent fifteen hundred Revolutionary Guards to the Bekaa Valley in order to train Hezbollah fighters. In the early years, Hezbollah's main base and area of operations were in the Bekaa Valley, specifically the city of Ba'albek. Only later did it move to southern Lebanon and some areas of Beirut (known as the "Belt of Misery"), especially after its battles with Amal.[18] In the city of Ba'albek, the Iranian Revolutionary Guards funneled huge amounts of money, weaponry, and expertise to train Hezbollah fighters in guerrilla warfare.[19] The terrain in Lebanon made guerrilla warfare a particularly effective type of combat, with its thick brush and vegetation, dense population, and hilly topography.[20] Up to that point Hezbollah had lacked the weapons and training to go along with its ideological zeal and calls for martyrdom.

NOTE

The group's initial goals were to lead the nascent Shiite insurgency against the Israelis and rid Lebanon of Western forces and influences. However, it also continued to associate itself with its ultimate goals that were listed in its 1985 Open Letter, including the creation of an Islamic state in Lebanon. To help achieve these goals, Hezbollah received the backing of the Iranians and the Syrians, who supported the group to varying degrees for their own purposes over time.[21] For Iran, having a proxy force in Lebanon allowed it to attack Israel, have a hand in the Arab-Israeli peace process (which it opposed), and expand Shiite influence in the Arab world.[22] Some experts believed that Iranian support for Hezbollah would weaken after the end of the Iran-Iraq War, yet that prediction proved false.[23] For the Syrians, its support initially aimed to provide a balance to other Lebanese groups (both Christian and Sunni) that it feared would become too powerful and would consequently block Syrian intervention or assistance. Syrian support for Hezbollah also made Israel and the West understand that it needed Syria if they ever wanted quiet along Israel's northern border or peace in the region.

During much of its existence, Hezbollah's relationship with non-Shiite Lebanese parties was very tense. As opposed to today when Hezbollah has been integrated into the Lebanese government and has assumed a Lebanese identity, in its earlier years Hezbollah was quite openly anti-Lebanese. Spokesperson Sayyid Ibrahim al-Amin explained at the time, "We in Lebanon do not consider ourselves as separate from the revolution in Iran, especially on the question of Jerusalem. We consider ourselves, and pray to God that it will become, part of the army which the Imam wishes to create in order to liberate Jerusalem. We obey his orders because we do not believe in geography but in change."[24] To be sure, in the early years Hezbollah officials and their allies stated numerous times that they did not recognize the legitimacy of the Lebanese government or its basis for existence, and they consequently refused to take part in the existing political system. As Tufayli once opined, "We do not work or think within the borders of Lebanon, this little geometric box, which is one of the legacies of imperialism. Rather, we seek to defend Muslims throughout the world."[25] To illustrate this point, in the past, Hezbollah rallies would include the party's flag as well as the flag of Iran, which it viewed as the flag of Islam and not just of the country of a sovereign state. Yet the Lebanese flag was conspicuously missing. In fact, Hezbollah rally participants frequently partook in the burning of the Lebanese flag, until this practice was ended by Sheikh Fadlallah, who believed that it was needlessly confrontational.[26] Although Iranian flags do not fly as prominently as they once did in Hezbollah-controlled zones such as south Lebanon, one can still find pictures of Iranian ayatollahs Khomeini and Khamenei in many Shiite homes and Hezbollah offices. Most recently, pictures of Venezuelan president Hugo Chavez have also begun showing up on street corners and posters, as his anti-American antics have made him a natural ally of Hezbollah and Iran.[27]

Examining Hezbollah's relations vis-à-vis the Lebanese government and people reveals significant changes from its earlier years. Just as Hezbollah used to burn the Lebanese flag and brandish the Iranian flag when it first emerged on the scene in Lebanon, it likewise engaged in other actions and attitudes toward all Lebanese that were much more openly extreme than they are today. Soon after it began to exert its influence in southern Lebanon, for example, Hezbollah enforced a strict code of Islamic behavior on the Shiite population. All actions considered to be prohibited by Islam were banned: sale of alcohol in restaurants and stores, participation in parties or other social gatherings, dancing, loud music, women in bathing suits, even coffee shops.[28] As one of the most moderate, diverse, and secular countries in the Arab world, these extreme interpretations of Sharia law imposed by Hezbollah were a shock to most Lebanese and resulted in a major backlash against the organization. At the same time, increasing attacks against Israeli forces and foreigners were leading to harsh retaliations and significant damage, resulting in an even greater level of dissatisfaction with Hezbollah among the Lebanese population. As a consequence of these policies, support for Hezbollah fell significantly toward the end of the civil war and before the organization's "political transition."[29]

Hezbollah's relationship with the Christian population had also been quite hostile in comparison to what it was later to become. The organization initially viewed Lebanon as being ruled by Christian "crusaders." As a result, cooperation with and assistance to the Christian population were limited to the restricted religious and social freedoms that Christians were to be allotted as *dhimmis*—members of a monotheistic faith that Muslims are required to grant a special status with limited rights and protections. Furthermore, Hezbollah members were supposed to urge the Christian population to convert to Islam. These actions raised the ire of the Christian community and diminished its otherwise growing support in some circles, which resulted from its "resistance" to Israeli occupation in southern Lebanon.[30]

In addition to these worries, in the 1980s Hezbollah had other concerns. Chief among these was its faltering relationship with Amal, as the Islamist group began to more effectively compete with its older and more secular sister organization. In terms of both military might and influence among portions of the Shiite population, Hezbollah emerged as the more significant Shiite party over time. As an ally and backer of Amal, the Syrians were also concerned about these changes. They had already lost much of their stature as a result of being badly beaten by the Israelis after the 1982 invasion, and they were increasingly worried that Hezbollah and Iran were on their way to creating another Islamist state in their most important backyard. As a result, Syrian troops initially backed Amal's attacks on the group and at times directly attacked Hezbollah forces themselves. These assaults helped reestablish the balance of power vis-à-vis Syria and Lebanon, as well as between Amal and Hezbollah.[31]

Hezbollah in Post-Taif Lebanon

In October 1989 members of Lebanon's various sects met in Taif, Saudi Arabia, to hammer out a more just allocation of government representation for Lebanese Muslims in order to help bring about an end to the civil war. The result of these negotiations was the ratification in November 1989 of the previously mentioned National Reconciliation Accord, better known as the Taif Accord. The agreement helped reorganize the government's power structure in Lebanon so that it would provide greater representation for what had become a majority Muslim population in Lebanon. It also reiterated Lebanese sovereignty over southern Lebanon, recognized and supported the Syrian role as power broker in the country, and called for Syria to facilitate the establishment of peace in Lebanon.[32] Finally, the accord demanded the complete disarmament of all Lebanese militias. Though the Taif Accord was never fully implemented, all but one of Lebanon's militias did by and large disarm, the exception of course being Hezbollah.[33]

Hezbollah not only remained armed but expanded its arsenal, training, and knowhow and became significantly more powerful during the fifteen years of Syrian tutelage. The organization has always argued that it was a "resistance" group and not a militia. It argued that it was consequently not in violation of the numerous UN resolutions or the Taif Accord, all of which called for a disarmament of all Lebanese militias. This view went generally unchallenged by the post-civil-war Lebanese government, which was due in part to Syria's endorsement of Hezbollah's right to retain its weapons. In the post-Taif political climate, when all of the primary, preexisting armed groups had been successfully dismantled, Hezbollah's strategy to preserve its military power focused on emphasizing its "exceptional" character and on reassuring all parties that its force existed solely to combat Israel and other foreign powers (aside from Syria and Iran)—and not to exert influence on other Lebanese groups or on the Lebanese government. Moreover, the fact that Hezbollah fighters (mostly) did not participate in the civil war and instead remained focused on fighting Israel also lent them a degree of legitimacy and respect within the various sects, while further contributing to the group's claim that it would not employ its weapons against other Lebanese citizens.[34]

Even though the post-civil-war arrangements allowed Hezbollah to keep its weapons arsenal and continue its armed "resistance" against Israel, the organization was still rather dissatisfied with the Taif Accord. Specifically, the group criticized the agreement for failing to repeal the confessional political system that had been a major factor in the eruption of the civil war in the first place. It also argued that Taif continued to favor the Christian and Sunni communities politically. Because the Shiites were believed to be the largest confessional group within Lebanon, they would benefit from the abolition of sectarianism and the introduction of a nonconfessional and proportional electoral system. Furthermore, although Syrian tutelage was mostly beneficial to Hezbollah, the new political arrangement nevertheless rendered the organization less autonomous and more restricted in its freedom of action because of the strict control that Syria exercised over the Lebanese polity.

Until the year 2005, Syria occupied and controlled much of Lebanon both politically and militarily, thereby also overseeing Iran's main channels of arms flow to Hezbollah. Furthermore, Syria had an interest in keeping Hezbollah in check, as it feared the Islamization and radicalization of the entire Lebanese Shiite community. In this sense, Syria consistently backed both Hezbollah and the group's main rival, the secular Amal. It was interested in preserving a balance of power between the two Shiite political organizations, mainly to prevent Hezbollah from becoming too strong. Overall, however, the Syrian presence was crucial for Hezbollah's growth, as it served both to contain the group's political enemies and to ensure that its weapons flow would not be questioned or threatened. As a result of this reality, during the 1990s and in the period leading up to the Syrian withdrawal in 2005, Hezbollah began to openly recognize the importance of its alliance with Syria in ensuring the Lebanese government's support for Hezbollah's military actions against Israel and its continued favored status.[35] Hezbollah's relationship with Damascus improved even further in the aftermath of the Israeli withdrawal in 2000 as a result of the internal leadership changes within Syria. After the death of Hafez al-Assad in 2000, his son Bashar proved to be a more sympathetic and vocal supporter of the group's anti-Israel activities and closer to Hezbollah's leadership on both a political and a personal level.[36]

This was the context for Hezbollah's open opposition to the Syrian withdrawal from Lebanon in 2005. Hezbollah was crucial in creating a political alliance with pro-Syrian parties and Amal, which in the winter of 2005 responded to the March 14–led protests that called for a Syrian withdrawal from Lebanon. Hezbollah was instrumental in organizing the pro-Syrian demonstrations in Beirut on March 8, 2005, that paralyzed the city. That event would later be chosen as the name of the Hezbollah-led opposition alliance, the March 8 coalition. In the aftermath of the Syrian withdrawal, Hezbollah has been a key party advocating for the restoration of a more solid political alliance with Damascus, and it has been very successful in this endeavor. Since the beginning of the wide protests against the Assad regime in early 2011, Hezbollah has taken a similarly supportive position, which has placed the group increasingly more at odds with ample sectors of the Lebanese population.

The Taif Accord not only marked the beginning of Hezbollah's alliance with Syria but also contributed to another fundamental change in the group's strategy: its formal entry into the political system and its direct participation in elections. In fact, Taif marked the end of hostilities and thus constituted a first incentive for all existing armed groups, including Hezbollah, to consider joining the post-civil-war political system. Hezbollah decided to follow the path of political integration when it chose to run in the 1992 parliamentary elections, which were the first to take place since the beginning of the civil war in 1975. That decision to run as a party was not an easy one for the organization, and it created a temporary internal rift. At the time, Hezbollah's second secretary-general, Sayyid Abbas al-Musawi was actively involved in pushing the group toward active domestic political involvement.[37] However, Musawi's views at the time were in sharp contrast to another "hardcore group" of Hezbollah supporters, led by the first secretary-general of the organization, Subhi al-Tufayli.[38]

Tufayli was openly against the prospects of joining the political system, and he claimed that running for office would mean renouncing the organization's resistance ethos and revolutionary structure. In the end, Tufayli's senior status and prestige within the organization were not powerful enough to overrule the will of those who advocated for political participation—a move that was supported by a dominant coalition within the organization and backed by Iran. As a result, Hezbollah decided to create a Parliamentary Council, which was placed under the supervision of the Central Council and the secretary-general. Hezbollah eventually participated in the 1992 elections, gaining 8 out of the 128 seats in the Lebanese Parliament. It ran again in the 1996, 2000, 2005, and 2009 parliamentary elections, as well as in the 1998 and 2004 municipal elections.[39] Before Hezbollah's participation in the elections, the organization had viewed cooperation with the Lebanese government as unacceptable because it opposed both the sectarian system and the concept of a government ruled by man-made laws (*al-qawanin al-wad'iyya*), such as a constitution and parliament. Before this transition, Hezbollah had refused to participate in any government other than one conceived around Islam and ruled according to Sharia law, like that of revolutionary Iran.

In this sense, joining the political system and accepting participation in a secular, confessional-based state represented a major watershed in Hezbollah's history. Consequently, the group's political participation led to many changes in how it related to other religious groups and political parties in Lebanon as well as in the way the group described its role domestically. First, Hezbollah adopted a Lebanon-oriented posture, accepting to participate in the local elections and to portray itself as a Lebanese nationalist movement—a stark change from its pre-1992 "revolutionary" phase.[40] Since the 1990s, Hezbollah had adopted a Lebanese and Arab undertone, and its rhetoric changed dramatically from rejecting and criticizing the Lebanese state to portraying the group as nationalistic and patriotic and even a savior of the Lebanese people.

Second, the organization started to rebuild relationships with other sectarian groups. In order to improve its standing among the Sunni and Christian communities, Hezbollah reversed course and removed most of its Islamic prohibitions that isolated it from so many of the Lebanese people. The organization also began to soften its rhetoric regarding the group's ambitions and its final goals for Lebanon. Although Hezbollah never accepted the Taif Accord and never failed to criticize its sectarian basis, the group became increasingly silent over its goals to establish an Islamic state. Similarly, Hezbollah actively reached out to other sectarian communities within Lebanon, reassuring them they would not attempt to modify the political order by force. In the months preceding the 1992 election, numerous interviews and statements from the secretary-general had precisely this purpose in mind. For instance, the secretary-general declared that "we never said we want to built an Islamic identity through oppression and compulsion at any level. . . . we should not build an Islamic government on oppression and coercion."[41] During the 1990s, the group also began to invest in cross-sectarian political alliances, and social-cultural exchanges to create a limited, yet existing network of supporters outside the Shiite community. At the same time, Hezbollah changed the direction in which it was heading with the Christian population and began a process of active engagement in an attempt to attain Christian cooperation in Lebanon and its support for guerrilla and terrorist activities against Israel. This policy became known as *infitah* (opening). Its new goal of a united front served to counter the Israelis, who had previously relied on the differences between the various Lebanese sects to increase their influence in the country.

Hezbollah's campaign to reach out to the Christians was multifaceted and included informal interfaith dialogues, meetings between Hezbollah-affiliated organizations and Christian groups (including youth movements), and formal political contacts between party members and Christian political and religious leaders.[42] The group also consistently relied on the achievements of its "resistance" against Israel to boost its support. In fact, following major Israeli attacks in Lebanon, the group was often able to improve relations with the Christian community.[43] Another episode that demonstrated Hezbollah's shift in its relations with Lebanon's Christians was the group's decision not to retaliate against pro-Israel Christian communities in the months after the Israeli withdrawal from its Security Zone in southern Lebanon. When Israel withdrew its military forces in 2000, many feared that Hezbollah would engage in bloody reprisals against former Israeli allies in the south. Yet such episodes of violence were almost nonexistent.[44]

Hezbollah also cultivated political relations with Christian parties and the community at large, evidenced by having Christians run on its tickets and winning elections in heavily Christian towns. Still, during the years of Syrian tutelage, Hezbollah and the Christian parties found themselves holding radically different views regarding the country's strategy and the political role of Syria in Lebanese affairs. Even during the protests leading up to the Syrian withdrawal, Sunni and the Christian communities basically coalesced in demanding the end of Syrian rule, whereas Hezbollah stood at the opposite extreme of the political spectrum by supporting it. As discussed in chapter 1, the situation changed in the aftermath of the withdrawal, when the Christian community split between March 14 and March 8 forces, and Hezbollah was able to create an alliance with General Michel Aoun.[45]

Allying with political parties that have radically different political platforms and visions is in line with Hezbollah's pragmatic approach to political participation. Hezbollah has exhibited a high level of pragmatism in creating ad hoc electoral alliances with a diverse range of political actors, including political opponent Rafik Hariri, and former military-foes-turned-political-allies such as the Christian Phalange Party.[46] Hezbollah and Amal have also participated in elections together, often running on the same ticket.[47] Although the two parties currently show substantial political affinity, the political alliance was largely a Syrian creation at first. In fact, after the prolonged armed confrontations between the two Shiite groups in the late 1980s, they were co-opted into a political coalition despite their reciprocal animosity. Though Amal was the dominant Shiite political party at the beginning of the 1990s, the situation has gradually changed, with the two groups now achieving substantial parity in their level of political representation, and with Hezbollah being the dominant force in dictating the political agenda for the Shiite community. This rise in popularity and importance is due both to the group's military activities and achievements against Israel and to the fact that since the end of the civil war Hezbollah has invested heavily in creating a vast social network of welfare services for the Lebanese Shiite population. Hezbollah's welfare system allowed the movement to develop strong social ties with the population, while also boosting public relations through its propaganda medium, delivered via the Internet and its popular satellite television station, Al-Manar. Another element that has contributed to Hezbollah's level of political support and popularity has been the group's pragmatism in devising political programs centered on social and economic development and emphasizing "bipartisan" social issues, such as social justice, anticorruption, and welfare reforms.[48]

Relying on these elements, Hezbollah has been able to successfully participate in the political system through its political party, and it has maintained a significant presence in government at the municipal, local, and central levels. Until 2005 Hezbollah restricted its political participation to Parliament, and refused to take part in the country's executive cabinet, regularly abstaining from awarding the vote of confidence to the elected prime minister.[49] In fact, Hezbollah wanted to remain strictly an opposition and "resistance" party and considered the possibility of joining the executive branch of government as problematic and at odds with both its ideological orientation and its critical view of the confessional political system in place within Lebanon.[50] The group was additionally concerned that joining the cabinet would somehow limit its autonomy and flexibility to continue its armed struggle. However, when Syria's grip on Lebanon collapsed and Hezbollah felt more vulnerable to attempts by political foes to disarm the organization, its position changed. The party finally joined the executive cabinet in Fouad Siniora's government, in which it held two cabinet posts.[51]

Even after joining the executive cabinet, however, Hezbollah's relations with the March 14–led government remained tense. The May 2008 armed clashes between Hezbollah and its political adversaries were the culmination of a political crisis that began in December 2006 between the March 14 majority coalition and the Hezbollah-led opposition. The hostilities were started over the March 14's efforts to establish an international mechanism to investigate and prosecute those responsible for killing Hariri, a process highly antagonized by Hezbollah and its allies. This lack of agreement led to the resignation of the March 8 opposition ministers from Fouad Siniora's cabinet in November 2006 and to a long-standing boycott that caused the de facto paralysis of the Lebanese government, which deeply impaired the decision-making process. The crisis escalated from peaceful protests to armed confrontation in May 2008, after the March 14 government attempted to remove Hezbollah sympathizer, Wafiq Shkeir, from his post as security chief at Beirut's Hariri International Airport and to shut down the organization's communication network that was run independently from the rest of the country. Because Hezbollah was unable to stop these reforms politically, it resorted to armed force and in May 2008 sent its gunmen to seize parts of West Beirut. This temporary takeover led to a series of bloody engagements between the different sectarian groups, leading to the worst episode of violence in Lebanon since the second civil war.[52]

Notably, the Lebanese military stayed above the fray in an effort to remain neutral. Hezbollah ultimately obtained the reversal of the provisions, and it agreed to enter a temporary "national unity" government after reaching an accord with the other Lebanese political parties in Doha, Qatar. Despite the popularity that Hezbollah enjoyed in many parts of the country and the efforts it made in the past two decades to improve relations with other sects, these episodes raised wide suspicion and discontent among sectors of the Sunni, Christian, and Druze communities. The May 2008 clashes also seemed to indicate that Hezbollah was increasingly willing to intimidate other Lebanese sects through the use of force, as its strength continued to grow with rising political, economic, and military support from Iran and Syria.

Observing Hezbollah's evolution and its increased participation in the political system, many scholars relate these changes to the organization's moderation, which on the surface may seemingly be the case. Domestically, the group abandoned some of its most divisive rhetoric. As it started to portray itself as a Lebanese and Arab nationalist movement, it came to be seen as a more mainstream political party and a widespread social movement, as it developed cross-sectarian relations and alliances. Although it is important to take all of these developments into consideration when analyzing Hezbollah's identity today, a different reading would suggest that the organization adopted a more Lebanese-oriented and accommodation-prone attitude for other reasons. Namely, after recognizing that the initially chosen route was not useful in reaching its goals, Hezbollah recognized that something drastic needed to be done. In other words, it did not act out of altruism or a desire to become a status quo, pacified political actor. As Joseph Alagha once explained, "Hizbullah's adherence to democratic principles and politics is not based on political-ideological grounds since its political ideology anathematized the Lebanese political system; rather [its adherence is based upon] advancing *al masalih* [interests]."[53] This reading suggests that though some have argued Hezbollah acts in such a manner because it has genuinely modified its stance with respect to its acceptance of democratic principles, it seems more accurate to argue that the group has simply modified its tactics to better reach its goals, while evolving and adapting to the changing political and security environment.

Regardless, it is undeniable that since 2005 the group's political activism has been rising steadily, not just as an opposition party but also as a full-fledged member of the executive. A case in point is certainly the party's role in both causing the collapse of the Saad Hariri government in January 2011 and backing the rise of a new, more pro-Syria government. In fact, in January

2011 Hezbollah and its political allies caused the collapse of the elected government after the resignation from the executive cabinet of the ten ministers of the Hezbollah-led March 8 coalition and of an "independent" minister who had been appointed by President Michel Suleiman. Hezbollah and its allies disagreed with the March 14 forces over how to continue Lebanon's cooperation with the UN Special Tribunal for Lebanon (STL), tasked with investigating the 2005 assassination of Rafik Hariri. Hezbollah had always ostracized and opposed the STL, but after rumors asserting that the tribunal would soon be issuing indictments against members of the Lebanese-Shiite militia in connection with the Hariri murder, the group's attitude with respect to the UN court became gradually more hostile. For example, in October 2010, Secretary-General Hassan Nasrallah declared: "Copies of whatever the international investigators collect are transferred to Israel . . . what is taking place is a violation. The investigation is over. The indictment that they say will be issued has been written since 2006. The issue is over." Furthermore, Nasrallah urged "every official in Lebanon and every citizen in Lebanon to boycott these investigations and not to cooperate with them," marking the peak of the anti-STL campaign.[54]

Not surprisingly, given the animosity Hezbollah had been expressing with respect to the tribunal, when the March 14 coalition refused to follow Hezbollah's lead in condemning the UN-led investigations and to open alternative domestic files, the opposition forces did not hesitate to resign from the cabinet, causing its collapse. Since then, Hezbollah has become a member of the parliamentary majority within the government, and it has been involved in the new cabinet created by Prime Minister Najib Mikati, thus becoming an increasingly prominent political force within Lebanon and further confirming its status as a *sui generis* hybrid armed and political organization. On June 30, 2011, the STL issued indictments and arrest warrants for four members of Hezbollah.[55] That reality, along with the Shiite organization's open support for the Assad regime in Syria, has led to increased polarization of support for Hezbollah in Lebanon.[56]

3   Ideals and Belief System

HEZBOLLAH'S IDEOLOGY and core principles are rooted in its religious beliefs and, as such, have remained constant throughout its political and military development. At the same time, the organization has shown a capacity to adapt its discourse to the changing security and political environment. To understand the evolution of Hezbollah's ideology, it is important to analyze the organization's main themes and narratives, as expressed by its two main declarations of principles: the 1985 Open Letter and the 2009 Manifesto.

The first declaration of principles, which many consider to be the foundational document of Hezbollah, was published on February 16, 1985, following the creation of the group in the early 1980s. Formulated in the midst of both the Lebanese civil war and the Israeli intervention in the country, the group's document reflected a Manichaean view of the world, divided between the forces of evil (namely, the West and its local allies) and the forces of good: the Party of God. The 2009 Manifesto was composed during the seventh political conference of the organization in the fall of 2009, and its creation was announced during a press conference in Beirut on November 30, 2009.[1] On that occasion, Hezbollah secretary-general Hassan Nasrallah personally read the organization's new Manifesto. The document is important because it is only the second ideological platform that Hezbollah has ever published and it was issued twenty-four years after the original Open Letter, which had been the main tool employed to convey the group's vision to the world over the preceding two decades. The document has four parts: an introduction, and three chapters on the state of the world ("Hegemony and Awakening"), the group's domestic policy ("Lebanon"), and its view on the Arab-Israeli conflict ("Palestine and the Settlement Negotiations"); it reflects the political and military evolution of the organization since the 1985 Open Letter and explains the group's strategic vision for the future. Although certain ideological pillars and central themes remain, such as the group's religious belief system and its assessment of its external enemies, the group's narrative and discourse—especially with respect to its role within Lebanon—has undergone a number of specific changes.

The Religious Pillars

Hezbollah is a self-described anti-imperialist and jihadi organization that views its battle against the West—led by the United States and spearheaded by Israel—as a fight for the very survival of Islam. Hezbollah's religious ideology consists of three pillars: belief in Shiite Islam, the *wilayat al-faqih* or the jurisconsult, and *jihad* in the way of God.[2] Shiite Islam—and Hezbollah in particular—holds that the average man lacks the intellect and moral capacity to fully understand the Quran, the Sunna (sayings of Mohammed), and the traditions of the imams. As a result, Shiite Islam traditionally holds that the imams serve as the "divine guides" of the community whom the people are encouraged to imitate. In the past, these imams had never been considered to be infallible, and members of the community had the option of choosing whom they would like to follow. With the rise of Ayatollah Khomeini's Iranian Revolution, and in sharp departure from more traditional notions of Shiite tradition, this all began to change.

Khomeini preached the theory of *wilayat al-faqih*, an elitist concept associated with the supremacy of senior Shiite clergy. According to this hierarchy of obedience, the *wali al-faqih* is the most divine source today on earth, appointed by the Prophet Mohammed himself. As such, "anybody who disobeys him [the *wali al-faqih*] or the jurists disobeys God himself."[3] This faith in strict obedience and unquestioning loyalty to the supreme religious clerics is unique to this sect of Shiite Islamists and provides their leadership with unprecedented powers. Previously, Shiite religious leaders had traditionally shied away from exercising their political strength. Hezbollah hopes that this belief system can unite the Sunni and Shiite communities. In actuality, however, the notion of divinity for the imams is antithetical to the Sunni belief system and is respected by few Sunni Islamist groups. The Palestinian Islamic Jihad is one group that adheres somewhat to this notion, and it should come as no surprise that PIJ is heavily supported by Iran, works closely with Hezbollah, and has been one of the Palestinian groups most radically opposed to any agreement, cease-fire or otherwise, with Israel.[4]

After the death of Khomeini in 1989, when Ali Khamenei was chosen to be the second supreme leader of Iran and the new *wali al-faqih*, fissures appeared within the Shiite Islamic leadership in Iran and Lebanon. Though he became the *wali al-faqih*, Khamenei had not held the important titles of *marja* or grand ayatollah before his ascension to the highest religious authority. As a result, many leading religious figures in Iran, such as Grand Ayatollah Hossein Al Montazeri—who had initially supported Khomeini—did not support his hand-picked successor, Khamenei. Leading Shiite Lebanese cleric Sheikh Fadlal-lah, who has been described as the spiritual leader of Hezbollah, neither pub-licly accepted nor challenged the notions of *wilayat al-faqih*, but it is known that he does not support them.[5] As a result of this difference of opinion with Hezbollah, the man who provided religious justification for attacking U.S. and other foreign targets while the Multinational Force (MNF) was deployed in Lebanon during its second civil war, and who had himself survived an assassination attempt as a result of his anti-American activities, distanced himself somewhat from Hezbollah for the past two decades.[6]

A View of the World: External Enemies and Allies

Hezbollah is an organization that seeks to emulate a revolutionary move-ment by searching for confrontation against Israel and the West in an effort to unite the Shiite community of Lebanon and in order to find a common pur-pose among its adherents and supporters. Hezbollah's core raison d'être lies in its "resistance" agenda with respect to Israel. In this sense, the group thrives on conflict, and it needs an ongoing confrontation with the Jewish state to maintain both external legitimacy and a wide supportive base. At the same time, the group's followers trust and support Hezbollah because of its success-ful record of providing a functioning welfare system to the Shiite community within Lebanon, in addition to its military activities.

The group aims to bring about a dramatic transformation in the inter-national order, starting with the destruction of Israel and a realignment of the power dynamic that the United States continues to lead.[7] Though it ultimately realizes that none of these changes will come overnight, Hezbollah patiently works within the system to help carry out its goals within Lebanon and abroad. Its policy of *infitah*, in its relations with other Lebanese political parties, is an example of one such tactic. While not supporting democracy as an ideal form of government, it uses the democratic system as a tool to strengthen the "re-sistance" in Lebanon. By building up its clout in terms of alliances with other sects and parties, as well as in its participation in both elections and actual government cabinet posts, Hezbollah attempts to implement its goals through other means when it finds that force is not a realistic option at that given time. Hezbollah has called for combating the enemy "by hand" or "by tongue"— whichever helps it better meet its goals.[8] Whenever possible, however, it will resort to the use of force or jihad against Israel, as this is one of the three central pillars of it existence. Hezbollah's members are encouraged to wage this struggle politically, economically, and spiritually. Within Lebanon and the political scene, it believes a struggle should be conducted through a bottom-up approach of working *within* the government to enhance its domestic position and its rights to hold weapons as well as to wage an ongoing war against Israel.[9] As a result, Hezbollah demonstrates that it is a multifaceted insurgency organization working both externally and internally.

Unlike Sunni Islamist groups such al Qaeda that support attacks against Arab regimes that are deemed un-Islamic (such as Jordan, Syria, Egypt and Saudi Arabia), Hezbollah traditionally does not publicly advocate for attacks against fellow Muslim and Arab states, although in recent years there are signs that this has begun to change as a result of Iranian influence.[10] It believes instead that once the more dangerous threats such as the United States and the rest of the West are defeated, the corrupt Arab regimes will lose their external support and thus fall by the wayside.[11] Hezbollah is quite fearful of the Salafi-extremist strain of jihad that is spreading throughout the Sunni Arab world, including strongholds in Lebanon. Unlike the rigid chain of command and control exhibited by Hezbollah fighters, Salafi-jihadists have very loose leadership and are not nearly as calculating in their spilling of blood. Hezbollah has sought to differentiate itself from al Qaeda, particularly in the post-9/11 era, as many have tried to highlight their similarities.[12] These differences have actually led to fighting between Sunni Islamist groups and Hezbollah fighters over the past few years, with Hezbollah calling for cease-fire agreements with different political strains of Salafi-jihadists.[13] Whereas Sunnis believe in the concept of the House of War (*Dar al-Harb*) and House of Islam (*Dar al-Islam*), Hezbollah views things more through the lens of the oppressed and the oppressor—in large part because of Shiite Islam's bloody history and centuries of discrimination.[14] This analysis of the world is present in both the 1985 Open Letter and the 2009 Manifesto. There is undoubtedly a deep continuity in both content and, to a lesser extent, language between the two documents. They both maintain the need to repeal the influence of the

West and its presence in the Islamic world, as well as to fight until the final destruction of the State of Israel.[15]

In addition to adopting and developing all of these concepts, the 2009 Manifesto showed a greater degree of political nuance. For instance, whereas the 1985 Letter referred to the United States and the West as an evil and oppressing force upon the Muslim world, the 2009 declaration of principles describes the United States' world plan in terms of seeking global "hegemony" and emphasized the negative impact of globalization on Muslim and Arab identity.[16] In other words, although completely similar in content, the 2009 document better reflects the organization's growing understanding of international politics and its attempt to employ terminology and notions that are commonly associated with the "antiglobalization," "leftist" movement. This is done in an effort to transcend its national and regional boundaries, identify itself as an international faction, and recruit these movements to its cause.

To support this endeavor to be increasingly "global," Hezbollah now clearly associates itself, for example, with the "independent and free endeavor that opposes hegemony in Latin American states" and notes the common contribution to "building a more balanced and just international system."[17] Similarly, the organization adopts a more nuanced approach toward Europe. Instead of openly attacking the continent as it did in 1985, it chooses instead to criticize Europeans for their "subjugation to U.S. policies," while reminding them of their "special responsibility pursuant to the colonial heritage" inflicted on the region, as well as Europe's "long history with resisting the occupier."[18]

In the 2009 platform, Hezbollah adds another important political element that was absent in the 1985 Open Letter, and one that signals that the group sees itself as part of the "regional resistance axis": it openly acknowledges its regional allies. The 2009 Manifesto praises Syria for its role in supporting the "resistance" against Israel and in lending continuous support to Hezbollah. It also openly advocated closer ties between Lebanon and Syria and remained a backer of the Assad regime.[19] While doing so, Hezbollah reiterates its political and ideological alliance with Iran, by stating that "Hezbollah considers Iran as a central state in the Islamic world since it is the state that dropped through its revolution the Shah's regime and its American-Israeli projects. It's also the state that supported the resistance movements in our region and stood with courage and determination at the side of the Arab and Islamic causes on top of which is the Palestinian cause."[20] Interestingly, however, the 2009 Manifesto remains silent with respect to the role that the Islamic Republic has been play-ing in supporting Hezbollah. The absence of references to this strategic part-nership between them is probably connected with Hezbollah's quest to be per-ceived, especially domestically, as a Lebanese national movement.

The other main theme that remains unaltered in content since 1985 is its view of the State of Israel. Israel had been the organization's primary enemy and its raison d'être since its founding in the early 1980s. In Hezbollah's world-view, the struggle against Israel is defined in existential-defensive terms: "Israel represents an eternal threat to Lebanon. . . . The role of the Resistance is a na-tional necessity as long as Israeli threats and ambitions to seize our lands and waters continue."[21]

As a result of Hezbollah's views on Israel, it believes that all acts of "resis-tance" against the Jewish state are legitimate and cannot be considered terror-ism. Whether or not these acts target civilians or soldiers, they are all seen as lawful because the Jews are "occupiers."[22] Hezbollah places a particular focus on the city of Jerusalem and the importance of liberating it from Israeli control. Jerusalem is Judaism's holiest city but is also Islam's third holiest, after Mecca and Medina. As a result, it is given particular importance by Hezbollah, as is the case in Palestinian and Arab narratives today.[23] Jerusalem (al Quds) Day is a day that Hezbollah uses to carry out parades and boast its military might, while using the theme of Jerusalem to tug at the hearts of Muslims worldwide in an effort to unite Sunnis and Shiites against Israeli and American policies.[24]

Hezbollah is more than just anti-Zionist; it also exhibits a rabid streak of anti-Semitism, replete with Nazi-like salutes and goose-step marches.[25] In ad-dition, like most other Islamist extremist and terrorist organizations, Hezbol-lah engages in pure Holocaust denial. It simply rejects any notion at all that the Jews were exterminated during the Holocaust. Some supporters of Hez-bollah, however, choose instead to deny the enormity of the Holocaust rather than its actual existence. Hezbollah's anti-Semitism, however, pervades the organization much more extensively than just Holocaust denial and conspir-acy theories. Despite the rare occasions where Hezbollah officials have stated they are anti-Zionist and not anti-Semitic, these words do not hold up upon closer examination. Hassan Nasrallah put it quite plainly when he said, "If we searched the entire world for a person more cowardly, despicable, weak and feeble in psyche, mind, ideology and religion, we would not find anyone like the Jew. Notice I do not say the Israeli."[26] Notably, during the 2006 war between Israel and Hezbollah, the Islamist group apologized only for killing Israeli Arabs, who are not Jewish.[27]

On this topic, it is clear that there has been no significant change, in either content or form, with Hezbollah's prime organizational duty, which remains "resistance." Similarly, almost three decades of organizational development and political integration have not led to any shift in Hezbollah's total opposition to a negotiated agreement between Israel and the Arab world. The group affirms its strong and absolute opposition to the principle of negotiations with the State of Israel and claims that negotiating with the Jewish state is tantamount to recognizing its "right to exist as a Jewish State"—a position that the PLO and Palestinian Authority, for example, do not see as mutually exclusive.[28] Hezbollah's initial raison d'être was to resist the Israeli occupation of southern Lebanon at all costs. The organization views Israel's very creation as an act of terrorism and sees Israel as the personification of state terrorism and Western imperialism.[29] In sum, Hezbollah's "foreign policy" has not changed in substance between 1985 to the time of publication, even if some of the terminology now employed by the organization shows a growing internal push to be recognized at the international level and transcend its regional identity.

Hezbollah in Lebanon: A Political and Military Platform

In contrast to Hezbollah's foreign policy, which has shown remarkable continuity throughout its development, the organization's view of its role within Lebanon has shifted considerably since its original formulation. In the 1985 Open Letter, Hezbollah called for the establishment of an Islamic state within Lebanon and rejected the possibility of participating in what it saw as the inherently corrupt existing political system.[30] In the organization's view of the world, the creation of this Lebanese Islamic state would be modeled after Iran and would be only the first step toward the establishment of a larger, pan-Islamic state that would unite all Muslims in the region under the same government.[31] Significantly, the 2009 Manifesto dropped all calls for creating an Islamic state; it failed to mention it even once in the entire text of the document and instead recognized that the Lebanese political system is the most suitable environment for Hezbollah's operations. Rather than openly calling for the creation of an Islamic state as was done in the Open Letter, the 2009 Manifesto called for the creation of a "political system that

truly represents the will of the people and their aspirations for justice, freedom, security, stability, well-being, and dignity."[32]

In truth, however, this shift in domestic priorities did not come as a surprise
to those who had observed Hezbollah's political evolution during the past decades. In fact, concurrent to the organization's first decision to take part in
the elections in the early 1990s, Hezbollah began to publicly refrain from
promoting the goal of creating an Islamic state, as it recognized that the political reality of Lebanon did not allow for the realization of an Islamic republic at this time.[33] Ever the keen observer of political currents, Hezbollah understood that it should not bite off more than it could chew. Notably, the 1985
Open Letter did clearly state that its leaders called "for the implementation
of the Islamic system based on a direct and free choice of the people, and not
through forceful imposition as may be assumed by some."[34] Hezbollah started
to increasingly emphasize this point over the years. It stressed its belief in the
principle of noncompulsion in Islam, declaring its opposition to an attempted
conversion of other Lebanese citizens by force.

Hezbollah's public renunciation of the goal of creating an Islamic state in
Lebanon was more a confirmation of an ongoing trend and a recognition of
Lebanon's political reality than it was a real strategic change. Needless to say,
the statement did not reveal the group's acceptance of Lebanon's parliamentary democracy as the final optimal system of government, but it was an important recognition that the group's discourse had shifted in the past two
decades, as it now adopted a more pragmatic and accommodative tone. Similarly, Hezbollah chose to refrain from publicly advocating for a pan-Islamist
state—another shift from 1985. In the 2009 Manifesto, the group stated that
"what we call for today is not a merging unity in the Arab or Islamic world.
We rather call for the unity between Arab and Islamic states which guards
these states' and nations' specifications and sovereignty."[35]

Similarly, the newer ideological platform gave prominence to a series of
political themes that Hezbollah had developed over the past two decades,
such as the importance of administrative decentralization and its open objec-
tion to both federalism and the current sectarian system.[36] As the document

affirmed, "The main problem in the Lebanese political system which prevents
its reform, development and constant updating is political sectarianism."[37]
While placing the abolition of confessionalism among its priorities, Hezbollah
also claimed that, until this goal was achieved, it would support a governance
model based on consensual democracy.[38] This point is particularly important,

for by reading between the lines one can find an expression of Hezbollah's new understanding of its political power and subsequent status in Lebanon. By stressing the need for a consensual democracy and a national unity government, the document's message was that Hezbollah sees itself as a major political player and that regardless of the electoral results, all elected governments should take this reality into consideration. It was this result that the 2009 elections produced, in which the majority coalition could not actually govern without a larger alliance with the Hezbollah-led opposition forces.[39] In the end, this arrangement did not prove to be enduring. The tensions between the March 14 forces and the opposition parties led by Hezbollah eventually resulted in a full-fledged political crisis, causing the collapse of the national unity government led by Saad Hariri in January 2011. In Lebanon, the majority March 14 coalition openly criticized the group's demands, emphasizing that Hezbollah's proposal for a consensual democracy went against the Lebanese Constitution, which declared the country to be a parliamentary democracy instead.[40]

An additional significant development in the 2009 Manifesto was Hezbollah's vision of its military role in Lebanon. On this front, the group was extremely clear about its intention to continue to maintain its armed structure and its refusal to even discuss disarmament. In a press conference following the release of the 2009 declaration, Secretary-General Nasrallah specified that national consensus over the "resistance" agenda is indeed desirable but not necessary, alluding to the fact that Hezbollah's armed struggle against Israel would continue despite domestic opposition arising against it.[41] Furthermore, on this topic, the document stated that "the continuous Israeli threats oblige Lebanon to endorse a defensive strategy that couples between popular resistance that participates in defending the country and an army that preserves the security of the country and safeguards its stability in a complementary process that has proved in the previous phase to be successful."[42]

The preceding statement is particularly interesting for a number of reasons. First, it showed Hezbollah's transition since 1985, from considering the Lebanese Army as an enemy to treating it as a de facto auxiliary force. In this sense, it challenged the expectation that Lebanon's armed forces would eventually have either the capacity or the interest in turning a cooperative relationship into a confrontational one, whereby it would pursue an eventual disarmament of the Lebanese-Shiite armed group. Second, the statement downplayed the efforts of the National Dialogue Council, which had been created to investigate issues such as finding national solutions to Hezbollah's independent arms cache and other projects calling for the group's dissolution into the army. Hezbollah had been adamant about its interest in conducting "resistance" in cooperation with the army only as long as its forces remained a separate and autonomous entity. This was another point that was criticized in a statement by the March 14 forces, as they explained that Hezbollah's claims to have a monopoly over the "resistance" and its treatment of the state and the army as the main supporting figures in the fight against Israel were highly problematic. Indeed, the statements directly contradicted the Taif Accord, which tasked the state of Lebanon as a whole with achieving "liberation."[43]

In a speech by Secretary-General Hassan Nasrallah in November 2009, he laid out Hezbollah's defense to this argument: "As for the decision of peace or war, it is exclusively in the hands of the state. . . . The problem is in the absence of the state and it being responsible. It is not enough to give the state this privilege. The state is absent." He added, "The state . . . will be responsible for protecting the country. There will be no need to have a public resistance."[44] Although it is certainly legitimate to question whether Hezbollah would be ready to follow through on its words and disarm, it is still significant to note how the organization's overall tone and discourse have developed since its original irredentist document back in 1985.

In conclusion, Hezbollah has shown a certain degree of change in terms of its domestic policy. The organization finally recognized that the Lebanese political system is the best arena for the organization to develop, thus removing all references to its goal of creating an Islamic state. However, its action should be interpreted not as a sign of weakness or retreat but rather as an indication that the group has become so entrenched in the political system that it now demands increased decision-making power. Finally, the group has maintained a "business as usual" posture with respect to its armed wing, by specifying its intention to remain a separate and autonomous armed group, whereby it can retain its weapons and its pose of "resistance." Thus, in essence, its 2009 Manifesto demonstrated the growing power of the organization and helped provide political cover by appearing to move toward moderation while simultaneously dismissing any internal talks about military integration, let alone disarmament.

4 Structure

AS LEBANON'S LARGEST and most powerful militia, whose strong political party is publicly backed by Syria and Iran, Hezbollah today has the luxury of maintaining a complex and relatively open leadership hierarchy in comparison to many of its Sunni-Islamist counterparts. For much of its history, however, the Shiite group was an underground organization. Though its military wing, the Islamic Resistance, is still hidden under a tight veil of secrecy, the organization as a whole enjoys a rather surprising openness today. From its headquarters in the Dahiyeh neighborhood of Beirut, Hezbollah operates everything from hospitals, schools, and construction companies to television channels, radio networks, and newspapers. It does all of this even as it oversees its military and "resistance" activities.

Political and Military Structure

As Hezbollah's secretary-general, Hassan Nasrallah sits at the head of the organization. The role of secretary-general had traditionally been somewhat of an honorary title, as the majority hold on power was collectively shared in the hands of the seven-member Shura Council (Majlis al-Shura) that is responsible for the "overall administration, planning and policy making" of the organization.[1] Members of the Shura Council are elected for a period of three years by the Central Council (Majlis al-Markazi), a group of nearly two hundred senior leaders and founders of the organization. Though it is not technically required, the Shura Council tends to be composed of one lay leader and six clerics, in keeping with a ratio that ensures that the group's religious ideology is never compromised.[2] When the Shura Council is convened, its members meet to elect the secretary-general and his deputy. Members of the Shura Council split responsibility for overseeing five executive groups: the Executive Council, Politburo, Parliamentary Council, Judicial Council, and the Jihad

Council. Of these, the first two units are the oldest and traditionally most powerful. These executive groups run the organization from the top down. All decisions by the Shura Council are taken either unanimously or by majority and are not only final but religiously binding for its members. In the event of a deadlock, the decision is passed on to the *wali al-faqih*, whose decision is also final and religiously binding.[3]

Before Hassan Nasrallah took control of the Office of the Secretary-General, the position had been much more collective and included a two-term limit, with each term lasting three years. Nasrallah assumed his position after the assassination of Abbas al-Musawi in an Israel Defense Forces helicopter strike. A charismatic, religious, intelligent leader and shrewd politician, Nasrallah has strong ties to Iran's Ayatollah Khamenei as well as to the Islamic Resistance. He has been in power since 1992 thanks to Khamenei's changing of the election rules in order to secure his continued leadership.[4] After the Israeli withdrawal from Lebanon in 2000 and the summer 2006 hostilities between Hezbollah and the Jewish state, Nasrallah became one of the most popular figures in the Arab and Muslim worlds and the face of Hezbollah.[5] His popularity was further magnified, and his position further legitimized, as a result of meetings held between him and many world leaders, including UN secretary-general Kofi Annan, who visited with him in 2000.[6] Nasrallah's popularity in the Muslim world is particularly impressive considering that he is Shiite—a fact not lost on the Sunni-dominated Arab leadership, which is increasingly wary of the Shiites' growing strength in concert with Syria and Iran. Admiration for Nasrallah pleases the Iranians greatly, as it serves to ingratiate them within the Sunni Arab street. Supporting the popular Nasrallah also serves Syrian interests, as he in turn legitimizes Syria's continued (albeit more concealed) presence in Lebanon.[7] While Hezbollah spokesmen accuse Israel and the West of continued interference in Lebanese affairs, they nonetheless continue to praise Syria and have publicly welcomed Syria's previous military and political presence in Lebanon.

Nasrallah's persona took on a life of its own after the 2006 war with Israel. From that point on, Nasrallah has provided the public face of the organization, though he is consequently constantly in hiding because of fear of assassination. Although he continues to play a critical role in the Islamic Resistance military wing, some of his powers have been removed by the Iranians because of what they felt was a miscalculation and poor performance during the 2006 war with Israel.[8] In fact, reports have indicated that a top Iranian

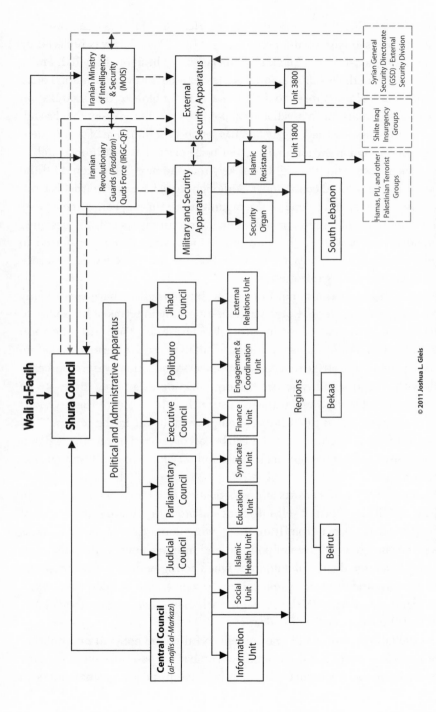

Hezbollah leadership structure. Based in part on Hamzeh, In the Path of Hizbullah, 46.

© 2011 Joshua L. Gleis

Revolutionary Guard Corps officer named Hossein Mahadavi had been installed to oversee Hezbollah operations and that Nasrallah was replaced by Deputy Secretary-General Sheikh Naim Qassem as head of Hezbollah's military wing.[9] Nonetheless, his removal as a leader—either by assassination or by internal political pressure—would cause a striking blow to the organization from both a military and a psychological point of view. In the event that Nasrallah were to be assassinated, Hezbollah has set up a continuation of government (COG) that would allow for a new leader to be elected almost immediately.[10] Yet in such a scenario it is highly unlikely that the next leader could fill the shoes of such a beloved commander. Although some have opined that Nasrallah's loss would spell the end of the organization, this appears to be a gross exaggeration, as the group's organizational structure is specifically designed to handle such problems, and control has increasingly been transferred to Iranian agents.[11] The reality is, however, that his departure would be a serious setback for the organization.

Nasrallah's influence is not lost on the Iranians. They have successfully limited his control over the organization, especially in terms of his ability to make decisions that can cause an outbreak of hostilities. Thus, after the 2006 war with Israel, the Iranians required Nasrallah to receive permission before carrying out a major strike that could cause the organization's vast resources— and, with it, Iran's ability to use the organization as a proxy force—to be squandered.[12] The Iranians want to ensure that they control the decisions that could mean the difference between peace and war in the region. They also want to make certain that the Hezbollah organization remains a deterrent against those who might seek to use military force to end Iran's nuclear program.

Hezbollah has made efforts at diversification of its financial revenues, investing heavily in efforts at self-sufficiency in order to achieve some degree of financial independence from Iran. Its growing domestic and regional status has given the group additional political and military power. Although Hezbollah has a large degree of autonomy when acting within the Lebanese domestic arena, and its military and political strength confers upon it an important regional role as well, the strategic partnership between Hezbollah and Iran is still the core of the organization.

Hezbollah relies on its Shura Council to fulfill the political and military decision-making processes. The organization has purposely removed as many intermediaries between the top military leadership and local commanders on the ground as a precaution against Israeli intelligence infiltration. Hezbollah's great respect for Israeli intelligence borders almost on paranoia. In general, once the green light for an operation is given, the small command involved in its planning, execution, and tactics handles all decision making.[13] Israeli intelligence officials have expressed their frustration with the ideologically driven Hezbollah fighters, who have been less susceptible to the lures that their fellow Arab and Muslim brethren have fallen victim to over the years, especially what are known in Israeli intelligence circles as the three "kafs" or Ks—*kesef* (money), *kavod* (respect), and *kussit* (a crude name for a woman), which are often used by intelligence agencies to attract potential spies.[14]

While the overall organization exhibits a formal hierarchical structure, its military wing is quite the opposite. In order to more effectively conduct irregular warfare, the military's fighters are covert, its operations are highly secretive, and its command-and-control incredibly mobile. Timur Goksel, formerly of UNIFIL, explained how Hezbollah's fighters do it: "They don't work in military hierarchies or military command levels. They don't have anything like that. There is one leader in Beirut and all the other units in the field are autonomous; they know what they are doing [by themselves]."[15]

In addition, no analysis of Hezbollah's organizational structure would be complete without at least a brief discussion of its shadowy External Security Apparatus. The ESA is a separate entity from the Islamic Resistance and is responsible for conducting terrorist attacks and other operations outside the immediate confines of the Lebanese-Syrian-Israeli borders. Working with the Iranian Revolutionary Guards Corps (IRGC) and the Iranian Ministry of Intelligence and Security (MOIS), and occasionally with Syrian intelligence, the group is tasked with being Hezbollah's long arm. It often works in conjunction with Iranian spies around the world, using Iranian diplomatic posts as part of its cover.[16] Although the ESA is not officially recognized as even existing—its mention is ignored by Hezbollah officials or dismissed as propaganda—it has played an important role in attacking Jewish, Western, and other targets around the world.[17]

Within the External Security Apparatus, there are various special units. The best-known is Unit 1800, tasked with conducting operations in Israel and the Palestinian territories. Unit 1800 establishes contact and works in conjunction with Palestinian groups, including the Palestinian Islamic Jihad, Hamas, and other terrorist organizations, in order to strike at Israeli targets. The unit provides military training, expertise, and funding to Palestinian groups and has also recruited Palestinians to conduct operations directly under its control.[18] Unit 3800 (formerly Unit 2800) is responsible for training Shiite fighters operating against U.S. and government forces in Iraq.[19]

The ESA was reportedly led by Imad Mughniyah until his assassination allegedly by the Israeli Mossad in February 2008 in Damascus. Mughniyah had been on the FBI's most-wanted terrorist list for decades, with a $25 million bounty on his head for his involvement in multiple attacks against U.S. citizens, including hijackings, kidnappings, tortures, and suicide bombings. Nicknamed "the Fox" for his ability to evade capture, he was believed to have been behind every major terrorist attack by Hezbollah over the past two decades, was considered a role model for Osama bin Laden, and helped coordinate operations with the Syrians and Iranians. Mughniyah helped plan terrorist attacks as far away as Argentina and as close as the bombing of the U.S. Marine Corps barracks in Beirut in 1983. His elimination was a significant loss to Hezbollah's planning capabilities. After many years of speculation, his successor is reported to be his protégé, Talal Hamiyah.[20]

Despite Hamiyah's appointment, Mughniyah's death changed the makeup of the external security apparatus forever. Secretary-General Nasrallah had reportedly feared the independence and power that Mughniyah had wielded and therefore watered down his successor's powers. By no means, however, has Mughniyah's demise spelled an end to the group's ability to carry out terrorist attacks. The ESA still has the potential to plan and perpetrate international operations abroad, and it continues to do so. Its men have been found conducting surveillance against U.S. targets in Southeast Asia and South America, as well as Jewish and Israeli targets in North America, Central Asia, Africa, and elsewhere around the world.[21] In the summer of 2010, U.S. representative Sue Merrick of North Carolina reported that there is a growing fear of Hezbollah operatives being smuggled into the United States. She explained that in prisons holding illegal immigrants who had crossed the U.S-Mexican border, there are gang members with tattoos in Farsi that demonstrate a "Persian influence that can likely be traced back to Iran and its proxy army, Hezbollah."[22]

Social Welfare

Hezbollah's social welfare network is another critically important part of its structure and one that, not surprisingly, was modeled after the Iranians. Beginning in 1984, Iran and Hezbollah teamed up to establish this network in order to transform Lebanon's poor Shiite neighborhoods into self-reliant districts, after years of neglect during the civil war by Lebanon's defunct central government. Most of the areas traditionally inhabited by the Shiite community, including southern Lebanon, the Bekaa Valley, and the southern suburbs of Beirut, were also Lebanon's poorest and most marginalized districts. The Lebanese state had failed to provide even basic services in these areas, and Hezbollah's intervention filled the gap created by the government's absence. In general, the Lebanese government did not regard Hezbollah's involvement in the delivery of social and political goods as a negative factor, as these interventions relieved substantial social pressure on the state itself. Accordingly, the unspoken understanding between Hezbollah and the government has been a reciprocal "noninterference" and mutual assurance: as long as Hezbollah does not negatively interfere in Lebanon's economic considerations, it is by and large left alone.[23] At the same time, there are also instances where the two parties cooperate on smaller-scale municipal projects and even work hand in hand on issues of shared interest.

Hezbollah is not the sole social movement and political organization that focuses its efforts on obtaining and providing social goods and services to its main constituency, which in the case of Hezbollah is the Shiite community. In fact, in the context of Lebanon's highly clientelist political system, the traditional role of confessional parties (and, during the civil war, of sectarian militias) included appropriating and distributing political and social goods along confessional lines as a way to boost a party's popularity within its own constituency. However, unlike the confessional groups, Hezbollah was able to fund its services independent of the state, making the organization stronger and more autonomous than its political and military counterparts and rivals.[24] Hezbollah's social welfare network extends to all of the Shiite areas in Lebanon, comprises a wide array of social services, and is managed through a network of numerous NGO-like organizations. The group focuses on poverty alleviation and economic and social development. Most of these interventions are implemented through the Construction Jihad (Jihad al-Binaa) organization, created specifically to help rebuild and revitalize Shiite communities. A complex and multifaceted NGO, Construction Jihad has been involved in water sanitation, rural development, and construction projects and traditionally also plays an important role in rebuilding the homes of Hezbollah members and supporters that have had them destroyed as a result of combat with Israel.

Hezbollah's social welfare system is also in charge of administering a network of basic social services, including education and health care. The group offers free schooling for children and adolescents and free medical services through the hospitals and clinics it runs. These Lebanese facilities were originally maintained solely for Hezbollah supporters but in many cases are now available to the Lebanese public at large. The organization also runs traditional charitable organizations that dispense financial aid to the most vulnerable groups within the Shiite community. The group's Relief Committee, for example, helps provide both financial and material aid to those it identifies as the neediest, including orphans, widowers, and the sick.[25] Importantly, Hezbollah is a participant in the Iranian Martyrs Foundation and other organizations established to assist fighters, their families, and civilians who have been either killed or injured in fighting with Hezbollah's adversaries, footing the vast majority of the bills for this group.[26] Hezbollah's support does not stop there. The organization not only acts as a traditional charity but also takes over many of the basic roles and tasks of local government. For instance, Hezbollah regularly runs garbage collection, waste management, water delivery, and other basic needs for Shiite Lebanese communities.

The programs administered by Hezbollah serve two critically important purposes. First, by supporting Lebanon's largest (and historically most neglected) sector of the population, Hezbollah ensures that it maintains the public's support, which is critical to the success of any insurgency movement. This has proved particularly useful as Hezbollah has demonstrated that it is considerably more organized and effective—not to mention less prone to corruption than the Lebanese government—in providing necessary social services. Accordingly, Hezbollah's successful track record in providing and maintaining an effective social welfare system to serve the Shiite community has earned the organization a certain degree of respect because of its transparency and efficiency in assisting its constituents. This reputation has helped Hezbollah in building its identity as a Lebanese national movement and in transitioning from a radical and isolated militia in the mid-1980s to the mainstream political organization that it represents today. Second, by maintaining its social welfare network and providing basic social services to the Shiite community, Hezbollah is able to disarm potential critics of the organization's more divisive policies related to its military affairs, allowing the group to continue to be less constrained by public pressure and norms.

Fundraising

Fundraising has become an increasingly important aspect of an insurgency's ability to effectively wage war both on and off the battlefield. More than a decade after 9/11, Hezbollah continues to be the largest state-sponsored terrorist organization in the world. Iranian funds have been critical in both creating and keeping the organization operational and have been crucial in supporting both the group's military activities and its political and social programs. It is impossible to determine with certainty the exact amount of financial support that Hezbollah receives from Iran; however, estimates range from a minimum of $200 million annually through official financial institutions to a much larger $1 billion a year—not including military assistance.[27] Under Iranian presidents Rafsanjani and Khatami, Hezbollah's funding was believed to have been cut by as much as 70 percent, but this number has since risen dramatically under the stewardship of Mahmoud Ahmadinejad.[28] It is not Ahmadinejad that is the real powerbroker in this case though but rather the *wali al-faqih*, Ali Khamenei. As supreme leader of Iran, Khamenei directs Iranian charities and foundations to pay Hezbollah without prior approval from the Ministry of Finance or the president. His ultimate control over Iran's Revolutionary Guard Corps (with whom his relations have traditionally been quite strong) and intelligence services allows him to direct further funding and expertise to Hezbollah's military branch, the Islamic Resistance.[29] Hezbollah's unyielding support for Khamenei's leadership has ingratiated the organization with the *wali al-faqih* and ensured its continued funding.

Most of Hezbollah's money is managed through Iranian state-owned banks, such as the Saderat, which was until the enactment of additional international sanctions less susceptible to U.S. pressure and international sanctions than other banks. They issue funds to Hezbollah through Lebanese and Gulf offices, where the money lies without collecting interest, as interest is banned under Islamic law.[30] Other sources of income come from a tithe known as *khums*, an Islamic tax that is supposed to correspond to one-fifth of people's annual income and that represents a form of *zakat*, or charity. In addition to these funds, many companies, banks, and other businesses from Lebanese and Shiite communities around the world donate money to the organization.[31] Although these "donations" are usually voluntary, they are sometimes forced upon the population, who pay out of fear of the repercussions they will suffer if they refuse.[32] Finally, Hezbollah is increasingly involved in a self-generation of revenues, by acquiring funds from investments it is making around the world. While some of these investments are legal and legitimate, many are highly illegal.[33]

Hezbollah's financial operations are extensive and global in their range. It is heavily involved in an area of South America known as the tri-border area or "triple frontier" region—a lawless corner of South America where Paraguay, Brazil, and Argentina meet. It also has an increasing political and military stronghold in Venezuela.[34] In addition to operating in South America, Hezbollah is very involved in the relatively lawless areas of Central and West Africa; two more regions where Shiite Lebanese expatriates live in large numbers. While its extensive involvement in Africa's illegal diamond trade is relatively well known, Hezbollah has more generally increased its involvement in West African commercial sectors. According to testimony before the U.S. House Subcommittee on International Terrorism and Proliferation, donations and other sources of funding in Africa are very difficult to track as they are made in cash and collected by Hezbollah couriers who make their way into and out of the country.[35] Hezbollah fundraising is not just prevalent in lawless areas but throughout the globe. In the United States, Hezbollah is well known for having run cigarette smuggling and credit card fraud operations.[36] Its members have attempted to purchase dual-use technologies and gain U.S. citizenship through staged marriages, green cards, and asylum applications.[37] The organization has generally been at the forefront of the nexus between criminal activity and terrorist groups.[38]

Hezbollah fundraising activities are banned in the United States, where the group has been classified as a foreign terrorist organization (FTO) since 1997. It was later further labeled a specially designated global terrorist (SDGT) entity in October 2001.[39] Yet, at the same time, the organization can still legally fundraise in much of Europe as well as nearly all other countries in the world. Indeed, few countries have labeled the Hezbollah organization in its entirety as a terrorist group.[40] Even in countries with strong antiterrorism laws, many of these states differentiate between Hezbollah's social welfare programs and its political party, treating those entities separately from Hezbollah's military wing. This is the position taken, for example, by most of the countries belonging to the European Union, where individual Hezbollah leaders have been classified as "terrorists" even while the group as a whole has not been labeled a terrorist organization. Consequently, many European states permit Hezbollah to collect funds on the basis that they are used to fund hospitals, schools, and other social welfare programs and not used for terrorist or insurgency activity. Ensuring that such moneys do not go to Hezbollah's military wing is very difficult to accomplish, as there is ultimately no real division between the coffers of Hezbollah's social welfare network and its military wings. Even when these fundraising activities are monitored to ensure a separation, it simply allows for moneys from other sources to be directly diverted for military purposes.[41]

Latin America and the Tri-Border Area as a Case Study

The tri-border area, which includes the Brazilian city of Foz de Iguazú, the Argentinean city of Puerto Iguazú, and Ciudad del Este in Paraguay, has served for the past twenty years as the operational and logistical center for international terrorist groups such as Hezbollah, along with a number of transnational criminal organizations. The area has a population of approximately 700,000 inhabitants, including roughly 30,000 of Arab descent. The Arab community constitutes one of the largest immigrant groups in the region and is predominantly made up of Shiite Lebanese, particularly in the cities of Ciudad del Este and Foz.[42] The tri-border region is one of the most important commercial centers of South America, with approximately 20,000 people transiting on a daily basis into the free-trade area of Ciudad del Este from neighboring states. The volume and variety of people and goods, together with its porous borders, are two important factors that originally attracted both criminal and armed groups to the region. The relative ease with which money is locally laundered and transferred to and from regions overseas also constitutes a powerful incentive to maintain a base of operation in the area. As a result, transnational criminal groups such as Mexican and Colombian drug cartels, Chinese and Russian mafias, and the Japanese *yakuza*, all appear to have a strongly rooted presence in this South American region. Within the tri-border area, the epicenter of organized crime can be found in Ciudad del Este—an important hub of drug and human trafficking and the smuggling of weapons, contraband, counterfeit products, and other goods.[43]

Hezbollah operatives and supporters are present in Ciudad del Este and have been active in the underground world that includes drug smuggling, gun running, and pirating.[44] According to Brazilian intelligence sources, an international terrorist presence in the tri-border area dates as far back as the early

1980s. It continued to grow during the following decades, becoming the "main focus of Islamic extremism in Latin America" by the end of the 1990s.[45]

Despite contradictory reports regarding the extent and nature of the international terrorist activities taking place in the tri-border area in the aftermath of 9/11, reports from both the U.S. Department of Treasury and the U.S. military's Southern Command (USSOUTHCOM) indicate that the tri-border area remains one of the main terrorism-financing hubs in Latin America.[46] In 2008 Israel's minister for internal security, Avi Dichter, reiterated his country's concerns over international terrorist cells operating in the area. This fear was further echoed by the Spanish Foundation for Analysis and Social Studies (FAES), which reported that the tri-border area is "a neuralgic center of Islamic terrorism financing, as well as of smuggling of weapons and contraband."[47]

Although the presence and activities of Hezbollah have been documented for years, the precise amount of money actually transferred to the group is more difficult to estimate, in part because a large portion of the money transfers are done through an informal monetary transfer arrangement, known as the *hawala* system. Because they take place outside the conventional banking marketplace, they are harder to identify and trace.[48] However, there are still some relevant data regarding the volume of monetary transfers that are made from this region for international terrorist and criminal organizations.

In 2007 the U.S. Department of State declared that tens of millions of dollars were laundered in the tri-border area on a yearly basis and disbursed to terrorist organizations.[49] A 2005 Paraguayan intelligence report claimed that roughly $20 million was collected in the tri-border area each year to finance Hezbollah and Hamas.[50] Hezbollah first established logistical and financial cells in the 1980s, taking advantage of the extensive network of immigrants of Lebanese origin residing there. In the 1990s Hezbollah operatives increased their activities, developing fully operational units. It is believed that part of the planning and execution of its terrorist attacks in Argentina took place in this frontier region. At the beginning of the investigations into the March 1992 bombing of the Israeli Embassy in Buenos Aires, it was reported that Hezbollah's senior operative at the time, Imad Mughniyah, entered Argentina through the tri-border area to oversee the execution of the attack, where he used the location as a safe haven.[51] Paraguayan intelligence sources also indicated that until at least the year 2000 more than forty-six known Hezbollah operatives lived in the region, including Ali Khalil Merhi, the regional fundraiser for Hezbollah.[52] Merhi was arrested in Ciudad del Este in 2001, when local law enforcement officials started to crack down on the regional network.[53] In June 2010 Paraguayan officials arrested a Lebanese American named Moussa Ali Hamdan on charges of conspiring to finance Hezbollah through the sale of stolen goods and counterfeit U.S. currency.[54]

Hezbollah's tri-border network has strong connections with local criminal activities, as illustrated by the uncovering of the Barakat Clan—a group of Lebanese residents involved in both criminal and terrorism-related financing. The clan revolved around the financial operations of Assad Ahmad Barakat, co-owner of one the largest malls in Ciudad del Este, the Galeria Page, which was a known front for Hezbollah financing and recruiting.[55] In raiding Barakat's apartment, the police found Hezbollah material and propaganda, including tapes praising suicide attacks and speeches of Secretary-General Hassan Nasrallah.[56] The U.S. Department of Treasury identified Ahmad Barakat as a SDGT in June of 2004, adding nine additional individuals and two enterprises to the list in 2006.[57] Muhammad Yusif Abdallah, the Hezbollah regional leader and another co-owner of the Galeria Page Mall, was also identified as an SDGT. He allegedly gave Hezbollah a percentage of the profits derived from his shopping center.[58]

The Barakat Clan also includes Ali Muhammad Kazan, who helped raise more than $500,000 for the organization, and Farouk Omairi, the owner of the travel agency and exchange house known as Piloto Turismo Ltda. Kazan, along with his son Khaled Omairi, was accused of involvement in narcotrafficking, money laundering, and terrorism financing.[59] In May 2003 the Paraguayan police arrested Lebanese merchant Hassan Abdallah Dayoub while in possession of 2.3 kilograms of cocaine. The investigations later revealed that Dayoub—a cousin of Ahmad Barakat—was in charge of the "wing of narcotraffickers" of the Barakat Clan, further proving the strong terror-criminal connection behind Hezbollah's fundraising operations in the region.[60]

Police operations have also revealed the existence of links between weapons smuggling and terrorist cells in the tri-border area. In 2004 three Paraguayans and an Argentinean citizen were arrested for possession of explosives and weapons.[61] Following the arrest, it was alleged that air-to-ground missiles were brought into the area and handed to terrorist cells operating nearby.[62] In 2007 Lebanese businessman Kassen Hijazi, a resident of Ciudad del Este and owner of Telefax Company, came under international scrutiny for his suspected money transfers to shadow enterprises in Beirut.[63] Finally, in 2008 news sources reported that the United States was looking for a group of terrorist suspects residing in the tri-border area who had been provided with U.S. visas by the former Paraguayan ambassador in Lebanon, Alejandro Hamed Franco.[64] In addition to these documented financial operations, it is also believed that Hezbollah used the region to run weapons-training and indoctrination camps for children and adults with Lebanese and Shiite backgrounds.[65] The tri-border area has been used by Hezbollah, Hamas, and a whole host of other nonstate armed groups for a plethora of illicit activities.

In the past few years, however, as a result of increased scrutiny of the area by Western intelligence agencies, Hezbollah has expanded its enterprises to other areas in Central and South America. Chief among these new locations is Venezuela, with some reports indicating that Hugo Chavez's government is providing training facilities and funding to Hezbollah.[66] With its Lebanese diaspora and anti-American government, Venezuela has been inching closer to Iran for quite some time.[67] In fact, a Spanish reporter named Antonio Salas (aka Mohammed Abdallah), who went deep undercover and underwent training at a Hezbollah base operating in Venezuela, managed to sneak out video footage of some of his experiences.[68] There is also a large Arab minority in the Guajira Peninsula, which is divided and controlled by Colombia and Venezuela. The peninsula is made up of numerous population centers, such as the village of Maicao, which is a hotbed for Islamists as well as a stronghold of Hezbollah.[69] However, Hezbollah is not just active in the shadowy backwaters of Venezuela. In fact, Venezuelan diplomat Ghazi Nasr al-Din has been designated by the U.S. Department of Treasury as a Hezbollah supporter, and other Venezuelan diplomats have been shown to support other terrorist groups, such as FARC and ETA.[70]

It is not just Venezuela that has seen a rise in Hezbollah activities in recent years. The Caribbean islands of Curacao and Cuba, for example, are also used by Hezbollah for drug trafficking and money laundering.[71] Ecuador has also seen Hezbollah involvement in drug trafficking in recent years. In 2005 Ecuadorian police broke up a drug trafficking ring that was operating out of the El Turco restaurant, where Rady Zaiter and Maher Hamajo helped ensure that Hezbollah received up to 70 percent of the drug profits.[72] Other areas of Central and South America have also been used by Hezbollah whenever possible. Panama's Free Trade Zone, for example, has proved to be a good location for both narcotics smuggling and money laundering.[73] As narcotrafficking and gang violence has increased in Mexico and along the U.S.-Mexico border, there has been growing concern about the possibility of a narcoterrorist nexus involving Mexican drug cartels and Hezbollah operatives.[74] While Hezbollah operatives have been reported to be in Mexico for some time, in the summer of 2010 Mexican authorities announced that they had shut down a Hezbollah network operating out of Tijuana.[75] If this connection proves to be accurate, it would indicate that Hezbollah and Iran's foothold in the Americas has expanded to the doorstep of the United States. It would also prove that they are capable of more easily perpetrating attacks on U.S. territory through the injection of operatives by way of traditional routes for illegal immigrants to enter the country. As evidenced by the multiple terrorist attacks against Jewish and Israeli targets in Buenos Aires in the 1990s, Hezbollah has been able to transform its existing financial networks into operational ones that can help carry out terrorist attacks in a given region. As an organization with the infrastructure, resources, and personnel to smuggle drugs, money, weapons, and counterfeit goods into countries in Central and South America, Africa, Central Asia, and North America, the fear is that it can again make use of these same resources to carry out terrorist attacks in other states as well.

5 Strategies and Tactics

"WE ARE NOT A REGULAR ARMY, and we don't fight like a regular army."[1] These were the words Secretary-General Hassan Nasrallah used to describe the organization's military wing, the Islamic Resistance. More generally, Hezbollah has defined a successful operation as one that kills, wounds, or expels an enemy force. It aims to confuse and spread panic while conducting attacks and thus recognizes the psychological as well as physical toll of its actions.[2]

Military Operations

Being both a national mainstream political party and an armed militia, Hezbollah straddles the line between being a civilian organization and a military organization. For instance, the group's political offices as well as military infrastructure are generally located below or among residential apartment buildings, often within a city or suburb that is sympathetic to its cause and that can assist it if needed.[3] Similarly, Hezbollah relies on numerous "part-time" fighters who are civilian workers during the day and warriors at night, thus making the distinction between civilian and combatant even more difficult to discern.

Hezbollah combatants do not wear uniforms while in combat, and their command structure is less pyramid-like and more horizontal in nature. Rather than having more prescribed military formations such as battalions, companies, and brigades, Hezbollah fighters operate in small teams of approximately 20 fighters, with few methods of identification.[4] Before Israel's withdrawal in 2000, at any given time no more than 500 Hezbollah fighters were usually involved in combat against the IDF and South Lebanon Army (SLA), who numbered approximately 1,500 and 2,500, respectively, in the Security Zone.[5]

Operating out of heavily populated areas weakened the IDF's and other potential adversaries' abilities to combat Hezbollah forces more effectively without being dragged into an urban warfare scenario. This tactic has proved extremely effective from a military perspective, but it also raises the potential costs for the civilian population, as civilians are often found at the center of potential battlefields or next to prominent military targets.[6] Hezbollah has also been found to operate in and around UNIFIL positions in prior years, seemingly to achieve similar results.[7] After Israel's withdrawal, Hezbollah stepped up its development of Vietcong-like tunnels for supplies, transport, and communications, all the while incorporating advanced weaponry such as antiship missiles, sophisticated night-vision goggles, unmanned aerial vehicles (UAVs), surface-to-surface missiles, and antitank missiles.[8] Since the Israeli withdrawal, Hezbollah technology and military hardware have become even more advanced, and Syria's border has been purposely kept porous to allow an easy flow of illegal weapons and personnel into and out of Lebanon. Since the conflict between Hezbollah and Israel in the summer of 2006, the Shiite Islamist group has been rearming at a feverish pace. It now reportedly has more than forty thousand rockets, operates fighters and command posts among civilian positions in Shiite villages on its southern border, and openly warns that it has a "precise bank of Israeli targets" to strike in the event of another war, which will likely see Tel Aviv targeted by its arsenal of rockets.[9]

The tactic of drawing in civilian casualties compliments the group's heavy indoctrination that emphasizes a love of death and desire for martyrdom— two elements that are infused into the training of Hezbollah fighters as well as Shiite youth, who begin such indoctrination in Hezbollah-sponsored schools, bands, and summer camps at a young age—they even have a Disney-like theme park called "Mleeta" known as the "Tourist Landmark of the Resistance."[10] It is also, of course, very difficult to counter someone who does not fear death. Hezbollah and Iranian officials are infamous for expressing their pride in the fact that, whereas Jews, Christians, and other "infidels" love life, the Shiites love and seek out death. These statements are reminiscent of the type of language used by al Qaeda, only it was used by Hezbollah decades beforehand. To quote the former commander of the Iranian Revolutionary Guards Corps, "We shall win and you, the Westerners, shall lose because we gave 200,000 victims, martyrs, in eight years of war with Iraq and we have 300,000 disabled and injured in this war—and we don't care about it. But you, the Westerners, are afraid to give 4,000 or 5,000 victims and casualties, so the final victory will be ours."[11]

Though the organization is quick to condemn attacks against its own civilians, it relies on targeting Israeli civilians in order to help establish a deterrent capability and gain popular support. Hezbollah's chief mode of attacking Israeli civilians both before and after Israel's departure from southern Lebanon in 2000 has been primarily through the launching of rockets, missiles, and mortars. When attempting to conduct kidnappings or other raids against Israelis, Hezbollah forces often fire a barrage of rockets across a length of the "Blue Line" of Israel's northern border, in order to spread IDF forces thin before infiltrating through a small, defined area to carry out a given operation.[12] Katyushas are short-range multiple-rocket launcher systems first developed for use by the Soviets during World War II. Although the number, size, distance, and potency of the rockets have advanced over the years, the concept is essentially the same: bombard your target with numerous rockets in a short period of time. While not particularly accurate, the rockets are cheap to produce and usually contain ball bearings that can spray up to one kilometer away on impact. As a result, they are not particularly effective against military forces but are perfect weapons for inflicting panic and casualties on an adversary's civilian population. Hezbollah first launched katyusha rockets at Israel's northern towns and cities following Secretary-General Musawi's assassination in 1992.[13] Israeli border towns had long before fallen under rocket; however, those had usually come from Palestinian groups, as they occasionally still do today. Hezbollah has also acquired longer-range and more accurate missiles, including the M-600/Fateh-110, the Zilzal I and II, and reportedly even Scud-D surface-to-surface missiles.[14] The bulk of these missiles were acquired from Syria after the 2006 war with Israel and greatly change the range, accuracy, and payload of Hezbollah's missile capabilities. This led U.S. secretary of defense Robert Gates to declare that Hezbollah "has far more rockets and missiles than most governments in the world."[15]

With regard to tactics, Hezbollah has evolved over time. Initially it relied solely on tactics that greatly limited the amount and types of engagements that its fighters could have in battle. As a result, most attacks took the form of kidnappings, roadside bombs, booby traps, and, of course, suicide bombings. Over time, however, Hezbollah attacks became bolder and more sophisticated. Today, their tactics could be described as ranging between low- and medium-intensity asymmetrical warfare that can incorporate more conventional methods and armaments. The group's military patterns have developed in the past decades, shifting in nature and scope in the years after the end of the civil

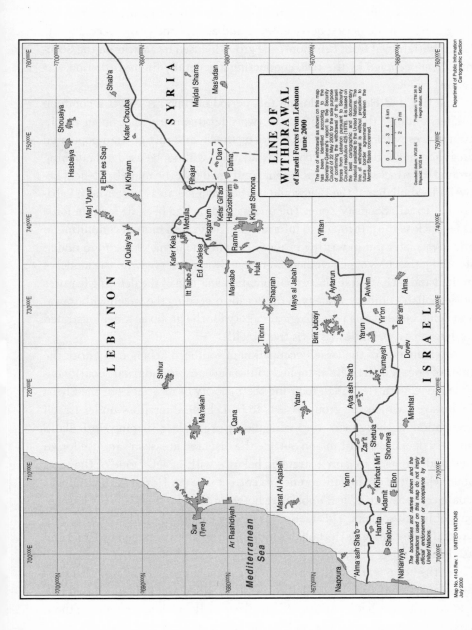

Department of Public Information
Cartographic Section

Blue Line delineating the border between Israel and Lebanon. United Nations map, Line of Withdrawal, Map No. 4143 Rev. 1, July 2000.

war. In fact, beginning in the 1990s Hezbollah's attacks against Israel started to develop according to what Daniel Sobelman defined as specific "rules of the game."[16] In the period between 1992 and 2000—the years preceding the Israeli withdrawal from Lebanon—the group focused its attacks on the Security Zone occupied by the IDF, conducting a generally limited attrition war against Israel.

The IDF and Hezbollah during this period of time arrived at a common "understanding" that committed the two sides to ensure "that under no circumstances will civilians be the target of attack, and that civilian populated areas and industrial and electrical installations will not be used as launching ground for attacks."[17] This agreement confirmed that the main battlefield between Hezbollah and the IDF would be the occupied areas in southern Lebanon, in Israel's Security Zone. The understanding had been de facto in force as far back as 1993, through an informal and unwritten mutual commitment, and it was later put in writing in 1996. Despite the terms of the 1996 understanding, the rules of engagement were not always observed. Yet the model of limited and reciprocal military confrontation was one of the defining features of Hezbollah's military strategy in the decade preceding the Israeli withdrawal and could be seen as a psychological victory for the group as it demonstrated its deterrent capabilities vis-à-vis the Israelis.

After the end of the Israeli occupation of southern Lebanon in 2000, the rules of engagement were reapplied to the new post-withdrawal security environment, with Hezbollah focusing the majority of its attacks in the Sheba Farms area, which the group asserts to be Lebanese territory under Israeli occupation. In those years, the main guiding principle in shaping Hezbollah's military operations within and outside the disputed areas was an "eye for an eye" and the need to gain a strategic balance with Israel.[18] One of the tools upon which the organization relied to correct what in Hezbollah's mind was a dangerous asymmetrical imbalance between the two sides was the kidnapping of Israeli soldiers. This tactic was mostly employed as a bargaining chip to obtain the release of Hezbollah's militants and allies detained by Israel and its allies.[19]

Yet the 2006 war saw the rules of the game change once again. That conflict was sparked after Hezbollah successfully killed and kidnapped two IDF soldiers in a cross-border attack. When all was said and done, there were thousands of Lebanese casualties and Hezbollah's personnel and weapons stockpile were severely depleted. The conflict also demonstrated utter confusion on the Israeli side, which led to a subsequent revamping of Israel's military and political structure. Furthermore, the hostilities resulted in a new understanding: despite Israel's tepid performance, the Jewish state's actions were enough to make it clear that it would no longer accept cross-border attacks by Hezbollah either in the Har Dov (Sheba Farms) region or elsewhere within Israel. UN Security Council Resolution 1701, which was passed in response to the conflict, also called for UNIFIL to expand its role in order to ensure that Hezbollah forces did not rearm south of the Litani River; an activity that the organization has not openly defied. It is indeed common knowledge that Hezbollah has been working very intensely to regroup and stockpile new weapons in preparation for the next round of hostilities with Israel. Recently, the Israeli government declassified a series of aerial images of southern Lebanon showing bunkers and arms caches located in the area next to the Lebanese-Israeli border to expose the organization's activities and warn it of the level of penetration of Israel's intelligence services.[20]

Israel remained in occupation of the border town of Ghajar, whose city lines cross the Israeli-incorporated Golan Heights, and whose citizens have Israeli citizenship. Hezbollah, however, today identifies all of Ghajar as part of Lebanese territory.

Hezbollah also helped pioneer and perfect the usage of suicide bombers or, in the group's own words, "martyrdom operations." Their skill and lethality—especially with regards to launching multiple, often simultaneous or back-to-back attacks to inflict maximum casualties—became a calling card of Hezbollah that has since been mimicked by groups ranging from Hamas to al Qaeda.[21] Even on this front, the group has evolved considerably in its usage of suicide operations specifically, and warfighting skills more generally. Starting around 1991, the organization began to take bolder initiatives. As its professionalism rose, its fighters grew more elite, and its intelligence and reconnaissance collection became more accurate. Its units came to include an organized infantry, an engineering division, an artillery force, a general staff, and a signals branch.[22] Hezbollah units began to launch raids on IDF and SLA emplacements, carried out more sophisticated assassinations and ambushes, and penetrated the ranks of the SLA and, occasionally, even the IDF. After Israel's withdrawal from Lebanon in 2000, those Hezbollah forces were augmented with Iranian intelligence agents from the IRGC. As much as Israel used its resources, including aircraft, artillery, tanks, and SIGINT, to try and hunt down Hezbollah forces, its fighters often managed to evade the

Israelis. Hezbollah itself had good intelligence and a better knowledge of the terrain.[23]

Hezbollah has become skilled not only at carrying out vehicle-borne (VBIEDs) and suicide vest (SVIEDs) strikes—two types of attacks it has significantly decreased its use of over time—but also at firing rocket-propelled grenades (RPGs) and more advanced antitank weapons, laying sophisticated booby traps, using improvised explosive devices (IEDs), and planting explosively formed penetrators (EFPs). One retired IDF Special Forces reconnaissance soldier told of his experience in the cat-and-mouse game the IDF conducted with Hezbollah. He explained that any time an Israeli soldier's item was found to have been left behind on a mission (e.g., a helmet, canteen), the unit was sent back to retrieve it. By the time it was located, it would inevitably have been booby-trapped, and the IDF would come to expect this. In general, the cat-and-mouse games continued, as Israel developed increasingly hi-tech weaponry to detect infiltration of enemy forces and jam explosive devices, while Hezbollah in turn found both advanced and sometimes rather simple ways of bypassing these technologies. These ideas included hanging IEDs on tree branches because the Israelis came to expect them to be on the ground, crawling along with sheep to avoid detection by sophisticated night vision or infrared goggles, and developing devices to counter Israel's jamming abilities for IEDs.[24] In more recent years, as Israeli military technology has further increased, the Shiite organization has tried to meet the challenges with the planting of more sophisticated ambushes and IEDs, often combined with the use of tunneling under Israeli borders and positions.

Hezbollah has become so sophisticated at planting IEDs and EFPs that its forces have trained Shiite Iraqi insurgents to do so in Iranian and Lebanese training camps. It has also assisted these insurgents in planning operations, procuring weapons, expanding communications, and developing hit squads.[25] With regard to Hezbollah's communications, the organization combines low-tech and high-tech methods. When messages are relayed, they often are done via motorcycle by men dressed in civilian clothing. Motorcycles are also used to transfer fighters from one area to another.[26] Riding in vehicles as part of a convoy of Lebanese civilians fleeing a given battle continues to be a common tactic for evading advancing forces during major IDF operations, as the IDF increasingly provides civilians (and Hezbollah forces) with ample warning before launching an attack on a given position. Aside from low-level technology for communication purposes, Hezbollah has been increasing what

E. V. Vandiver of the Center for Army Analysis described as "sophisticated computer and communications networks [used] to relay messages to different groups of fighters."[27] It even has developed its own internal private telephone and communications network.[28]

The summer 2006 war between Israel and Hezbollah provided additional glimpses into the group's military strategy and its warfighting skills. Although there is consistent evidence that Hezbollah heavily miscalculated Israel's reaction to the kidnapping operation of two Israeli soldiers in July 2006, the group's actual conduct during the war showed a remarkable level of organizational capacity.[29] Among other things, it demonstrated the evolution from a marginal militia to a powerful armed group, which was able to employ both conventional and nonconventional military tactics and survive a massive air assault by one of the most powerful air forces in the world. Hezbollah relied heavily on short-range rockets to inflict damage upon its adversary and raise the costs of war for the Israeli side. To protect these rockets and their launching sites from Israeli forces, the organization devised a system that prioritized defending and holding ground in a way that is most uncommon for the classic "hit-and-run" tactics employed by traditional guerrilla organizations.[30] In this sense, Hezbollah's tactics did always not conform to those of a traditional nonstate, armed group fighting a nonconventional war, as it "put too much emphasis on holding ground."[31] Yet it also failed to comply with the standard for conventional warfare, as the organization "relied too extensively on harassing fires and unattended minefields; it put too much emphasis on coercion."[32] One of the lessons it implemented after the 2006 conflict with Israel was to remove its rocket launchers from forests and other densely wooded areas where they could be more easily targeted by air strikes and rely increasingly on hiding them under the cover of civilian infrastructure.

On balance, the group has shown the capacity to adopt both conventional and nonconventional tactics and to act as a hybrid military organization—an unequivocal sign of the organizational evolution of the militia since its creation in the early 1980s. As a result, Hezbollah's use of irregular warfare can no longer be considered solely in the realm of low-intensity conflict. Rather, Hezbollah today is able to mix guerrilla and conventional warfare tactics and, as a result, can successfully conduct medium-intensity conflict as well. Evidence of this evolution was clear in its war against Israel in 2006, when the group made use of high technology such as UAVs, SIGINT, and precision guided weapons. More advanced technology and tactics will undoubtedly be on display by Hezbollah during any future conflict with Israel, which it has promised will bring the fight to its enemy by attacking and holding Israeli territory. These realities mark the first time that a nonstate armed group has so effectively implemented such advanced tactics and reciprocal deterrence vis-à-vis a state, leaving Major General (ret.) Robert Scales to call Hezbollah's tactics a "revolution in warfare."[33] This has also resulted in some American officials coming to fear that traditional counterinsurgency doctrine would not be enough to cope with the violence in Iraq and Afghanistan if Hezbollah's lessons are more fully transferred to, and implemented by, Islamists in those parts of the world, as we are beginning to see.[34]

Terrorism

Long before al Qaeda was being formed, when Osama bin Laden was just another son of another wealthy Arab tycoon, Hezbollah was wreaking havoc around the world. On April 18, 1983, a suicide bomber rammed his bomb-laden truck into the U.S. Embassy in Beirut, killing 63 people, including 17 Americans. Many were members of the Central Intelligence Agency's Beirut station, who had been meeting during the time of the attack. Six months later another truck, this time laden with six tons of TNT, was driven into the U.S. Marine Corps barracks in Beirut, killing 241 Americans. Just a few miles away at nearly the same time, 58 French paratroopers were killed in another suicide attack. Although an organization calling itself Islamic Jihad claimed responsibility for those bombings, and Hezbollah has maintained that it was not involved in those attacks, U.S. intelligence determined that Hezbollah forces were in fact responsible.[35] By September 1984, Hezbollah had struck again, this time bombing the U.S. embassy annex in Beirut, killing eleven more people. The attacks were only a handful of a series of acts perpetrated by the Shiite organization during the years of Lebanon's civil war, contributing significantly to its dossier on terrorism.

In alliance with the IRGC and the Iranian Ministry of Intelligence and Security (MOIS), Hezbollah continued to conduct kidnappings, suicide attacks, and hijackings. It was not long before the U.S. Department of State put out a $5 million bounty on Imad Mughniyah's head; he was the man held responsible for the death of more Americans in terrorist attacks until Osama bin Laden on 9/11. Although terrorist attacks and kidnappings of foreigners within Lebanon generally ceased at the end of its second civil war, the group remained involved in several international terrorist plots during the 1990s, targeting Israeli and Jewish interests abroad. In 1992 a Hezbollah suicide blew up his pickup truck by the Israeli Embassy in Buenos Aires, killing 29 people and wounding another 200. The attack destroyed the embassy as well as a nearby Catholic Church and school building. Two years later, in coordination with Iranian intelligence, Hezbollah struck again, destroying the building that housed the Jewish community center (AMIA) in Buenos Aires, killing 85 people and wounding over 300 more.[36] That attack was an apparent response to the Israeli assassination of Hezbollah's secretary-general, Musawi, who was killed by Israeli forces in 1992.[37] The brazen attack was a strong indication of the terrorist group's willingness to strike "soft target" Jewish sites around the world, as more hardened Israeli government facilities were no longer as easily available. Although the organization officially denied any involvement in the Buenos Aires attacks, Argentinean investigators confirmed the group's hand in plotting and carrying out both operations.

Since the mid-1990s, the organization's direct involvement in kidnappings and other international attacks has ceased, but Hezbollah is still operationally present abroad and, in recent years, has on multiple occasions tried to fulfill numerous stated vows to retaliate for Mughniyah's assassination. Israeli sites have consequently been unsuccessfully targeted in West Africa, Azerbaijan, Morocco, and Egypt. In the Moroccan plot, Hezbollah recruited an Israeli Arab named Rawi Sultani to help track and kill the IDF chief of staff as he was returning from a visit to Morocco. An Egyptian plot led to the arrest and conviction of dozens of Hezbollah members, including its operational unit head, Sami Hani Shihab. Senior Hezbollah leader Mohammed Qabalan was also implicated in that attack, and it is believed that some of the members were part of Hezbollah's Unit 1800, which had resided in the area for years and had trained in Libya and Sudan.[38] There was also an attempted attack in Turkey in December 2009, which was thwarted by Turkish security forces.[39] Home to a sizable Lebanese expat community as well as a large Jewish population, Canadian officials reportedly caught Hezbollah operatives conducting surveillance on the Israeli Embassy in Ottawa, several synagogues in Toronto, and numerous members of Israel's El Al Airline operating out of Toronto's Pearson Airport.[40] While all of these attempts have been unsuccessful, they indicate a continued desire on the part of Hezbollah to exact revenge against Israel, which it has openly blamed for the assassination of Mughniyah—a man whose very existence and association with Hezbollah was denied until after he was killed. Notably, these foiled plots can also be seen as an increasingly effective penetration of Hezbollah by Israeli intelligence, and closer cooperation with allied intelligence agencies.

Regional Involvement: A Growing Trend

Hezbollah has always been an important regional player because of its political power in Lebanon, its strategic relations with Iran and Syria, its capacity to influence the Arab-Israeli conflict, and its ability to directly challenge Israel. The organization's strategy of regional involvement has generally been focused on the Israeli-Palestinian conflict, through both direct military engagements with Israel and indirect support for Palestinian armed groups. During the second Intifada that closely followed Israel's withdrawal from Lebanon in 2000, Hezbollah attacks against Israel were often related to military developments in the Palestinian territories. For instance, the group chose to escalate its military attacks on the eve of Israel's Operation Defensive Shield in the West Bank in the spring of 2002, in solidarity with its "Palestinian brothers."[41]

More recently, Hezbollah played a significant role in the December 2008 Israeli incursions into the Gaza Strip. While ensuring it did not get directly involved, Hezbollah maintained a certain degree of participation in the war by maintaining continuous communication with Hamas throughout the conflict. In December 2009, just a few days before the expiration of a cease-fire between Hamas and Israel, Nasrallah launched a pan-Arab campaign to bring an end to the military embargo of the Gaza Strip that was being enforced by Israel and Egypt. The timing of these announcements indicated the existence of an open channel of communication between the two groups, as well as a minimum level of interorganizational coordination.[42] Even more interestingly, Hezbollah MP Mohammad Raad affirmed that his organization was able to share its tactical knowledge with Hamas, influencing the conduct of the war. This was evidenced by Hamas's increased reliance and deployment of Iranian versions of the katyusha and grad rockets, with longer ranges than Hamas's own homemade "Qassams."[43] Moreover, according to the Iranian newspaper *Hemayat*, Hezbollah also trained Hamas to attack Merkava tanks, the IDF's heavily armored main battle tank.[44] The group did not, however, militarily intervene directly in support of Hamas.

Hezbollah was also an important regional player in the context of the three-week battle in the Gaza Strip between Israeli and Hamas forces, which took place in late 2008 and early 2009. The Shiite group effectively utilized its media for propaganda and psychological warfare purposes, mobilizing the Arab population across the Middle East. Moreover, the organization openly attacked the leaders of Arab regimes that had assumed a more critical posture vis-à-vis Hamas. Hezbollah's outspoken criticisms against the so-called moderate Arab states, such as Jordan, Egypt, Saudi Arabia, and Arab Gulf countries, were specifically targeted by Hezbollah officials, including Hezbollah MP Nawaf Mousawi, who repeatedly lamented the "suspicious silence" of Arab leaders during that conflict.[45] Similarly, the group lashed out at Saudi Arabia for its alleged lack of leadership and questioned that state's role in the context of the Arab-Israeli conflict.

Hezbollah's criticism of "moderate" regional regimes, however, continued long after an unofficial cease-fire was reached in Gaza. For example, on September 18, 2009, Hassan Nasrallah stressed that the organization viewed the region as divided between "allies" and "enemies" of the "resistance" and emphasized the need to change the status quo. Referring to more pro-Western Arab regimes, he stated that "we have to replace the regimes in the Arab countries with other regimes that are convinced of war in order to send their armies to war."[46] Recognizing that such an option was not realistic in the short term, Nasrallah stressed the need to boost popular resistance throughout the region and added that the entire Middle East should follow the steps of Iran and Syria.

These statements indicated Hezbollah's increased regional involvement as well as the group's use of its political and military status to affect the policies of other regional players, while also influencing the Arab-Israeli conflict through means other than direct military conflict. Similarly, the Gaza War also represented the beginning of a harsh political confrontation between Hezbollah and Egypt. Specifically, Nasrallah criticized Egypt for not opening the Rafah border crossing during the Gaza flare up in late 2008 to early 2009 and called on the Egyptian people to protest against their governments. "Let this Egyptian people take to the streets in the millions. Can the Egyptian police kill millions of Egyptians? No, they cannot."[47] These statements, which were immediately supported by Egypt's traditional adversary, Iran, signaled a growing hostility toward the Egyptian regime as well as an attempt to weaken its stature as a leader among the Arab and Muslim worlds.[48] More recently, in the wake of the protests of the "Arab street," Hezbollah's stance with respect to the ongoing protest movements in the Middle East has been one of unequivocal support, with the organization openly celebrating the end of the

Mubarak regime. In the group's discourse, the demise of Mubarak is described as tantamount to the beginning of the "ousting" of U.S. allies from region and to the parallel rise of the "resistance axis." In his February 16, 2011, speech, Nasrallah eloquently explained this paradigm by stating: "The major blow to the resistance . . . was the participation of the Egyptian regime in the Camp David Agreement and consequently the emergence of Egypt from the Arab-Israeli struggle."[49] The fall of Mubarak is then seen as marking the end of the Israeli-Egyptian détente, which will in turn change the balance of power in the Arab-Israeli conflict in favor of the "resistance."

Besides the increased political confrontation with "moderate" Arab regimes, Hezbollah's regional involvement included an increased operational presence outside of Lebanon. This is not an entirely new development, as noted in the case study on the tri-border region earlier in this study. Hezbollah is believed to have bases as far away as Nigeria, where it not only trains local forces on military matters but indoctrinates them as well.[50] Similarly, the organization had been accused of arming and training other Islamist forces into its ranks, with Somali Islamist insurgents being a prime example of these activities.[51] In this context, Arab media widely covered the aforementioned discovery of a Hezbollah network operating clandestinely within Egypt. The investigation began in April 2009 with the arrest of forty-nine Egyptians, Palestinians, and Lebanese who were allegedly Hezbollah-affiliated operatives working in Egypt.[52] Local authorities later confirmed the arrests of twenty-six individuals, who were charged with assisting Hezbollah and brought to trial in front of the State Security Emergency Court.[53] As the investigations unfolded, Egyptian cabinet minister Mufed Shehab under Mubarak disclosed that local authorities had seized explosive belts from the Hezbollah cell and revealed that the group had been monitoring tourist resorts in the Sinai, an area with a high concentration of international and Israeli tourists,[54] as well as keeping track of ship schedules in the Suez Canal.[55] In Lebanon, Hezbollah denied its connections to the local cell,[56] but later the secretary-general admitted that at least one of the arrested militants, the alleged ringleader Sami Hani Shihab, was a Hezbollah agent dispatched to Egypt. Hezbollah claimed his role was to aid Hamas in smuggling weapons through the Egyptian-Palestinian border. During the 2011 revolution in Egypt, most of those arrested by Egyptian authorities escaped from jail, while the post-Mubarak regime released the remaining prisoners.

The existence of an organized clandestine Hezbollah presence in Egypt signals a trend of increased operational involvement and boldness in the region. This trend seems to also be confirmed by Kuwaiti reports that described the growing visibility and activism of the local Hezbollah branch, allegedly attempting to enhance its political role and increase its internal strength.[57] News reports from the Gulf States in late 2009 confirmed that as many as three Hezbollah militants were killed during a confrontation in Yemen between government troops and the Houthist rebels in the Saada region in the north of the country.[58]

Despite the difficulty in accurately assessing Hezbollah's actual operational presence outside of Lebanon, its activities have clearly taken on a new dimension. The fact that the group has been remarkably more visible outside its traditional areas of operation is of particular note. That reality, along with the more active role it has taken in supporting local "resistance" cells and its increasingly vociferous disapproval of more "moderate Arab regimes," represents a significant development, one that may signal that the group is seeking a more prominent, powerful, and permanent role in the region.

Propaganda and Psychological Warfare

Whether by shaping or simply by reflecting reality, the media have both a global and a local impact that both state and nonstate actors alike must take into consideration when devising their strategies and tactics. Nonstate armed groups such as Hezbollah have understood that this new trend has a substantial impact on their agenda. As Joseph Nye has explained, "The current struggle is not only about whose army wins, but also whose story wins."[59]

Groups like Hezbollah use the media for multiple reasons: to communicate with its followers, to draw support for its cause, to recruit, and to influence the opponent's perception of reality. Shahar defines the last tactic as psychological warfare.[60] Alternatively, John Arquilla and David Ronfeldt from RAND define it as "*netwar*":

> Netwar refers to information-related conflict at a grand level between nations or societies. It means trying to disrupt, damage, or modify what a target population "knows" or thinks it knows about itself and the world around it. A netwar may focus on public or elite opinion, or both.[61]

Hezbollah has become adept and understanding the importance of effective propaganda, public diplomacy, and psychological warfare and in many ways conducts them more effectively than its adversaries, including Israel and the United States. The organization has skillfully been able to record attacks on IDF soldiers and get those images uploaded and on the air the very same day, just in time for the evening news, ensuring maximum propaganda effectiveness for its target audiences. The organization is all too aware of Israeli society's sensitivity to casualties, in part because the IDF is a conscription army in a small country.[62] It exaggerates the number of Israeli casualties it causes, inflates the number of Lebanese civilians killed or injured by Israel, and underreports its own losses.[63]

Like all conflicts that involve Israel, Hezbollah's battles have taken on a life of their own in terms of using and abusing the world's media, which have increasingly become effective tools of war available to each side.[64] For some perspective, the Israeli Foreign Ministry's public diplomacy, or Hasbara budget, is smaller than Hezbollah's Al-Manar satellite television station. Al-Manar's budget stands at approximately $15 million with three hundred employees. Although this may not sound like a lot in comparison to CNN or Fox News, it is around half the size of the budget of Al Jazeera.[65] Hezbollah and Israel both must contend with the biases present in the world's media that present instant news around the world, and unlike the 1990s when cable television made news available to people twenty-four-hours a day, today each side must also deal with the proliferation of online news sites and blogs that seek ever shorter sound bites to get their messages across as quickly as possible. Furthermore, each side has devoted time and effort to prove accusations of bias and portray itself as the victim in the conflict.[66] While the pro-Arab camp attempts to influence the media by portraying the Arab world as victims of Israeli, U.S., and other Western aggression, the pro-Israel camp increasingly attempts to tie its conflicts to the U.S. "War on Terror." Both have seen moderate success, depending on what part of the globe you examine.[67]

Hezbollah has a number of media outlets at its disposal to spread its message of propaganda that focuses on anti-Israeli, anti-Semitic, and anti-American rhetoric. These include Al-Manar (the Beacon), multiple radio stations, including its largest, Al-Nour (the Light), newspapers such as *al-Intiqad* (the Criticism), and a plethora of Web sites that are run independently as well as by the previously mentioned outlets.[68] Al-Manar's first broadcast took place in 1989, when it televised Ayatollah Khomeini's funeral.[69] It calls itself the "Station of

Resistance" and admits that its primary goal is to wage "effective psychological warfare against the Zionist enemy [the term it uses to refer to Israel]."[70]
To reach this goal, Hezbollah caters its programming appropriately, with its
terrestrial channel differing slightly from its satellite one, because they target
different audiences. In addition to its primary audience in the Lebanese, Arab,
and Muslim worlds, its secondary audience has become the Israeli military
and people (both Jewish and Arab), with reports made in Hebrew to "undermine the morale" of the IDF and Israeli society.[71]

Al-Manar is a consistently popular network in the Middle East, but during
times of conflict that involve Hezbollah, it becomes the top channel to watch
in the Arab world as it provides coverage of Hezbollah that no other station
can. When unable to find a real image to meet its needs, there have been cases
where Hezbollah media simply create ones to their liking. These photos are
often picked up by the international news media and can make front-page
news before they are found to be false, too often resulting in just a small correction made a few days later.[72] Furthermore, Al-Manar has been a key tool
in spreading Hezbollah's political and military analysis of the world, as well
as expanding the group's understanding of the Arab-Israeli conflict and its
enemies. By articulating and promoting Hezbollah's ideology both regionally
and globally, Al-Manar directly boosts the popularity and legitimacy of Hezbollah, thus having a real impact on public opinion.

An analysis of Al-Manar news coverage for the 2008–9 Israeli military
operations in the Gaza Strip can provide powerful insight into Hezbollah's
media-savvy approach and impact. Since the beginning of the hostilities, the
group embarked in a massive media campaign to link the fighting in Gaza to
the 2006 war in Lebanon, affirming that the 2008 campaign continued Israel's military decline in the region. On Al-Manar, Hezbollah secretary-general
Nasrallah explained: "What is taking place in the Gaza Strip is a Palestinian
version of what took place in Lebanon in July 2006." He added, "The Israelis
said they learnt lessons from the second war in Lebanon, but it seems that the
resistance in Gaza benefited from these lessons more than the Israelis. Actually, the lessons are making the Israelis appear weak and hesitant. . . . They
[the Israelis] are afraid of failure."[73]

This kind of rhetoric was crucial in shaping the regional understanding of
the war, and irrespective of the military results on the ground, Hezbollah ran
a well-planned media campaign to assert the weakness of the Israeli deterrence
paradigm. After the IDF's pullout from Gaza in 2009, the group congratulated

Hamas "on the victory they have achieved in the face of the Zionist ruthless aggression against the Gaza Strip."[74] This tactic was similarly employed in the aftermath of the war in Lebanon in July 2006, when Hezbollah media ran a sophisticated campaign to promote the idea of "divine victory" that the group had allegedly inflicted upon the IDF. In the end, Hezbollah's media campaigns contributed to boosting the group's image and creating a narrative of victory as much as the organization's actual fighting on the ground. Although this narrative was generally not as well accepted as it was after the 2006 war between Israel and Hezbollah, its pervasiveness was nonetheless significant.

The United States is also an increasing target of Hezbollah media, particularly since the U.S. invasions of Afghanistan and Iraq. Referring to the United States in Iraq, Hezbollah uses nearly identical messages of hate and images of death that it used to refer to Israeli activities in Lebanon. While the organization has stated that its battle is not against the American people but rather against the American government and its foreign policy, it continues to view the United States as a terrorist state and the world's greatest oppressor, which acts as "judge of the world" and conducts "crimes against humanity."[75] Hezbollah's propaganda arm, spearheaded by its savvy Al-Manar television station as well as its professional looking Web sites, are increasingly mimicked by other Islamist organizations, including al Qaeda, which recognize the benefits of such technology in reaching audiences around the world.[76] Although Al-Manar television has been banned in the United States since 2004, it is available in many other places around the world.[77] As a result, Hezbollah's anti-American, anti-Israeli, and anti-Semitic messages continue to spread and resonate among Arabs and Muslims worldwide.

PART II HAMAS AND MILITANCY IN THE PALESTINIAN TERRITORIES

6 The Palestinian Players

A Background

FOLLOWING ISRAEL'S BIRTH on May 14, 1948, neighboring Arab armies joined the already engaged Palestinian fighters in an effort to quash the nascent Jewish state. With rallying cries that included "Slaughter the Jews" and "Drive the Jews into the sea," the invading Arabs declared that the fight would be "a war of extermination," in an attempt to stop what they saw as a continuation of Western colonialism in the region. Their attempts were unsuccessful, however, and an armistice agreement in 1949 brought an end to the 1948 Arab-Israeli War. This war, celebrated by Israel as its War of Independence and known to Palestinian and Israeli Arabs as the *al nakba*, or "catastrophe," was the result of the decision by the United Nations to partition British Mandate Palestine in 1947. In truth, the partition actually took place in two stages. British Mandate Palestine originally included the territories that today include modern-day Israel, the West Bank, and the Gaza Strip, as well as the Hashemite Kingdom of Jordan. In 1922, in an effort to appease the Arab world's displeasure with the Balfour Declaration that had recognized a Jewish homeland in Palestine, the British decided to break away 76 percent of Mandate Palestine and create a new area solely for Arab use and settlement, known as Transjordan. This territory, which would later be renamed the Hashemite Kingdom of Jordan, became off limits to Jewish immigration. The Hashemites were given control over Transjordan largely as a thank-you gesture from the British for their assistance in ousting the Ottomans during World War I. This left the remaining 23 percent of original Mandate Palestine to be divvied up.[1] That second partition took place as part of the 1947 UN Partition Plan, which was approved by the UN General Assembly under Resolution 181 on November 29, 1947, and called for a further division of the remaining land into two states: one Jewish and one Arab.

The results of the 1948 Arab-Israeli War saw an expansion of the land originally apportioned to the Jews, which at some points had been less than a mile wide and was considered largely impossible to defend. The war also resulted in a large number of Palestinian Arab refugees who either left of their own accord or were forced out of their homes. These refugees, who numbered anywhere from 450,000 (by some Israeli estimates) to 800,000 (by some Arab estimates), generally settled in the West Bank (under Jordanian control), the Gaza Strip (under Egyptian occupation), Jordan, Syria, and Lebanon.[2] In the years just before, during, and immediately after the 1948 Arab-Israeli War, approximately 800,000 Jewish refugees either left or were more generally expelled from Arab countries, with thousands more killed in pogroms.[3] Most of these Jewish refugees were either absorbed into Israel or moved to the West. This reality prompted Israeli officials to argue that the two massive movements of refugees—one Palestinian and one Jewish—resulted in an "exchange of population" similar to those that had been carried out by other countries, such as India and Pakistan, or Turkey and Greece.[4] For the Arab world, this thesis was flatly rejected, however, as the war was viewed as an attempt to install a foreign people onto Arab soil, in continuation of past colonialist and imperialist policies.

Having rejected the creation of Israel, the invading Arab armies occupied the remaining portions of Mandate Palestine that had been apportioned to the Palestinian Arabs. The Egyptians conquered the Gaza Strip and put it under military administration, which severely restricted the Palestinian Arabs living in the area. As the Egyptian representative to the armistice talks with Israel would later say, "We don't care if all the refugees will die. There are enough Arabs around."[5] In this phase, the Arab world did not show a high degree of sensitivity with respect to the Palestinians and their case for statehood. From the beginning, Palestinian refugees were treated more as political tools against Israel than as fellow Arab brothers in need of real assistance. For this reason, certain countries within the Arab world backed withholding citizenship to Palestinian refugees and supporting the creation of the Palestinians' own UN refugee agency, known as the United Nations Relief and Works Agency (UNRWA). UNRWA is separate from the agency in charge of the rest of the world's refugees, the Office of the United Nations High Commissioner for Refugees (UNHCR), and maintains a separate definition for "refugee."

During the Egyptian occupation of Gaza from 1949 to 1967, the Muslim Brotherhood (al-Ikhwan al-Muslimeen) in Gaza was twice banned from any activities, the first time being in 1949. The second ban took place in 1954, after an assassination attempt on Egyptian leader Gamal Abdel Nasser.[6]

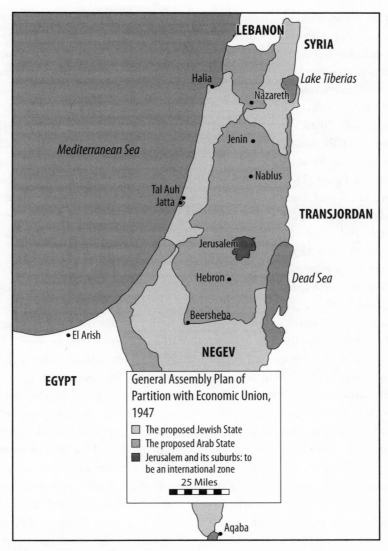

United Nations Partition Plan for Palestine, 1947. Courtesy of MidEastWeb (accessed October 31, 2011). Available from www.mideastweb.org/unpartition.htm.

After an apparent coup attempt against the ruling "Free Officers" in Egypt in 1965, a vicious clampdown on the Muslim Brotherhood's activities was conducted. It was during this time that the revered radical Islamist leader, Sayyid Qutb, was executed by the Egyptian government, and the future leader of Hamas, Ahmed Yassin, was arrested for Islamist activities.[7]

The West Bank on the other hand had been conquered by the Jordanians in the 1948 war. In an effort to support its claim over all of Mandate Palestine, Jordan officially annexed the West Bank in 1950.[8] The Jordanian approach to governing the West Bank was radically different from the model implemented by Egypt. The Kingdom of Jordan assumed a more moderate stance toward Israel and Zionism, while it also tolerated and even supported the political manifestations of the Muslim Brotherhood in the West Bank. The Jordanians, and other monarchies such as Saudi Arabia, used Islam and Islamic movements such as the Muslim Brotherhood to legitimate their rule. This alliance also became a powerful tool against the secular pan-Arab nationalism that would be led by the Egyptians, who were critical of the Arab monarchies.[9] As a result, the Jordanian regime granted much greater freedom of operation to its branch of the Muslim Brotherhood than did the Egyptians.[10]

The positive relationship between Jordan and Islamist groups would later continue after the creation of Hamas, which was permitted to have its headquarters in Jordan for many years. At the same time, however, both Egypt and Jordan supported the activities of Palestinian organizations fighting against Israel. Yet, in both the Egyptian and Jordanian cases, the ongoing support for the Palestinians did not go hand in hand with the promotion of the Palestinian national cause (especially in the Jordanian case), and the idea of creating a state of Palestine in the West Bank and Gaza Strip was never seriously considered by these countries. Rather, at this stage, Arab governments promoted the destruction of Israel and supported Palestinian organizations that worked toward that goal. As long as Palestinians did not threaten their own governments and instead focused their efforts outward, toward targeting the nascent Jewish state, their activities were tolerated. Support for Palestinian activities ranged from mere lip service to financial and military aid for their Arab fighters, known as the *fedayeen*.

Both Jordanian and Egyptian control over the West Bank and Gaza Strip ended after the 1967 Six-Day War, when Israel conquered and occupied those territories along with the Sinai Peninsula and the Golan Heights, thus deeply shifting the dynamics of the conflict. The war was, at first, considered a great victory for the Jewish state, which at that stage had set about developing a policy it hoped would strike a balance between protecting its own interests and still leaving the door open for the possibility of peace with its Arab neighbors. The war, however, created new facts on the ground, including the Israeli occupation of the West Bank and Gaza Strip, and Israel's direct control over the Palestinian residents of those areas. This reality initiated a process that in the long term would make both the maintenance of that balance and the achievement of a resolution to the ongoing conflict increasingly challenging.

A similar situation would also arise from Israel's control over East Jerusalem, which had been previously held by the Jordanians. Upon conquering the eastern half of the city, the Jewish State declared the entire city of Jerusalem would henceforth be considered Israel's capital. From an Israeli perspective, the "reunification" of Jerusalem under Israeli authority was a reaffirmation of the strong religious and ideological connection between the holy city and its Jewish roots. Israel set about reclaiming synagogues and other Jewish sites that had been either destroyed or converted to mosques while under Jordanian occupation. It allowed Jews to return to ancient sites where they had been banned by the Jordanians and mandated that each religious site be administered instead by its respective religion. Israel ultimately decided that control over Judaism's holiest site, which is also Islam's third holiest site—known to the Jews as the Temple Mount and to the Muslims as the Haram el-Sharif—would be administered by the Muslim religious body known as the *waqf*, under the continued guidance of the Jordanian monarchy, which assumed the role of protectorate.[11] From an international law perspective, the Israeli takeover of East Jerusalem and the subsequent steps the Jewish state took to extend its de facto control over the city were highly controversial. The international community immediately protested these actions, affirming that "acquisition of territory by military conquest is inadmissible."[12] The UN position on the matter, unaltered since 1967, has in fact been that "all legislative and administrative measures and actions taken by Israel, including expropriation of land and properties thereon, which tend to change the legal status of Jerusalem are invalid and cannot change that status."[13] This is a position that the international body would reiterate following Israel's official incorporation of the eastern part of the city, after the passage of a 1980 law declaring Jerusalem its "undivided" capital, a position that it holds to this day.

In the Israeli mindset, the policies implemented in the aftermath of the 1967 war were developed out of the assumption that its occupation of Arab areas could provide it with an unprecedented opportunity to reach a final lasting peace accord with its Arab neighbors.[14] As Minister Yigal Allon, one of the Israeli architects of the 1967 war would say at the time, "This is an historic opportunity. We can get comprehensive peace or separate treaties."[15] At the same time, Israel's occupation and extension of military control over the West Bank and Gaza Strip led to the establishment of the country's direct ruling over approximately one million Palestinians, further complicating the dynamics of the conflict.

During the first few months after the end of the 1967 war, Israel's military administration over the West Bank and Gaza Strip maintained the preexisting Arab civil service, allowing Jordanian law to remain and temporarily pulling the majority of its forces from major Arab population centers. At the same time, it also lifted roadblocks and curfews, which allowed Palestinians to travel into Israel proper as well as into Jordan, and reopened trade routes with both Jordan and Israel. No settlements were built during these earliest months, but rather the first years of Israel's occupation saw schools and hospitals built, utilities expanded and in many cases tied to Israel's own grid, and trade significantly increased.

In the wake of the 1967 Six-Day War, the Arab world reacted to Israel's ongoing policies and to its extended military occupation with the Arab League's now infamous September 1967 Khartoum declaration, which rejected the possibility of signing a peace treaty with Israel, of directly engaging in negotiations with the Jewish state, and of accepting Israel's de jure existence. A few months later, in November 1967, the UN Security Council passed Resolution 242, urging Israel to withdraw from territories occupied during the preceding war.[16] Notably, the resolution purposely left out which territories exactly Israel needed to withdraw from, leaving open the possibility that Israel could remain in control of some land. UNSCR 242, which formed the basis for a two-state solution, was publicly rejected by most of the Arab world for many years. Israel's prime minister Levi Eshkol outlined his country's willingness to give up the West Bank, Gaza Strip, Sinai Peninsula, and Golan Heights in return for peace with its Arab neighbors. Such a move would have been rather simple at the time, as no settlements were yet built and thus little pressure could be exerted by constituents. As long as peace was not a viable option, the Israeli government found it useful to first develop "facts" on the ground, under the argument laid out by Defense Minister Moshe Dayan at the time:

"If the Arabs refuse to make peace . . . we cannot stand still. If we are denied their cooperation, let us act on our own."[17]

These "facts" came largely in the form of settlements, which in the years that followed would be built in the West Bank, Gaza Strip, Golan Heights, and parts of Sinai, through the specialized agricultural-military infantry force known as Nahal, which had already helped establish many villages and cities in Israel proper.[18] These Nahal settlements would serve not only military objectives but ideological ones as well. The West Bank, also known as Judea and Samaria, is home to a number of Judaism's and Christianity's holiest sites. Some of these settlements would be built on lands that had previously been Jewish towns prior to their destruction before and during the 1948 war, while many others would be built on land expropriated or confiscated from the Palestinian population. Many would later be handed over to Israeli citizens and further developed, settled, and expanded significantly. Israel's settlement policy from the beginning was one of the most controversial aspects of its occupation of the Palestinian territories, and it has continuously been rejected by the international community, both because it is held to be in violation of international humanitarian law and because it is seen as creating Jewish-only enclaves in Palestinian areas, thus rendering future withdrawals and removal of the military occupation more challenging.

The Gaza Strip in particular was at first very sparsely settled by Israel. No settlements were initially built in Gaza, with the exception of Kfar Darom in 1970, which had been rebuilt on the same plot where it had originally stood both in 1936 and again in 1946 (after having been overrun and destroyed in 1939).[19] The majority of Gaza's settlements were built in the 1980s, with some established as late as the 1990s.[20] This was mainly the result of Israel's initial uncertainty over what to do with Gaza. The Egyptians made clear during peace negotiations that they did not want it back, and Prime Minister Levi Eshkol would quickly come to realize that it was "a bone stuck in our [Israelis'] throats."[21]

From the Palestinians' perspective, the post-1967 military occupation represented a second collective trauma, after the 1948 Nakba, and a continuation of Israel's denial of their right to self-determination. Although in some aspects the lot of the Palestinians may have improved after the 1967 war, they were still living under military occupation, only this time by a state and people that they viewed had destroyed their own. Palestinians living in the West Bank and Gaza Strip were put under Israeli military rule, and as such, their freedoms and rights were severely impaired. In the West Bank, Israel decided against formally annexing the area, as such a move would require granting citizenship to so many Palestinian Arabs that it would risk the Jewish nature of the state. Consequently, the Palestinians who worked in Israel proper would grow increasingly resentful of the clear disparity in standards of living and rights between themselves and the Israelis. In less populated areas such as the Golan Heights, the land was officially incorporated, and the local Arab populations were offered Israeli citizenship, thus ending the legal occupation of that land in the eyes of the Israeli government. For all of these reasons, Palestinian nationalist sentiment and the right to self-determination through the use of armed struggle took on a major role after 1967.[22]

Another important consequence of Israel's rule of the Palestinian territories was the renewed freedom that was awarded to Islamic and Islamist organizations. This was especially significant in Gaza, where the Muslim Brotherhood had been banned and forced to operate clandestinely under Egyptian control. From the late 1960s to the mid-1980s, Israel went out of its way to support these Muslim groups in order for them to serve as a counterweight to the PLO and its secular brand of nationalism.[23] This initial Israeli support is what has led many to assert rather erroneously that Israel "created" Hamas. In reality, as long as these organizations were not found to support anti-Israeli activities, they were largely left alone to operate their social welfare systems. First developed by the Muslim Brotherhood in Gaza in 1946, the Islamic Charitable League, or al Mujamma al-Islami (hitherto referred to as the Mujamma), was a "network of social, charitable, and educational institutions linked to the local mosques."[24] Such Islamic charities existed throughout the Muslim world, providing social welfare to needy Muslims in line with the Islamic instruction to give charity, or *zakat*. Following Israel's takeover of the West Bank and Gaza Strip, these Islamist groups slowly were able to upgrade their operations and thus increase their popularity. At the same time, they gradually began to be more involved in political activities against Israel. As many of these charities began to support anti-Israeli political and military operations, Israel increasingly monitored and prohibited many of their actions.[25]

Israel's occupation of Gaza was, however, not the only reason why Palestinian Islamist groups, including the Muslim Brotherhood, began to develop and gain popularity in the years following the 1967 war. Israel's tremendous victory in 1967 resulted in a clear failure for Nasser's secular pan-Arabism. The progressive decline of pan-Arabism in the Arab world and the sense of frustration and disappointment as a consequence of the military defeat of 1967 would lead to a major rise in Islamist ideology among the Palestinians, who were traditionally a rather secular people.

Additional events would lead to increased Islamist sentiment among Palestinians. The improved result of the 1973 Yom Kippur Arab-Israeli War and the later jolt to the oil markets around the world were the first additional stimuli. This new environment provided Islamists with not only a massive infusion of funding but also an increase in adherents who felt out of step with the ever-wealthier Arab elite.[26] Additionally, although the Palestinian Muslim population was nearly completely Sunni, the 1979 Iranian revolution further radicalized them, as did the Soviet invasion of Afghanistan.[27] Finally, the defeat and expulsion of the PLO from Lebanon in 1982 further helped to increase the number of Islamists among Palestinians. The year 1982 also led to a resurgence in Islamist ideology, as the Palestinians' loss in Lebanon was blamed on their lack of adherence to Islamic thought and doctrine.[28] Despite their rise in popularity, Palestinian Islamists continued to be challenged by secular groups for the hearts and minds of the Palestinian people.[29] No group was more emblematic of this than the Palestine Liberation Organization (PLO), and in particular Yasser Arafat's dominant Fatah party. Arafat, Fatah, the PLO, and the later Palestinian Authority (PA) all took steps to minimize support for Islamist organizations, chief among them Hamas.

The PLO and Fatah

The rise of Islamism following the 1967 defeat was part of a greater trend toward growing Palestinian nationalist movements. Palestinian nationalism overall continued to be fundamentally secular in nature, with leftist ideologies such as Marxism playing a major role and religion providing a more private character to Palestinian identity.[30] Secular groups such as Arafat's Fatah party did, however, also use Islamic symbolism for popularity purposes. In fact, the name Fatah itself is a reverse acronym for Harakat al-Tahrar al-Filistini, or "Liberation Movement of Palestine," which refers to the historical period of expansion within Islam and was thus a very appealing name.[31] Additionally, drafts of a constitution for a future Palestinian state explicitly affirmed that "Arabic and Islam are the official Palestinian language and religion."[32]

Since its founding in 1964, the PLO served as an umbrella organization for Palestinian "resistance" groups that attacked Israelis. Following the 1967 war, it became increasingly clear to Palestinians that they could not rely on the greater Arab world to bring about Israel's destruction. They came to recognize that a more autonomous movement was needed to carry on the armed struggle against Israel even more directly. In this sense, armed attacks and terrorism as a tool began to increase significantly, as the Palestinians simultaneously began to call for their right to self-determination. It was during this time that Yasser Arafat became chairman of the PLO, and his Fatah faction the dominant party in the organization. Arafat used his newfound platform to plan spectacular "blind terrorism" attacks during the 1970s as a way to effectively bring the Palestinian cause to international consciousness and arouse support for it in the Arab and Muslim worlds.[33] Despite, or perhaps as a result of, the horrific nature of these attacks, which included assassinations, bombings, kidnappings, and airplane hijackings around the world, Arafat and Palestinians such as PFLP head George Habash, were very effective at raising the plight of the Palestinians to the world's consciousness.[34]

By 1974 the Arab League had named the PLO as the "sole legitimate representative of the Palestinian people," yet it was not until July 1988 that Jordan dropped its claim to the West Bank, thereby conceding much of its role as representative of the Palestinian people.[35] In 1989 the PLO recognized UN resolutions 242 and 338, essentially accepting the notion of negotiations with Israel based on a two-state solution to the Palestinian-Israeli conflict. This acceptance also allowed for a significant rise in acceptance of the PLO by the international community.[36] Arafat, who had previously been perhaps the best-known terrorist in the world, was able to make over his reputation into that of a pragmatic revolutionary, freedom fighter, and statesman. This policy change would also become a major source of contention with groups such as Hamas, which from their onset criticized the PLO because of its "moderate" drive toward independence. Yet, despite the Islamist and radical leftist groups' rejection of a two-state solution with Israel, the majority of the Palestinian population backed Fatah and its political evolution. Following the signing of the 1993 Oslo Accords, Arafat rode a wave of immense popularity amongst Palestinians. When he returned to the West Bank in 1994 after decades in exile, he returned as leader of the newly formed Palestinian Authority. The exuberant crowds who rejoiced at his return were evidence of just how much support he had amassed.

The Oslo Accords appeared for many to be the dawn of a new era in the Middle East, one that would transform the region and relations between

Arabs and Israelis. The Cold War had just ended and peace talks had the backing of the sole remaining superpower, thus further raising the hopes of all involved parties. By 1994, Israel and Jordan signed a peace agreement long in the making, while negotiations between the Israelis and Palestinians continued. However, the Declaration of Principles agreed upon in Oslo and the subsequent creation of the Palestinian Authority did not provide a stable platform to solve the conflict between the Israelis and Palestinians.

From an Israeli perspective, there was an issue of trust on whether Fatah's recognition of Israel's right to exist was genuine, and whether there was a real acceptance of Israel as a Jewish state. Furthermore, soon after Israel handed over control of parts of the West Bank to the newly created Palestinian Authority, suicide attacks appeared in Israel for the first time, thus further hindering many Israelis' trust in their Palestinian counterparts. Yet, from the Palestinians' perspective, the self-government formula agreed upon in Oslo was not extensive or effective enough. As they saw it, the February 1994 terrorist attack at the Cave of the Patriarchs in Hebron by a Jewish settler was a major impetus for the suicide bombing campaign against Israelis. Israel's continued settlement expansion activities even in the aftermath of the accords further undermined the level of trust in the Israeli government. Although settlement expansion was not explicitly forbidden in the accords, it was generally viewed as unacceptable by the international community and led to an increasing wariness between the two sides. This was only exacerbated in the years that followed, as both Palestinian attacks on Israeli civilians and Israeli reprisals and settlement building continued.

As the euphoria of the moment seemed to pass, so did the feelings of goodwill on both sides. Following the collapse of the Camp David II Summit in July of 2000, violence began to spiral out of control. By September, the second Intifada, dubbed the Al Aqsa Intifada by the Palestinians, had commenced. Unlike the first Intifada in 1987, this second uprising was marked by greater force, more weaponry, and sophisticated low-intensity warfare tactics throughout the West Bank and Gaza Strip. Furthermore, whereas the first uprising was largely spontaneous, Israeli sources claimed that the second round of fighting was planned and sponsored by Arafat, in conjunction with other groups such as Hamas and the Palestinian Islamic Jihad (PIJ). Palestinian sources have asserted that Ariel Sharon's controversial visit to the Temple Mount in Jerusalem when he was a sitting member of the Knesset spurred the violence. An American fact-finding commission, headed by Senator

George J. Mitchell, reported that "we have no basis on which to conclude that there was a deliberate plan by the PA to initiate a campaign of violence at the first opportunity; or to conclude that there was a deliberate plan by the GOI [Government of Israel] to respond with lethal force. However, there is also no evidence on which to conclude that the PA made a consistent effort to contain the demonstrations and control the violence once it began; or that the GOI made a consistent effort to use non-lethal means to control demonstrations of unarmed Palestinians. Amid rising anger, fear, and mistrust, each side assumed the worst about the other and acted accordingly."[37]

The second Intifada also marked the beginning of the decline of Fatah within the Palestinian territories and the progressive rise of Hamas's popularity and credibility. In parallel, as the situation on the ground deteriorated, so did the relations between Arafat, Israel, and the United States, as both the Sharon and Bush administrations refused to have any contact with him, further weakening both Fatah and the Palestinian Authority. By the time he fell ill before his death in November 2004, he had been isolated in his damaged Muqata headquarters compound in Ramallah, surrounded by Israeli forces and largely shunned by members of the international community.[38]

The outbreak of violence during the second Intifada highlighted important divisions within secular Palestinian society more generally and the Fatah leadership in particular. The Palestinian population as a whole is divided by those who live within Mandate Palestine (excluding Jordan), known as the "insiders," or *al-dakhil*, and those in the diaspora known as the "outsiders," or *al-kharij*. The insiders were further separated according to whether they lived as Israeli citizens in Israel proper, or whether they lived in the West Bank or Gaza Strip.[39] Yet a further division existed between Palestinian Arabs who lived in refugee camps after 1948 and those not considered refugees until Israel's takeover of the land in 1967.

Within Fatah itself, three major divisions existed that have resulted in increasing tensions within the organization. The first group, made up most famously of Arafat, Mahmoud Abbas, and Ahmed Qureia, were known as the "old guard" of Fatah. These men came from the founding generation but were largely absent during the first Intifada as they were far away from the conflict during that time. The second, middle generation arose during the first Intifada and helped form the more hard-core and locally rooted militia known as the Tanzim, led by Marwan Barghouti. It was during the first Intifada that Palestinian groups began to realize that if they wished to remain acceptable to the international conscience, they would need to move their focus from international terrorism to attacks that were isolated to the West Bank and Gaza Strip. This group had a key role in organizing Fatah's presence during the second Intifada.[40] The third group was made up of the youngest generation and emerged during the second Intifada. It was associated with, and often participated in, the Fatah-affiliated terrorist group known as the Al Aqsa Martyrs Brigades (sponsored by Marwan Barghouti), as well as the Popular Resistance Committees (PRC). Both organizations were involved in anti-Israeli terrorist activities more so than most other Fatah factions were during the second uprising.[41] For Arafat, the Al Aqsa Martyrs Brigades was used to compete with Hamas, the PIJ, and the PFLP, by attracting Palestinians who largely supported the "armed struggle" against Israel. In this sense, he was trying to cope with the ongoing political decline of Fatah and reassert its popularity and credibility within the Palestinian population, which had become largely discouraged and exasperated by the failure of the Fatah-backed "peace process." Following Arafat's death and Barghouti's arrest by Israeli forces, however, the Al Aqsa Martyrs Brigades proved more difficult to control for leaders such as Mahmoud Abbas.

While the Al Aqsa Martyrs Brigades is considered a splinter or offshoot of Fatah, there is significant evidence that Arafat and his followers refrained from controlling and at times even supported terrorist activities following the outbreak of the second Intifada.[42] At the beginning of the second Intifada, in fact, the various Palestinian factions tried to put their differences aside and pool their resources against Israel.[43] Although Fatah and Hamas had been fierce competitors during the period of the Oslo talks, they temporarily cooperated during this initial phase of the uprising.[44] Following the outbreak of hostilities in late 2000, Arafat also sheltered and assisted terrorists wanted by Israel, hiding them in his own Muqata compound and releasing Hamas fighters that the Palestinian Authority had previously arrested under past agreements with Israel.[45] However, as the Intifada progressed, Arafat's ability to cooperate with, control, and contain other Palestinian armed factions— especially Hamas and the Islamic Jihad—started to diminish, especially in the aftermath of Israel's 2002 Operation Defensive Shield, which further placed PA political and security institutions in a state of disarray. As a result, while loosening the situation and the ability to control Palestinian violence, Arafat's status within the international community simultaneously began to deteriorate.

For the American administration under President George W. Bush, two actions in particular are said to have led him to shun Arafat altogether. The first was a roadside bombing of a U.S. diplomatic convoy in Gaza that killed three Americans.[46] The second act was the capture by Israeli naval commandos of the Lebanese ship named the *Karine A* in January 2002. The ship had been sailing under the command of Arafat's cohorts and carried fifty tons of Iranian-supplied weapons that were prohibited under the Oslo Accords. The capture of this ship, along with documentation captured in West Bank raids by the IDF, appeared to prove—despite Arafat's denial of any involvement in the shipment—that he had been purchasing arms to carry out attacks at the same time he was denying and condemning violence against Israelis.[47] Just months after 9/11, when President Bush had outlined his "with us or with the terrorists" position, the *Karine A* capture was yet another strike against the Palestinians, one that left them diplomatically isolated as long as Arafat remained in power.[48]

A final point regarding the PLO and Fatah is the high levels of corruption within these organizations, as well as in the Palestinian Authority, which had dominated the Palestinian Territories. According to the World Bank, between 1993 and 2004 international aid for the Palestinian community reached $10 billion, "the highest per capita aid transfer in the history of foreign aid anywhere."[49] An IMF study in 2003 discovered that only 8 percent of the funds allocated had been used appropriately, with the rest doled out according to Arafat's whim, often to pay off supporters and control monopolies. Israeli intelligence would estimate his personal fortune in the "billions of dollars," while *Forbes* listed him as one of the wealthiest in the world in its 2003 report on "Billionaires: Kings, Queens and Despots."[50] It was this high level of corruption and inefficiency within Fatah and the Palestinian Authority that further contributed to their political decline in the past decade and to the parallel rise of Hamas. The rise in corruption also saw the demand by Western contributing states for a more financially responsible Palestinian leader. This resulted in the appointment of economist Salam Fayyad to the position of prime minister for the Palestinian Authority in 2007. A relative outsider and member of the small "Third Way" political party, Fayyad's more financially lucid character and the support he enjoys by Western states has led to increased tension with Fatah, Hamas, and the PLO. Although Fayyad did an excellent job at improving the lot of the Palestinians in the West Bank, in cooperation with Israel, Jordan, and the West, he remained unpopular with the Palestinian leadership of both Fatah and Hamas because of his outsider status. Consequently, after a new unity government was announced between Hamas and Fatah, Fayyad was not renominated for the position of prime minister.[51]

Despite the political flaws of the Palestinian Authority and Fatah, support for Arafat continues to this day among many Palestinians, as he is revered as the father of the Palestinian national movement. While this reality leaves some Western observers baffled, many of these analysts fail to understand that Arafat is respected for having helped elevate the Palestinian cause to the world's attention, even if his efforts fell short of delivering the Palestinians a sovereign state. Thus, while Palestinians increasingly turned to the less corrupt and more effective social welfare organizations offered by Islamist groups like Hamas, Arafat loyalists remained. It took Hamas's own criticisms of Arafat and the corruption of Fatah to help turn many Palestinians away from the secular group. This became particularly evident in the Gaza Strip, the traditional stronghold of Hamas and Islamism among Palestinians.

Palestinian Islamic Jihad

The early 1980s saw the emergence of the Palestinian Islamic Jihad as the first major militant Islamist faction in the Palestinian territories to target Israel. The PIJ, or Harakat al-Jihad al-Islami al-Filastini, is designated as a foreign terrorist organization (FTO) by the United States, and together with Hamas it has led the Palestinian "armed struggle" against Israel over the past few decades.[52] While the PIJ is considered to be a violent offshoot of the Muslim Brotherhood, the organization was formed out of the merging of four like-minded factions: the Islamic Jihad, the Islamic Jihad Jerusalem Brigade, the Islamic Jihad Battalions, and Islamic Jihad Palestine.[53] It first became active in the late 1970s and early 1980s under the influence of the Iranian Revolution. Although many groups in the Muslim world have taken on the generic name "Islamic Jihad" in the past (most notably in Lebanon), the Palestinian Islamic Jihad is the longest running, largest, and most permanent of these groups. The PIJ was founded by two Palestinians from the Gaza Strip who had been influenced by Egyptian jihadi groups: Sheikh Abd al-Aziz Awda and a physician named Fathi Shiqaqi, who would become the group's leader.[54]

Although the PIJ shares with Hamas the goal of establishing an Islamic state in the entire "liberated" Palestine and also rejects both the existence of the State of Israel and the notion of negotiations and agreements with the Jewish state, the ideological differences between the two organizations are still quite substantial. Similarly, despite the fact that Hamas and the Palestinian Islamic Jihad have employed similar tactics in conducting their fight against Israel—including the use of suicide bombings against civilian and military targets and the launching of rocket attacks—the activities of the PIJ are far more restricted than those of Hamas and do not include social and political activism at nearly the same level.

Ideologically, the PIJ was influenced by the beliefs of both the Egyptian Muslim Brotherhood and the Iranian Revolution. It developed a tighter ideological and practical connection with Iran more quickly than did Hamas. Although technically Sunni, the PIJ adheres to the Khomeini-Shiite principle of a *wilayat al-faqih*—a fact that clearly differentiates it from Hamas and nearly every other Palestinian Islamist group. The PIJ also rejects the Palestinian Muslim Brotherhood's notion that jihad against Israel could come only after the resolution of the "internal jihad" among its followers in the Islamic world—a disagreement that spurred the creation of PIJ as a splinter group in the first place.[55] The Mujamma had previously stated that until Muslim adherents were ideologically sound and sufficiently learned, they should not wage jihad against Israel. Shiqaqi rejected this idea and called for the unification and mobilization of Sunnis and Shiites in order to liberate historic Palestine. He argued that the fight against Israel needed to be the first defensive jihad undertaken by Muslims, as Islamic land was currently being ruled by Jews in violation of Islamic law.

Since its creation, the PIJ has focused almost exclusively on violence and terrorism against Israeli civilians and soldiers and has generally ignored the need for an effective social welfare system, thus differing itself from Hamas both ideologically and operationally.[56] As the ultimate goal of the organization is the creation of an Islamist state in historic Palestine as part of a first step toward the Islamization of the world, jihad against Israel has been, and will remain, the PIJ's primary objective.

Although founded in the early 1980s, PIJ stepped up its operational activism around 1985, when it began to regularly conduct attacks against Israel.[57] The PIJ has since rejected nearly all truces established between Israel and other Palestinian factions and has continued to carry out strikes even when groups such as Hamas have been able to reach cease-fires, demonstrating a lack of the political pragmatism and flexibility that Hamas has achieved.[58]

The PIJ's focus on violence over indoctrination or ideology on the eve of the 1987 Intifada would come to inspire many new Palestinian Islamist jihadi groups. This violence would be conducted through the group's "military wing," known as the Al Quds (Jerusalem) Brigades.[59] Al Quds Brigades' members received financing from Iran, Syria, and Saudi Arabia, along with training from the Iranian Revolutionary Guards Corps (IRGC) at Hezbollah-run training camps in Lebanon.[60] Although the PIJ did carry out some joint attacks with Hezbollah, it focused much more of its attention on attacking targets in Israel proper, the West Bank, and Gaza Strip. After the signing of the Oslo Accords as well as during ongoing peace talks between Israeli and Palestinian officials, the PIJ often acted as a spoiler, launching some of the deadliest suicide bombing campaigns against Israeli civilians.[61] After Shiqaqi's assassination by Israeli agents in Malta in October 1995, the organization's activities slowed to a near standstill. However, by the second Intifada the group had bounced back, and today is once again responsible for some of the worst attacks inflicted on Israel, occasionally in conjunction with Hamas, the Al Aqsa Martyrs Brigades, and other Palestinian rejectionist groups.[62]

Despite the ideological differences with Hamas, the two organizations have shown the ability to cooperate with one another, even while competing for members and support from many of the same sources, especially during the years of the second Intifada.[63] In the aftermath of Hamas's electoral victory in 2006 and its armed takeover of Gaza in 2007, however, the relationship between the two organizations progressively deteriorated. Unlike Hamas, the PIJ never had any serious political platform or substantial interest in taking part in the political process, even though it did not have any real opposition to Hamas's political participation. On the contrary, it urged the group to stay in power while maintaining its right to armed jihad and its firm rejection of the State of Israel.[64] Yet the group's posture gradually shifted and assumed more confrontational tones after Hamas's takeover of Gaza, a move that the PIJ condemned. It urged Hamas to focus on jihad against Israel instead of fighting fellow Palestinians.[65]

Among the reasons that led the PIJ to oppose Hamas's takeover was the group's opposition to Hamas's increasing degree of control within Gaza and its desire to effectively hold a monopoly of force within the Strip—two realities that threatened the PIJ's freedom of action. To prevent this occurrence, the PIJ did not hesitate to create short-term alliances with both former Fatah members and Qassam Brigades' militants in order to enhance its strength in the Gaza Strip and to challenge Hamas's monopoly of force.[66] Similarly, the group has publicly defied Hamas's authority. For example, between June and December 2008 it repeatedly fired rockets into Israel while Hamas was urging all factions to respect the temporary cease-fire it had agreed to establish with the Jewish state. These events led to increasing tensions between the two organizations, occasionally escalating into armed clashes and leading to Hamas's repeated attempts to curb the group's autonomy and power in Gaza.[67] Consequently, the PIJ emerged as another Islamist group challenging Hamas on the basis of its "moderate" political trajectory as well as its alleged accommodation with respect to Israel. In this sense, in the unlikely event that Hamas would come to terms with its anti-Israeli Islamist ideology and accept a peace agreement, the PIJ would most likely emerge as the leading Islamist rejectionist group and spoiler among Palestinian organizations.

Salafi-Jihadist Groups in Gaza

The recent rise in tensions between Hamas and the Palestinian Islamic Jihad can be considered as part of a larger trend within Palestinian society at large—namely, the ongoing internal radicalization process. An important indicator of this development is represented by the emergence of splinter groups with a Salafi-jihadist orientation, which have stated goals and rhetoric more closely associated with global jihadists groups and less with the Palestinian struggle.

Most of these new groups are composed of former members of Fatah, Hamas, and the Palestinian Islamic Jihad, who further radicalized and left their original organizations. The number of Salafi-jihadist militants is unknown, although estimates range from a few hundreds[68] of militants to five thousand.[69] The movement is predominantly Palestinian, although more recently a few dozen foreign militants—some of them returnees from Iraq—are believed to have entered the Gaza Strip through Egypt in an effort to join local jihadist movements.[70]

In truth, Salafism is not entirely a new phenomenon in Gaza, as non-violent Salafi organizations that focused on social work and proselytism first emerged there in the early 1980s.[71] At that time, the movement was led by clerics such as Sheikh Salim Sharab, who had undergone religious training in Saudi Arabia and subsequently returned to the Palestinian territories with the purpose of spreading its radical understanding of Islam. The movement continued to grow during the 1980s and received an additional boost in the 1990s following the establishment of the Palestinian Authority.[72] Yet it never became a mainstream actor within the Palestinian political arena. These types of nonviolent, political-Salafist groups are still present in Gaza, as evidenced by the Liberation Party (Hizb ut-Tahrir), which advocates for the establishment of an Islamic Caliphate of Palestine and politically opposes the Hamas government.[73]

Yet the more interesting trend taking place in the past few years is the gradual development of a Salafi-jihadist camp within Gaza. These groups started to mushroom in the months leading up to and following the 2005 Israeli withdrawal from Gaza, and their presence additionally increased in the months following Hamas's electoral victory and its armed takeover in 2007.[74] Since then, the Salafi-jihadist movement has steadily grown within the Gaza Strip, and it now represents a loosely affiliated network of small organizations and operational cells whose main focus has been both attacking Israel and attempting to "Islamize" Palestinian society by force. This has resulted in Hamas making its own efforts to further Islamize the Palestinian population of Gaza, in order both to appease the Salafis and to compete for their supporters.[75]

Ideologically, these groups have adopted an international jihadist agenda that is aligned with al Qaeda's ideology. They have dramatically shifted away from framing the Palestinian struggle under nationalist terms, thus strongly differentiating themselves from groups such as Hamas. The Salafi-jihadist groups have also harshly criticized Hamas for joining the Palestinian political system, condemning the organization's administration of the Gaza Strip, accusing Hamas of having moderated its struggle against Israel, and implying that it has not implemented Sharia law within Gaza. However, despite the strong ideological connection with the transnational jihadist movement, the Gaza-based Salafi-jihadist movement is largely a local phenomenon that lacks direct organizational and operational links with al Qaeda.[76]

Early reports of Salafi-jihadist activities in the Gaza Strip go back to 2005, when the first operational cells were starting to emerge. An example of these early groups was the Jundullah group (Allah's Brigades), allegedly composed of former Hamas and Fatah members and claiming to be affiliated with al Qaeda.[77] Despite the lack of a direct connection, the group's platform was nonetheless shaped by Bin Laden's call for international jihad. The organization's spokesman, Abu Abdallah al-Khattab, also declared that it was interested in targeting U.S. interests in the region.[78]

Since then, a substantial number of new jihadist groups has developed within Gaza, including Swords of Righteousness (Suyuf al-Haq), the Army of Islam (Jaish al-Islam), the Army of the Nation (Jaish al-Ummah), the Army of Allah's Supporters (Jund Ansar Allah), and Jaljalat (also known as Ansar al-Sunnah). The Swords of Righteousness is one of Gaza's first Salafi-jihadist groups, operating even before the 2007 Hamas takeover of the Gaza Strip, and is concentrated in the Beit Hanoun area. The group was allegedly founded by former Hamas cleric Abu Suheib al Maqdisi, who left that organization to protest its decision to take part in the 2006 Palestinian legislative elections.[79] The Swords of Righteousness has been active in Gaza ever since and has focused mostly on internal targets, trying to Islamize society by force and to punish those involved in activities deemed as "corrupt" or "immoral."[80] The group has in the past systematically bombed Gaza's Internet cafés and music shops, attacked the local al-Arabiya television facilities,[81] and assaulted and kidnapped individuals who defied their calls to live a more Islamist lifestyle.[82] This group has also repeatedly threatened the small Gaza-based Christian community. In 2006, for example, it announced its intention to blow up local churches in response to the publication in Denmark of cartoons depicting the Prophet Mohammed.[83]

Another veteran group, the Army of Islam, similarly developed in the period following Hamas's electoral victory and its subsequent takeover, but it chose to focus more on external targets, both Israeli and international. The organization's first real operation was as a participant together with Hamas's Qassam Brigades and the Salah al-Din Brigades in the kidnapping of IDF soldier Gilad Shalit in June 2006.[84] The Army of Islam took credit for that operation through an al Qaeda–affiliated online forum, and it introduced itself as a jihadist Palestinian organization waging a religious, not nationalist, war on Israel.[85]

In truth, the Army of Islam is a product of both the growing Salafist influence within Gaza and internal clan politics. The group was created by former Popular Resistance Committee member Mumtaz Dughmush and, since its inception, has been linked to the powerful Dughmush clan in Gaza.[86] In this sense, the organization also had the objective of challenging Hamas's authority in the Gaza Strip, which has led to armed clashes between the two groups.

In March 2007 the Army of Islam orchestrated the kidnapping of BBC correspondent Alan Johnston and held him captive for more than four months in an attempt to emphasize its capacity to prevent Hamas from properly ruling Gaza.[87] The Army of Islam's actions were also motivated by an international jihadist agenda; the group had initially decided to condition Johnston's release on the simultaneous release of al Qaeda cleric Abu Qatada, who was being held in the United Kingdom—again stressing its ideological closeness to al Qaeda.[88] However, the kidnapping of the BBC correspondent backfired for the Army of Islam, as it led Hamas to severely crackdown on the group, which significantly reduced its size and importance. Since that time, the Salafi organization has continued to conduct internal attacks against "corrupt" businesses in Gaza while recurrently clashing with Hamas.[89] In 2009, for example, it was involved in the training of Egyptian jihadists of the al-Zeitun cell, an al Qaeda–inspired group that was planning to assassinate the Israeli ambassador to Egypt.[90]

A third main Salafi-jihadist group in Gaza is the Army of the Nation (Jaish al-Ummah), operational since June 2007.[91] It is focused predominantly on targeting Israel,[92] while largely avoiding claims of responsibility for attacks against internal Palestinian targets.[93] The organization, led by Abu Hafs al-Maqdisi,[94] demonstrated its interest in pursuing an international jihadist agenda when in January 2008 it announced its intention to assassinate U.S. president George W. Bush during a forthcoming trip to the region.[95] The Army of the Nation maintains a close ideological, albeit not operational, link with al Qaeda, together with a very critical stance on Hamas.[96] Its leader, Abu Hafs, has stated: "We believe that Hamas does not implement the rule of God on earth, and does not implement or enforce any ruling of the Islamic Shariah."[97] Not surprisingly, the relations between Hamas and the Jaish al-Ummah have been reciprocally hostile, with the Salafi group recurrently defying Hamas's calls to preserve a cease-fire with Israel,[98] and with Hamas periodically arresting the group's fighters and leaders.[99]

To date, the worst episodes of violence between Hamas and Salafi-jihadist groups took place with the Rafah-based Army of Allah's Supporters (Jund Ansar Allah). The group, funded by Syrian-born Abu-Abdallah al-Muhajir, had been active mostly against Israel since 2008.[100] It is allegedly composed of former Hamas and Fatah members,[101] as well as a few Egyptians, Yemenis, Pakistanis, and Afghanis.[102] The Army of Allah's Supporters and Hamas clashed in August 2009, when Abd-al-Latif Musa, one the organization's leaders and the imam of the Ibn Taymiyah Mosque in the Gazan city of Rafah, called for a rebellion against Hamas and for the creation of an Islamic Emirate in Rafah.[103] These declarations prompted Hamas to intervene militarily, killing both Abd-al-Latif Musa and the group's military leader, Abu-Abdallah al-Suri, in the course of a military engagement that led to more than twenty-two casualties.[104] In the aftermath of this bloody confrontation, the group's activism has been substantially curbed, although it appears to still be operational. In October 2009 and March 2010, for example, the group resurfaced and claimed responsibility for firing rockets against Israel.[105]

A final important Salafi-jihadist organization is the so-called Jaljalat (Thunder),[106] a loosely structured group led by Mahmud Talib, a former leader within Hamas's military wing. Jaljalat is largely composed of former and current Hamas militants who are critical of the group's "moderate" drive.[107] Talib has declared his group's intention to officially pledge its allegiance to al Qaeda by way of a future terrorist operation.[108] Jaljalat has targeted Israelis, other Palestinians, and international targets. Its operations include two foiled attempts to assassinate both former U.S. president Jimmy Carter and former British prime minister Tony Blair when the two visited Gaza.[109] Within the Gaza Strip, Jaljalat has also claimed responsibility for the bombing of the house of Dr. Marwan Abu-Ras, a Hamas member of the Palestinian Legislative Council,[110] as well as for the bombings against Hamas's security buildings in August 2009, following Hamas's crackdown on Salafis in Rafah.[111] In response to these attacks, Hamas has tried to curb Jaljalat's activities, and in March 2010 it was able to arrest Jaljalat's leader, Talib, thus weakening but not destroying the group's operational capacity.[112]

This brief examination of Gaza's Salafi-jihadist activism, however, admittedly falls short of covering all of the existing operational cells and groups. In fact, in addition to these better-established groups, there are now a growing number of smaller, more loosely affiliated cells that have adopted a variety of front names to perpetrate attacks against Israelis and Palestinians alike, making it more difficult to determine who is behind each operation.[113] Indeed, new Salafist groups and cells keep mushrooming within Gaza and continue to challenge the Hamas government. The last major confrontation between the Salafists and the Gaza government occurred in April 2011, when an Italian member of the pro-Palestinian International Solidarity Movement (ISM) was kidnapped and assassinated by a small cell of militants belonging to different local Salafist groups. This led to a bloody confrontation with the Hamas security forces who tracked down the killers.[114]

Describing the recent rise of jihadist activities within the Gaza Strip still serves the purpose of illustrating the growing impact of the Salafi-jihadist movement and confirms the existence of an internal Palestinian movement pushing to further Islamize and transnationalize the Palestinian struggle. This reality clearly represents a direct challenge to Hamas and its authority in Gaza, especially given that the local jihadist factions have grown more defiant of Hamas over time.[115] At the time of writing, the Salafi-jihadist movement lacked the military strength to effectively challenge Hamas's authority. Yet their role should not be underestimated, especially considering the ongoing defection of disenchanted Hamas fighters, who have left the group's military brigades to join some of the new jihadi formations.[116]

7 Hamas
History and Development

HAMAS EMERGED FROM within the Muslim Brotherhood as a way to accommodate the group's need to become more involved in both Palestinian politics and the Palestinian struggle against Israel. The Palestinian Islamic Jihad had opposed the Muslim Brotherhood's lack of political activities and its focus on implementing a social agenda for the Palestinians in the early 1980s, and Hamas became the answer to fill this void. The organization was essentially a product of the first Intifada, which provided it with the impetus to bring itself into the Palestinian political scene and become part of the "resistance" camp. It offered an alternative to the more conventional, secular-minded political thought of the Palestine Liberation Organization, arguing that the PLO's failures in Lebanon were a result of its disconnection from and failure to adhere to Islamic tenets.[1] Hamas also rose, however, in part as a competitor to the Palestinian Islamic Jihad, which had broken from the Muslim Brotherhood because of its disagreement over when jihad against Israel could be waged. Unlike the PIJ, the Muslim Brotherhood advocated for proper indoctrination and understanding of an individual Muslim's own "internal jihad" before an external defensive jihad against Israel could commence.

The Beginning

When the first Intifada erupted, Sheikh Ahmed Yassin had already been an established Islamist leader in the Gaza Strip, as a prominent principal of the Brotherhood and the founder and first president of the Mujamma since 1983.[2] The PIJ's participation in jihad against Israel threatened the Muslim Brotherhood's base, many of whose members were turning to the PIJ in order to be able to participate in the armed struggle as the uprising began. As a result, after some hesitation Yassin and his inner cabal established a separate wing of the Brotherhood in 1988, known as the Islamic Resistance Movement, or Hamas. After all, it was Yassin who had been one of the first members of the Muslim Brotherhood to conceive of the idea of the destruction of Israel through jihad and its replacement with an Islamist state.[3] Yassin, who had become a paraplegic because of a sporting accident he sustained when he was a young boy, had still managed to study at the esteemed Al Azhar University in Cairo. He was a charismatic and clever leader of the organization who served not just as its spiritual head but also as its overall director. During his time in Egypt, Yassin first joined the Muslim Brotherhood and became familiar with Salafi influences. However, Hamas would differentiate itself from other Islamist groups around the world in focusing foremost on the fight against Israel and in adopting a mix of nationalist and Islamist rhetoric to promote its cause of liberating all of historic Palestine. Unlike the PIJ, Hamas rejected the Khomeini-Shiite notion of the *wilayat al-faqih* and developed a vast social welfare system that not only helped Palestinian Muslims in need but also provided indoctrination, funding, and membership for the militant organization.

In its charter, Hamas identified itself as a wing of the Muslim Brotherhood in Palestine, which accurately highlighted the organizational and ideological roots of the movement. However, since its creation, Hamas was conceived to be autonomous from the Brotherhood, in order to have the operational and ideological freedom to openly join the Intifada and take part in armed clashes against Israel. In this sense, Hamas's self-identification with the Brotherhood, as with other declarations it would make, was indicative of the group's efforts to strike a balance between its ideological roots based in the Muslim Brotherhood and its desire to become a leading Palestinian nationalist movement. In truth, the creation of Hamas as a separate entity from the Muslim Brotherhood was done precisely to prevent Israeli authorities from targeting the organizations' greater activities, in the hopes that it would leave them relatively immune. Moreover, Hamas was created essentially because the Islamists connected to the Muslim Brotherhood feared that without their direct participation in the first Intifada, they would lose supporters to both the PIJ and the PLO, the latter of which was anxious to reassert itself in the Palestinian territories after being marginalized following its expulsion from Lebanon.[4] As authors Mishal and Sela explain, "The Mujamma's decision to adopt a 'jihad now' policy against 'enemies of Allah' [through the creation of Hamas] was thus largely a matter of survival."[5]

Although Hamas is Sunni and does not adhere to Khomeini's and Hezbollah's ideology, it was nevertheless influenced early on by the Iranian Revolution in 1979, as were most Palestinian Islamists. The revolution provided proof that the Islamists could use the power and ideology of jihad to bring about real change. This offered important encouragement for Islamist groups to wage jihad against Israel, and it probably had an impact in accelerating the rise of organizations such as Hamas and the PIJ, as well as facilitating their increased importance early on in the Intifada. Thus, although initial ties between the young Islamic Republic of Iran and the new Hamas organization were weak, Iran's ideological influence was still important for Hamas, as the experience of the Iranian Revolution had a profound effect throughout the region.

The outbreak of the first Intifada in 1987 launched Hamas as an autonomous player in Palestinian politics, through its smaller-scale armed campaigns against the Israeli presence, such as the "knives war," which involved stabbing individual Israelis.[6] At this stage, however, its role was not as important as the one played by its secular-nationalist rival, the PLO. From the outset, the relationship between the PLO and Hamas was characterized by competition and reciprocal distrust, but the degree of open hostility between the two groups was substantially lower than what it would later become. When Hamas was founded, it went out of its way to explain its natural alliance and affinity toward the larger and more powerful PLO. In its charter, the group explicitly stated that the PLO "is the closest to the heart of the Islamic Resistance Movement [Hamas]," that it "contains the father and the brother, the next of kin and the friend," and that "the day the Palestinian Liberation Organization adopts Islam as its way of life, we will become its soldiers, and fuel for its fire that will burn the enemies."[7] Although Hamas openly acknowledged the PLO's role in the Palestinian struggle, the two organizations did not initially cooperate directly or assist each other. Concurrently, they also refrained from openly hostile behavior and interference in each other's operations.

However, despite these supportive statements, many differences between the two groups continued to exist, and these divergences were only heightened after the PLO's acceptance of a two-state solution. Regarding the diverging ideological views of the organizations, Sheikh Yassin explained the difference between his fighters and those of Fatah and other non-Islamist groups as follows: "Those in the Palestinian movement have no commitment to Islamic values. . . . I do not believe that a person who joins Fatah is a Muslim militant when at the same time he does not pray. He is like a Muslim who drinks wine and eats pork. Loyalty is acceptable only when it is devotion to God."[8]

The degree of competition and hostility would additionally rise as Hamas started to become an increasingly important player in both Palestinian domestic politics and the greater context of the Arab-Israeli conflict. Specifically, in the early 1990s the political and military rise of Hamas was boosted by the group's growing degree of international and regional recognition, mostly because of Hamas's role (or lack thereof) during the first Gulf War in Iraq. After Saddam Hussein's invasion of Kuwait, nearly the entire Arab world lined up behind the U.S. coalition and condemned the action. Arafat and the PLO, however, continued to publicly side with Saddam Hussein. Because of the PLO's stance, once power was restored to the Kuwaitis, much of the Arab world significantly cut funding to Arafat, and the Gulf States expelled hundreds of thousands of Palestinians whom they had employed, which caused a severe blow to the Palestinian economy back home. As the most significant competitor to Fatah, Hamas was able to step in and gain a foothold in the deep pockets of the oil-rich Arab world and, in particular, the coffers of Saudi Arabia.[9] At the same time, Hamas's opposition to Saddam Hussein's invasion of Kuwait also helped the group in improving its ties and strategic relations with Iran. In fact, whereas the relationship with the Islamic Republic was rather cool during Hamas's formative years, it gradually shifted after the defeat of Iraq in the 1991 Gulf War.

With its historic Iraqi enemy neutralized, Iran recognized it had an opportunity to increase its influence in the region and decided to start backing Hamas politically and financially. By 1992, Iran had accepted a Hamas delegation, to which it pledged $30 million in annual funding as well weapons and advanced training at Iranian Revolutionary Guards Corps (IRGC) camps that existed in Iran, Lebanon, and Sudan. By 1993, Hamas had opened an office in Tehran.[10] This was a watershed moment for Hamas, which was able to capitalize on its newly acquired political and financial support to assert a greater role within Palestinian politics. Slowly but surely, Hamas began to rise as a realistic political, social, and military alternative to Fatah and the PLO.

The year 1991 also saw Zakaria Walid Akhel establish the Izz al-Din al-Qassam Brigades, Hamas's military wing.[11] It was an additional indication of Hamas's growing organizational sophistication and domestic strength. This development also led Israel to become increasingly alarmed with the new Islamist organization. At the outset of the Intifada, Hamas's religious nature, revivalist-social background, and lesser role in the uprising had led the Israeli government to believe that it might emerge as a better alternative to the PLO. By 1991, however, Israel's assessment of Hamas had changed drastically, which led Prime Minister Yitzhak Rabin to attempt the dismantling of the organization by expelling 415 members of Hamas and the Palestinian Islamic Jihad from the West Bank and Gaza Strip in 1992. This group was mostly exiled to southern Lebanon, where it remained in limbo on the border until it was later readmitted by Israel in 1993 after significant media attention and outside pressure.[12] During their time in partial exile, the militants received training and support from Hezbollah, so that by the time they returned to the West Bank and Gaza they were able to integrate Hezbollah's terrorist tactics, such as the successful deployment of suicide bombers.[13]

Between the signing of the Declaration of Principles in Oslo in 1993 and the outbreak of the second Intifada in September 2000, Hamas intensified its attacks against Israel, ensuring its role as a leading terrorist organization. Following the February 1994 attack at the Cave of the Patriarchs in Hebron by a radical Jewish settler named Baruch Goldstein, Hamas chose to escalate the violence it used against Israel, shifting from individual killings and kidnappings to large-scale terrorist attacks. The first such assault occurred on April 6, 1994, when a bomb was detonated on a bus in the center of the Israeli city of Afula, killing eight civilians.[14] At the same time, while increasing its attacks against Israel, Hamas assumed a more confrontational and critical position vis-à-vis the newly established Palestinian Authority (PA), rejecting and endangering the successful outcome of the peace negotiations. In turn, this led to a deterioration of the group's relationship with the PLO. Specifically, when the PLO assumed control over the Palestinian Authority, relations between the two groups further eroded as sporadic clashes erupted. Fatah was in charge of the provisional government set up under the Oslo Accords, and its job was to maintain law, order, and security in Palestinian areas under its control. This included preventing terrorist attacks against Israel. While the PA's record in this regard was mixed, when it did act to prevent anti-Israeli activities, its forces usually had to confront members of Hamas. Hamas's role in the context of the Arab-Israeli conflict and the inter-Palestinian political arena would increase even further with the outbreak of the second Intifada in 2000, when the organization took the lead in organizing and implementing attacks against the Jewish state and its citizens.

Political and Social Development

Hamas's attitude toward democracy and its institutions and procedures, such as elections, have been ambivalent and characterized by a pragmatic cost-benefit evaluation. On the one hand, Hamas has since its very beginning expressed its acceptance of the electoral principle and has on several occasions made it clear that it would be willing to accept the concept of democratic elections. In a 1989 interview for the Palestinian newspaper *Al Nahar-that*, Hamas leader Ahmed Yassin said that the organization would accept any electoral result, including the victory of a non-Islamist force. He added, "There is no other way to choose representatives of the people except the way of elections."[15] Two years later, a Hamas communiqué also stated the same principle and made clear that no political force should be able to represent the "masses" without having won "free, honest, and neutral elections." However, even if the organization seemed to have accepted the principle of electoral democracy, it nevertheless is questionable at best whether it believes in the content and values of democracy.

Hamas's interest in elections and in the Palestinian political system dates back to the organization's formative years. Its first direct involvement in the issue of elections occurred in April 1989, after Israeli prime minister Yitzhak Shamir's call for elections in the Palestinian territories to mitigate the tensions caused by the Intifada. On that occasion, Hamas conducted a public campaign to reject the idea of elections.[16] At the time, although the organization did not reject elections or political representation per se, it believed that, under the existing situation, elections were going to be manipulated by Israel and therefore rejected such a proposal. Even in this period, however, when it was reluctant to get involved in "official and high politics," Hamas was nevertheless very active politically at the grass-roots level, through its participation in the elections of student and professional associations, which play an important role in Palestinian society.[17]

Internal discussions regarding the creation of an official political party began as early as the summer preceding the September 1993 Oslo Accords. Supporters of this idea argued that a political shift would allow the organization to gain popularity and visibility while diminishing the chances of open persecution by the PLO.[18] Calls for more active political participation grew stronger in the following two years. Those who argued for this option claimed that the creation of an official political branch would not weaken the jihadist struggle, as opponents had argued.[19] Rather, they affirmed that the new party would effectively co-opt all Islamist sympathizers in the Palestinian territories, weakening the secular PLO. Moreover, they claimed that by promoting political organizations such as student and professional organizations, they could more effectively spread their idea of creating an Islamic state.[20]

Hamas's external leadership, however, was initially opposed to joining the political system, because it was worried that direct participation would be interpreted as de facto acceptance of the Oslo process and that Arafat might later more easily succeed in co-opting it into the system, thereby weakening its Islamic appeal.[21] In the end, Hamas decided not to participate in the 1996 PA elections, both because of its ideological opposition to Oslo and because it was mostly concerned with the fact that the electoral and political Palestinian system was basically shaped by Arafat, which meant that Fatah had an unfair advantage.[22] At this stage, according to Hamas's evaluation, its real political power came through its *dawa* (social welfare) network, its grassroot level political machine, and its terrorist apparatus. Through these means Hamas believed that it could have more influence on Palestinian internal politics than through participation in the "democratic" elections, which would put the group at greater risk of becoming a puppet of Arafat and his cohorts.

Hamas maintained this same posture and political calculation all throughout the "Arafat era." In 1998 Arafat again tried to co-opt the main anti-PLO Islamic factions into the political process by consulting with Hamas and the PIJ and trying to make them part of the Palestinian Authority administration.[23] Again, both parties refused to participate in any government that recognized Israel or the utility of the peace negotiations, maintaining the same ideological argument.[24] But Hamas's motivations were well beyond ideological at that point; they were largely founded upon political realism. Hamas believed that there was no real opportunity to affect public policy within the centralist political system that Arafat had created.[25]

With the death of Arafat in November 2004 and the subsequent partial internal opening of the political system, Hamas perceived a unique opportunity to challenge Fatah's leadership and hegemony. In this case, although the organization had not gone through ideological changes and was still dedicated to the creation of an Islamic state, the continuation of jihad against Israel, and the rejection of all peace agreements, a political and pragmatic consideration led it to participate officially in the municipal elections of 2005. This position demonstrated just how calculating and rational the group could be, for, despite its ideological premise, it still found ways to mold its core ideology to meet its needs as it became an important political actor in Palestinian politics.[26] Consequently, because of pragmatic reasons, in January 2005 Hamas contested the Palestinian municipal elections and performed extremely well, winning 77 of the 118 available seats in the Gaza Strip.[27] This satisfactory electoral performance led Hamas to announce its intention to participate in the January 2006 Legislative Council elections.

Israel reacted to this announcement by stating that it would not interfere in the Palestinian elections but that it would also not negotiate with elected representatives of Hamas as long as they did not recognize past Israeli-Palestinian agreements.[28] Specifically, Israel expressed concern that Hamas would undermine the peace process by refusing to comply with the requirement of dismantling armed groups, negotiating with Israel, and ending terror as set out in the "roadmap."[29] As it explained, "The participation of Hamas in the PA elections would be nothing more than a bid by this group of Islamist extremists to seize power from moderate Palestinians who are interested in coexistence with Israel. It would be an abuse of democracy, in order to promote terrorism and violence as political tools."[30]

Publicly, PA chairman Mahmoud Abbas (aka Abu Mazen) expressed his unequivocal intention to allow Hamas in the elections: "Democracy would be meaningless once we start banning any faction from taking part in the democratic process. We reject any attempt or pressure in this regard and see them as a flagrant interference in the internal affairs of the Palestinians. We won't allow anyone to harm our democratic experience."[31] Privately, however, Abbas was in favor of postponing elections until such time as Fatah's popularity increased. With his calls for spreading democracy to the Middle East and around the world, U.S. president Bush rejected this idea and pressed the Israelis and Palestinians for elections to take place immediately.[32]

Despite his hesitations, Abbas never foresaw the Hamas victory that was to come. The veteran Fatah leader had just won the PA presidential elections the previous year with a wide 62 percent of the electoral vote and had calculated that his party would continue to be the majority party in the Legislative Council.[33] If anything, he hoped that Hamas's participation would provide him with the leverage to co-opt and influence the Islamist group and had hoped to be able to include it in the newly born political system. Abbas and the other Fatah leadership, however, grossly miscalculated the popularity that Hamas had, as well as the resentment that had built up against Fatah through the years.

The Palestinian Authority was characterized by an inherent deficiency in influence, as it lacked the means to obtain a monopoly of force and to exercise coercion, mostly because of the fragmented nature of Palestinian society and the permanence of armed groups, militias, clans, and private armies. Furthermore, the PA was plagued by a chronic inability to effectively deliver the political goods and maintain services and infrastructure; it was inherently corrupt from its very birth. Additionally, the Fatah-sponsored peace process of the 1990s had visibly failed to deliver, falling short of improving the lives of Palestinians on the ground or of significantly advancing toward the end of the Israeli occupation. For all of these reasons, Fatah's once unquestioned hegemony over the Palestinian political arena crumbled concurrently with the rise of Hamas, which could also count on its honest and uncorrupt reputation to attract political supporters among the Palestinian population. In addition, Hamas's effective and extensive welfare system, along with its impressive record in terms of delivering social services to Palestinians, also contributed to its increased level of popular consent and legitimacy.

For all of these reasons Hamas's electoral bid was a sweeping success. Its "Change and Reform" block obtained 74 of the 132 seats in the Legislative Council, gaining the majority of the legislative branch, becoming the majority party in Palestinian politics, and ending forty-years of Fatah domination in the Palestinian territories.[34] For a radical Islamist organization to ascend to power through a democratic process was almost without precedent.[35] Its impressive electoral victory left the PLO and Fatah shocked and changed forever. Additionally, the elections resulted in the two organizations becoming direct competitors for the support of the Palestinian people. Increased internal polarization and political fragmentation was one of the first consequences of Hamas's victory, along with a deepening political crisis in the Palestinian political system. In the immediate aftermath of the January 2006 legislative elections, Hamas's assumption of control of the PA's Legislative Council led to a representational crisis for the Palestinian people.[36]

Hamas's cabinet was announced on March 29, 2006, and mostly included Hamas officials and ideological sympathizers.[37] It was not approved by Fatah representatives, as they had chosen to boycott the Parliament.[38] As a result, the Palestinian political system was divided between Fatah, which remained in control of the executive branch of the PA government, and Hamas and its Gaza-based leader Ismail Haniyeh, the new Palestinian prime minister who was the leading political force in the Legislative Council. In turn, this led the two parties to engage in a political and military struggle, each to assert its political dominance over the other, hindering internal stability. Political clashes followed by temporary cease-fires and attempts to embark on national reconciliation dialogue with Fatah characterized the Hamas government during its introduction into the Palestinian political fold.

Significantly, the political confrontation between Hamas and Fatah soon became an armed one as well. The situation was worsened by the lack of control and efficiency of PA security forces. In May 2006, for example, Hamas decided to fill the ranks of PA security forces with units from its own militia. This caused resentment from Fatah militants, who had dominated the Palestinian security services since their creation.[39] Hamas's decision to use its own militias in support of the existing security apparatus created significant friction between the pro-Fatah and pro-Hamas units, spilling out into open clashes of light urban warfare.

In parallel with the deterioration of the relations between Hamas and Fatah, the newly elected Hamas government had to face an additional challenge: the progressive drying up of its financial revenues. In the months following Hamas's victory, Israel began to withhold its monthly transfer of approximately $50–60 million in Palestinian taxes and fees that it collected, cutting one of the government's main sources of income.[40] At the same time, both the United States and the European Union decided to cut off direct aid payments to the Hamas-led Palestinian government because of its refusal to renounce violence and recognize Israel.[41] These provisions considerably hindered the Hamas government's capacity to function and enormously impacted the daily lives of the Palestinian population—especially within Gaza. Because of the substantial state of disarray of the Palestinian economy and the paucity of private investments and enterprises, government is the primary employer within the Palestinian territories. As a result, when it became impossible for the Hamas government to pay the salaries of its employees, this had a direct economic impact upon the civilian population. According to UNRWA, there was an increase in "the number of deep poor [Palestinians] from an average of 650,800 in second-half 2005 to an average of 1,069,200 in first-half 2006—a 64.3 percent increase."[42] Eventually the Quartet (encompassing the United States, European Union, United Nations, and Russia) devised a system to deliver aid to the Palestinians while bypassing the Hamas government, partially alleviating the social pressure on the Palestinian territories while continuing to refuse to fund Hamas.[43]

While dealing with the fiscal and economic crises, as well as the rising tensions with Fatah, in the months following its victory in the January 2006 elections, Hamas became involved in another round of military confrontations with Israel. Tensions culminated in June 2006, with Israel's first full-fledged military operation into the Gaza Strip since its unilateral withdrawal back in 2005. The IDF's main objective in invading Gaza was to put a stop to the launching of rockets from the Gaza Strip into the south of Israel, which had increased by more than 100 percent after Israel's 2005 withdrawal. It secondary objective was to pressure Hamas into releasing kidnapped IDF soldier, Gilad Shalit, who was captured on June 25, 2006, and not released until 2011.[44] In the course of the hostilities in Gaza, the Hamas government was further undermined by Israel's direct attack on its members, which culminated in the arrest of 64 senior Hamas officials, ministers, and legislators on June 29, 2006.[45] The clashes lasted until November 26, 2006, when Israel agreed to withdraw from Gaza in exchange for a cessation of rocket attacks from the Gaza Strip into Israel.[46]

With the beginning of a cease-fire between Hamas and the State of Israel, the group also initiated a round of negotiations with Fatah, attempting to solve the stalemate between the two parties. Between November 2006 and February 2007, Hamas and Fatah would alternate between armed clashes and political negotiations, until they finally reached an agreement. Known as the Mecca Agreement, the understanding was based upon the June 2006 National Conciliation Document. It called for the creation of a national unity government based on the January 2006 electoral result, along with recognizing the parties' common goal of creating a Palestinian state in the pre-1967 borders.[47] In Mecca, on February 8, 2007, Hamas and Fatah also agreed on how to divide up the seats in the executive cabinet, agreeing that Hamas's senior leader Ismail Haniyeh would continue to sit as prime minister of the new unity government. Haniyeh would be tasked with forming a new government, to be then approved by the Palestinian Legislative Council. PA president Abbas would nominate a deputy prime minister.[48]

The new agreement, however, failed to pacify the animosity that existed on the ground between Fatah and Hamas fighters. And so as early as May 2007, armed clashes between the two parties recommenced. This time the violence spiraled out of control relatively quickly, and within Gaza it would turn into a full-fledged internal war over what side would control the Gaza Strip. In the end, with superior numbers and combat skills, Hamas was able to defeat its opponent and gain control of the Gaza Strip, leading to the permanent collapse of the unity government as well as to the creation of a parallel Fatah-led government in the West Bank, under the leadership of Chairman Mahmoud Abbas and Prime Minister Salam Fayyad.[49]

With the creation of an alternative government in the West Bank and the rise of Hamas as the sole authority in Gaza, the state of isolation of both the Hamas government and the citizens of the Gaza Strip increased exponentially. Israel gradually began to tighten the cross-border movements of people and goods, ultimately leading to a total blockade of the Gaza Strip in January 2008 that lasted nearly a year and a half before it was eased but not ended.[50] Since then, Hamas has been able to take advantage of the isolation to occupy all positions of power within Gaza, tighten its grip on the population there, and tax those smuggling goods via tunnels that span from the Sinai. In 2011, after the demise of the Mubarak regime in Egypt and the gradual rise of a new political order, Egypt promised to ease the restrictions and to open the border with Gaza, although, to date, the situation has not substantially improved.[51]

After the creation of a Fatah-led Palestinian government in the West Bank, President Abbas ordered all police and security forces active in Gaza not to report for duty, a measure that soon extended to all public employees that received PA-funded salaries.[52] In response, Hamas filled the temporary vacuum by employing its own Executive Force, staffed by members of the Qassam Brigades units, to establish law and order.[53] This expanded the actual degree of direct control that Hamas had over Gaza, resulting in a temporary improvement of the local security situation, as Hamas effectively cracked down on petty crime, clan warfare, and locally armed groups.[54] This was evidenced by Hamas's prompt release of abducted BBC journalist Alan Johnston, who had been kidnapped by the group Army of Islam before Hamas had gained control over Gaza. After this operation, Hamas's deputy of the political bureau, Mousa Abu Marzook, explained: "We did not deliver up Alan Johnston as some obsequious boon to Western powers. It was done as part of our effort to secure Gaza from the lawlessness of militias and violence, no matter what the source. Gaza will be calm and under the rule of law." This statement made explicit Hamas's goal to impose social order in areas under its controls.[55]

At the same time, Hamas's control of Gaza also facilitated the group's crackdown on civil, social, and political opposition, often through extralegal means and the engagement in human rights violations ranging from abductions to arbitrary detentions and unlawful killings.[56] In fact, one the most worrisome effects of the rise in power of Hamas within Gaza had been the impact of this dynamic upon Palestinian society's pluralism. Hamas's stated goal is to create an Islamic state of Palestine and to restructure society according to Sharia law, an objective that can hardly be reconciled with the plurality of Palestinian identities. Palestinian society is inherently pluralistic: affiliation and identity range from strong political associations to particular loyalties for warlords and armed groups, along with more traditional affiliations such as extended families and clans. Trying to suppress these societal relationships and impose a monolithic religious identity represents a very dangerous dynamic and an additional source of future domestic tension.

One of the main targets of Hamas's campaign to suppress internal dissent in the Gaza Strip has been the members of its main political opponent, Fatah. This has resulted in massive repression against Fatah leaders, activists, and supporters alike, further exacerbating the tensions between the two parties. Between 2007 and 2011, Fatah and Hamas remained unable to repair their relationship and to reestablish a unity government to function in both the West Bank and Gaza. In March 2008 Hamas and Fatah agreed to resume dialogue in the Yemenite-brokered Sanaa Declaration and committed to a Yemeni plan that envisioned resuming the Mecca Accord, attempting to re-create a new unity government, and proposing a comprehensive reform of Palestinian security forces.[57] Despite the formal commitment of the parties, this initial agreement never developed into concrete steps to change the status quo. Since that time, Egypt took over the role of main mediator between Hamas and Fatah, and numerous rounds of negotiations took place in Cairo, under the auspices of Egyptian president Hosni Mubarak in 2008, 2009, and 2010. In October 2010, things seemed to start moving in the right direction when Fatah agreed to an Egyptian-drafted plan to overcome internal divisions within the Palestinian territories. However, at that time, Hamas rejected the

Egyptian plan—a position that it would reverse only in April 2011 when the group finally decided to accept the reconciliation plan, moving toward ending the rift with Fatah.[58] According to the approved plan, Fatah and Hamas agreed to end their conflict and to move toward forming a national unity government. Similarly, the parties agreed to hold presidential, Legislative Council, and Palestine National Council (PNC) elections in 2012, as well as to create a joint security committee, and release each other's political prisoners.[59] In reality, the ideological and historical tensions between the two groups remain very strong, even in the aftermath of the agreement. It will be particularly challenging for both parties to concretely implement the plan and to permanently end the territorial and political division between Gaza and the West Bank.

At the same time, Hamas's relations with Israel in the aftermath of the June 2007 takeover were characterized by waves of renewed military confrontation between the two parties, followed by extended periods of relative calm. The main episode of violence in the period after the takeover was the December 2008–January 2009 Gaza War, which Israel dubbed Operation Cast Lead. This conflict exploded in unison with Hamas's refusal to extend the Egyptian-brokered cease-fire between Israel and most militant factions in Gaza, an act that led the Egyptian government to openly criticize Hamas's decision.[60] The key conditions for the cease-fire had been Israel's demand for a complete halt of armed attacks from the Gaza Strip into Israel as well as an end to the smuggling of weapons into Gaza through Egypt. In return, Hamas had demanded the end of Israeli military operations within the Gaza Strip as well as the progressive lifting of the economic blockade. Although both parties had failed to comply fully with the terms of the cease-fire, it had brought significant quiet to both sides. Yet when the six months' cease-fire agreement ended on December 19, 2008, Egypt was unable to convince Hamas to renew or extend it. Instead, Hamas escalated its launching of rockets against the south of Israel, which was met by a full-fledged Israeli military operation into Gaza. After approximately three weeks of combat, Israel declared a unilateral cease-fire on January 17, 2009, entering a period of relative calm between the Jewish state and Hamas in Gaza.

To date, Hamas remains firmly in power in the Gaza Strip, although it still remains under Israeli, Egyptian, and international sanctions and is largely isolated from the international community. This trend may change in light of the May 2011 agreement between Fatah and Hamas, which could lead to a rapprochement between the two groups as well as to the creation of a new national unity government, thus ending the de facto separation of the Gaza Strip and the West Bank. However, in the short term, Hamas remains isolated. In fact, since Hamas's forced takeover of Gaza in June 2007, the organization has even become increasingly isolated by its traditional allies in the Arab world, who viewed the rise of an Islamist group as a threat to their own regimes—a posture fostered and encouraged by the Palestinian Authority, Israel, Saudi Arabia, and the United States. Notable exceptions to this trend have been Syria and its non-Arab ally, Iran. In fact, following Israel's withdrawal from the Gaza Strip and Hamas's later rise to political office, relations between Hamas, Iran, and Hezbollah grew substantially.[61] In the context of Hamas's growing isolation, Iran saw an opportunity to step in and develop a stronger alliance with Hamas, leading to the group's increased dependence on Iran and, consequently, to even greater isolation with respect to most of the Arab world. One reason for this was the realization by Iran that Hamas was a growing power and potential ally whose relationship it needed to foster. It also recognized the strategic importance of having another avenue to threaten Israel, in an effort to further deter the Jewish state from using a military option to attack its nuclear program.

Hamas's rise to power was supported by Iran, which invested in building an alliance with both Hamas's leadership abroad and those in power in the Palestinian territories. In January 2006 Iranian president Mahmoud Ahmadinejad called Damascus-based Hamas political leader Khaled Meshaal to congratulate him on his electoral victory.[62] One month later Meshaal paid a visit to Iran, where he expressed his support for the Iranian regime and its stand on Israel.[63] Meshaal's trip was followed by the official visit of a Palestinian governmental delegation to Iran, led by Palestinian deputy speaker of Parliament Ahmed Bahar in April 2006.[64] Besides the renewed diplomatic relations between the two nations, Iran also increased its financial ties with the Hamas government. Since April 2006, when it first pledged $50 million in aid, Iran's financial contributions to Hamas have been increasing.[65] As early as December 2006, Iran had pledged $120 million to the Hamas government.[66] Since that time, Iran has become one of the chief donors and financial partners to the Hamas government.[67] Its role in supporting and financing Hamas was boosted by the international boycott against the organization, which left Hamas politically isolated and in dire need of political and financial partners.

However, in the aftermath of the wave of political and social turmoil that spread across the Middle East in 2011, Hamas was weakening its ties with both Iran and Syria, and it now sees the potential to gradually shift its relations with other regional actors. An example of this trend is the partial process of warming ties between Hamas and post-Mubarak Egypt.

8   Ideals and Belief System

ISLAMISM IN HISTORIC PALESTINE can be traced back to Sheikh Izz ad-Din al-Qassam, the man whose name and example Hamas would adopt for its militant wing, the Izz ad-Din al-Qassam Brigade. Al-Qassam, whose full name was Muhammad Izz ad-Din bin Abdul Qadar bin Mustafa al-Qassam, is largely credited as being the Palestinians' first Salafi Islamist leader, as well as the first local Palestinian leader to carry out jihad against the British in the 1930s.[1] Born in Jebla, Syria, al-Qassam fled to Haifa in modern-day Israel after being sentenced to death by French powers for subversion. Using Islam as a rallying cry for poor and rural Palestinian Arabs to rise up against the British and Zionists, he traveled the region spreading his message of pan-Islamist nationalism. An internal British police report would describe his methods as follows:

> His interpretation of the parts of the Qur'an which sanction the use of physical violence, was unorthodox . . . but by his policy of selecting from amongst the poor, ignorant and the more violently disposed of the pious, he was able . . . to obtain a small following.[2]

In November 1935, following multiple murders of British and Jews by al-Qassam and his band of fighters (known as Qassamites), British authorities finally tracked down the "brigand sheikh" and killed him after an extended firefight.[3] Although his following was relatively small, his message, struggle, and ultimately his "martyrdom" would become an important example to Islamist groups such as Hamas.

Islamist Roots and Religious Pillars

After al-Qassam's assassination, the Arab rebellion against the British did not wane as they had hoped, but rather it increased. Although the uprising was eventually quelled, al-Qassam's memory and story lives on in the hearts and minds of Palestinian Islamists. Yet Islamism was not a prominent sociopolitical force among the Palestinian population until the late 1960s. In fact, it was not until the 1967 Arab-Israeli War that Islamism received its next major boost. That war saw the defeat of Egypt's Gamal Abdel Nasser, the popular Arab leader who led a secular pan-Arab style of nationalism that was the primary competition for Islamists. In the eyes of Islamists, Israel's decisive victory in 1967 served as evidence of the inability of pan-Arabism to succeed without a proper commitment to Islam. As a result, in the aftermath of the Arab defeat the Islamist alternative to secular pan-Arabism began to emerge as an increasingly significant and influential political and social current. Of course, the 1967 Six-Day War was not the only historical event that helped boost the credibility and popularity of the Islamist alternative: the 1973 Yom Kippur War, the 1979 Iranian Revolution, the Russian-Afghan War, and the 1982 Israeli-Lebanese War all further contributed to shaping not just Islamism in general but Palestinian Islamism in particular.

Hamas emerged from the late 1980s as the main social, political, and military Islamist movement in the Palestinian arena, and as such it shares several characteristics and goals with other Islamist movements worldwide, including the desire to build a state and society modeled after the values and beliefs of Islam. At the same time, Hamas is a distinctively Palestinian movement, and therefore it focuses its rhetoric and actions on a specifically nationalist agenda.

Hamas's historic ideological document is the organization's 1988 Charter of the Islamic Resistance Movement, although the group has over time developed and become increasingly sophisticated in terms of both its political ideology and its analysis of the outside world.[4] Nevertheless, the principles and goals expressed in its charter still constitute an important basis in understanding Hamas and its ideology. First, the style of the charter is highly indicative of Hamas's ideological background as an Islamist revivalist movement and of its militant dimension. In this sense, the group's ideology, as originally formulated in the charter, is similar to that of other militant religious political movements as it is universalistic, exclusionist, and militant.[5] Moreover, the charter's numerous references to the past, its use of verses from the Quran and the Sunna, and its millenarian tone radically differ from the secular charter of the PLO. This emphasizes the ideological differences between the two movements and the secular-religious divide that to this day still defines the relations between Fatah and Hamas.

Second, the charter clearly identifies the two main pillars of Hamas's ideology: nationalism and Islamism. Religion in particular is a powerful ideological construct, and it is crucial to analyzing Hamas's rhetoric. Again, similar to other militant religious political movements, religion is often invoked by the group as a justification for its actions and goals and is simultaneously employed as a social construct to define identity, regulate inner-group behavior, and provide a source of legitimacy for the organization and its raison d'être.[6]

Third, the charter directly identifies the group's main religious and philosophical inspirations. As explained in the previous chapter, Hamas strongly associates itself and its ideology with that of the Muslim Brotherhood, and in the opening of the charter there is a quote from that movement's founder, Hassan al-Banna: "Israel will exist and will continue to exist until Islam will obliterate it, just as it obliterated others before it." Hamas was strongly inspired by the work of al-Banna, who was a prominent revivalist concerned with inducing internal transformations within Muslim societies, while promoting Islam and the study of Islamic texts.[7] Another important source in defining Hamas's vision is Sayyid Qutb, a major advocate of the concept of individual obligation to wage *jihad*. Qutb's books, *In the Shadow of the Quran* and *Milestones along the Way*, as well as his teachings about the universality, practicality, and importance of embracing jihad against the corrupted Arab regimes, Crusaders, Zionists, and Communists, played an important role in shaping the radical Sunni shift in the aftermath of the 1967 war.[8] This first occurred in Egypt and later in the Gaza Strip.[9] The link between Qutb and Hamas is evident, for example, in Article 12 of the Hamas Charter, where the organization calls on every member of society to perform his duty and participate in the jihad against Israel, in line with Qutb's vision.

Another important concept in shaping Hamas's ideology is that of the *shaheed* (martyr or, literally, witness). According to Islamic tradition, martyrs were identified with those who died in battle to defend Islam, and the tradition rewards them with eternal life in the afterworld.[10] For those who perished as martyrs, Qutb emphasized: "After their death they remain an active force in shaping the life of their community and giving it direction. It is in this sense that such people, having sacrificed their lives for the sake of God, retain their active existence in everyday life."[11] Furthermore, Hamas stresses the idea of martyrdom as honorable and desirable, and it uses the concept of *bassamat-al-Farh* (the joy of martyrdom)—a concept borrowed from Shiite tradition.[12] This theological elaboration is indeed crucial to Hamas's strategy, because it allows it to distinguish the concept of martyrdom from that of suicide, which is condemned as a mortal sin in the traditions of Mohammed. With regard to suicide, the Muslim Prophet had clearly stated, "Whoever kills himself in any way will be tormented in that way in hell."[13] Hamas's and other Islamists' ideologies use this framework to justify and promote both the waging of violent jihad against Israel and the use of "suicide operations."

However, in its charter Hamas does not limit itself to incorporating Islamist beliefs but also adds a strongly nationalist dimension to its Islamist discourse, focusing both its message and its goals toward Palestinian society. In this sense, Hamas created a cohesive dialogue that combined a millenary vision rooted in the Islamic tradition of the Muslim Brotherhood with a nationalist-patriotic appeal, in which ethnicity, religion, and universalism converge to generate a platform that effectively draws support to the organization.

Notably, Hamas shares its Muslim Brotherhood roots with more internationally focused groups such as al Qaeda. That group's founder, a Palestinian named Abdullah Azzam, is believed by some to have been a driving force behind Hamas's creation as well. There are other links between the two Sunni Islamists aside from their shared roots and common anti-Semitic and anti-Western rhetoric.[14] For example, al Qaeda operative Richard Reid, the man who would later become infamously known as the "Shoe Bomber," visited Israel and the Palestinian territories in August 2001 using his British passport to gain access. He was given sanctuary in Gaza by Nabil Awqil, a man who was himself supported by Hamas leader Ahmed Yassin.[15] Awqil had been trained in Pakistani-controlled Kashmir and later in al Qaeda camps as well. While Reid's visit was in part to test the security of Israel's national airline, El Al (which he deemed too secure to risk the shoe bomb plot), his activities in Gaza are largely unknown. What's more, after the assassination of Osama bin Laden, the Hamas leadership in Gaza and Damascus condemned the United States' operation, calling his death an "atrocity" and praising the al Qaeda leader as a "holy warrior," even while noting the differences in "interpretation" between Hamas and al Qaeda.[16] To date, Hamas is the only government in the world to have publicly spoken out in support of Bin Laden.

Overall, however, despite the more general ideological connections, the two groups are operationally quite distant—something Hamas goes out of its way to make clear. Unlike Hamas, al Qaeda holds a universalist agenda and less accommodating foreign and domestic policy approach.[17] As former director of the Mossad Efraim Halevy has explained, Hamas has aspirations "to be

NOTE

part of the system and not, as Al Qaeda aspires, to destroy it."[18] In fact, although Palestinian Islamist organizations can at times have a more difficult time reconciling their Palestinian nationalism with the more universalistic Islamist message that transcends international borders, Hamas has been able to maintain a distinctively Palestinian identify.[19] Similarly, both the group's actions and goals have remained solely focused on the Palestinian level, and the organization has not been involved in any operation that did not officially target the Jewish state or its citizens. Hamas's decision to join the Palestinian political system and participate in Palestinian elections was harshly criticized by al Qaeda, which accused it of "moderation" and of taking part in "polytheistic councils."[20] For these reasons, especially in the aftermath of the June 2006 Palestinian elections, al Qaeda has been openly hostile to what it has viewed as some of Hamas's more "moderate" positions. This more vocal criticism is in part believed to be due to the more Salafist elements within Hamas, who have gradually drifted away from that organization and allegedly reached out to other Salafi-jihadist elements within Gaza as well as international jihadist networks, in an effort to further radicalize Hamas and other Palestinian groups.[21] This may be one reason why in a 2011 Pew Global Attitudes poll regard for Osama bin Laden was higher among Palestinians than any other group, with 34 percent expressing confidence in bin Laden to "do the right thing in world affairs."[22]

A View of the World and of the State of Israel

The 1988 charter is extremely clear in identifying Hamas's original goal: to take control over not just the West Bank and Gaza Strip but indeed the entire country of Israel. To date, some studies dispute the notion that the group would still be seeking the original goal of "liberating" Palestine in its entirety and argue instead that Hamas has de facto accepted a future Palestinian state within the 1967 borders. However, although some in the Hamas organization may privately be open to settling in just East Jerusalem, the West Bank, and the Gaza Strip, its official perspective as formulated in its charter clearly states otherwise.

In Hamas's view, the land of Israel exists on what had once been part of an Islamic caliphate and is in its entirety considered a religious trust (*waqf*), thus belonging to the Muslim community as a whole. As such, the existence of a Jewish state is in deep contrast with the principles of Islam and is therefore not a negotiable condition. In the worldview of Hamas, Israeli withdrawals can be viewed only as steps toward the eventual complete destruction of a state whose right to exist cannot be accepted. Similarly, the official ideology rejects any compromise in dealing with the State of Israel as stated in Article 13 of the charter: "Initiatives, and so-called peaceful solutions and international conferences, are in contradiction to the principles of the Islamic Resistance Movement."[23]

In terms of other Palestinian groups, Hamas's opposition to negotiations and partial settlements with Israel has put it directly at odds with Fatah, which Hamas accuses of having betrayed the Palestinian cause by moderating and accepting the platform of a two-state solution with Israel. Similarly, this ideological rejection of Israel and any attempt to reconcile differences with the Jewish State have recurrently provided Hamas with the leading role as "spoiler" of any potential peace agreement between the Palestinian and Israeli peoples. In order to stall such agreements, Hamas has in the past agreed to cooperate with other Palestinian rejectionist groups, despite the existence of ideological differences, in order to prevent any real progress vis-à-vis the Israeli and Palestinian peace talks.[24] This attitude toward creating broad political alliances is also supported by the ideological premises espoused in the founding charter, which states that Hamas "views other Islamic movements with respect and appreciation. Even when it disagrees with them on a particular aspect or viewpoint."

If from an ideological point of view Hamas has remained consistent in its denial of Israel's right to exist and in maintaining the goals advocated in the charter, the practical and political behavior of the group has substantially evolved since 1988. Hamas has elaborated a political discourse marked by pragmatism and cost-benefit analysis. For example, along with an ideological rejection of Israel's right to exist, Hamas has developed a de facto political acceptance of its existence as a fait accompli of Israel for the time being. Without amending the charter or altering its basic opposition to the creation of the State of Israel, Hamas has in parallel stated: "There will remain a state called Israel. This is a matter of fact." Hamas Political Bureau leader Khaled Meshaal clearly stated this concept in an interview with Reuters on January 11, 2007, adding: "The problem is not that there is an entity called Israel. . . . The problem is that the Palestinian state is non-existent."[25] In other words, although the group refuses to grant or recognize acceptance of Israel, it could still be prepared to deal with the reality of a State of Israel. Additionally,

Hamas has been able to transition from its earlier position of a complete refusal toward any negotiated settlement or agreement with Israel to a gradual acceptance of short-term truces and even long-term (albeit still temporary) ones, provided there is a fulfillment of a series of political conditions. Senior Hamas leader Mahmoud Zahar explained as much in an interview with the Palestinian Maan news agency in May 2011, when he explained that recognizing Israel would "preclude the right of the next generations to liberate the lands." He added that for the time being Hamas would recognize a Palestinian state "on any part of Palestine," even as he wondered, "What will be the fate of the five million Palestinians in the diaspora" if the organization were to recognize the Jewish state and reach a final peace agreement?[26]

The idea of implementing a ten- or twenty-year truce (*hudna*) with Israel was advocated by Sheikh Yassin as early as 1993, provided that Israel agreed to withdraw from Gaza, the West Bank, and East Jerusalem, and that the Palestinians would be able to exercise autonomous self-governance in such a nascent Palestinian state.[27] Without agreeing to recognize Israel and its Jewish character, Yassin's proposal laid down the foundation for Hamas's political stance on a future Palestinian state, known as the so-called "phased solution." Accordingly, Hamas would accept the idea of entering into a long-term *hudna* with the Jewish state and to establish and participate in a Palestinian country established along the 1967 borders. Such acceptance would not be seen as tantamount to recognition or the achievement of a final and stable peace accord between an Israel and a Palestine but rather as a temporary phase in the long-term fight toward the complete destruction of the Jewish state and the "liberation" of all of historic Palestine. The "phased solution," therefore, grants Hamas the political flexibility to temporarily accept and participate in a Palestinian state, without forcing the organization to revise its ideological charter, thus ensuring political pragmatism and ideological continuity. In the immediate aftermath of the 2006 elections, senior Hamas leader-in-exile Mousa Abu Marzook released an interview to an Israeli radio station, which reiterated these concepts and indicating Hamas's posture vis-à-vis Israel and future negotiations. He said that Hamas was considering making changes according to reality, "but there are three principles we will not compromise on: government according to the laws of the sharia (Islamic law), our right to live in Palestine, and our right to resist the occupation."[28] Marzook explicitly addressed the issue of the recognition of Israel: "We cannot recognize Israel, as that violates our principles and our election platform of resistance, reform and change. . . . You don't run on a platform and then reverse it when you win."[29] However, he conceded that the Palestinian government's responsibility for the well-being of its people would eventually require a higher degree of flexibility: "Relations with the Jewish State are inevitable as the existence of Israel is a fact, but recognizing its legal legitimacy is another thing. . . . Hamas may recognize Israel's legitimacy, under certain conditions, such as the establishment of a Palestinian state in '67 borders in the West Bank and Gaza with Jerusalem as its capital and the return of millions of refugees to their homes in Israel."[30]

Hamas's leadership, however, is somewhat split over how far it is willing to go to establish a long-term cease-fire with Israel and thus institute a de facto, albeit temporary, acceptance of Israel's existence.[31] Although no Hamas leader has gone so far as to accept the notion of peace with Israel, its Gaza leadership had generally been more open to the idea of establishing a long-term (though temporary) cease-fire than has its exiled political leadership based in Damascus.

Hamas in the Palestinian Territories: Political Agenda and Activities

In parallel to this vision of its external enemies and to its political stance with respect to the establishment of a Palestinian state, Hamas's ideological charter also sheds light on the group's domestic ambitions within Palestine. In this respect, the document proposed a radical transformation of the status quo and the restoration of an "authentic Islam" within Palestinian society. Again in line with the Muslim Brotherhood's agenda, Hamas's objective as expressed in the charter is the creation of a society and state based on the principles and teachings of Islam.

Much of Hamas's ideology is learned through its social welfare network, which spans everything from mosques, schools, food banks, clinics, summer camps, and hospitals. As is clearly outlined under Article 16 (Education of the [Young] Generation) of its charter, one of its major goals is to instill Islamist values into Palestinian children from a young age.[32] At the same time, Hamas employs this wide social network to promote the group and its militant agenda with respect to Israel. This manifests itself in military activities for children in summer camps, indoctrination of kindergarteners to praise suicide attackers and wish to be like them, the reenactment of suicide bombings, and the use of schoolbooks laced with Islamist, anti-Semitic, and anti-Western propaganda.[33] From just one Hamas affiliated youth soccer team, for example, multiple terrorists were recruited, including suicide bombers.[34]

Hamas also relies on its activities as a social movement to spread an anti-Israeli and, at times, anti-Semitic agenda. As with other Islamist and anti-Israeli organizations, Jews as a people and not just Israelis in general are portrayed as the driving force behind most of the wrongs in the world, including most recently the 2008 recession and world economic crises.[35] Israeli activities are often compared to those of the Nazis, as can be seen in Article 20 of Hamas's charter, where it states: "The Nazism of the Jews includes [even] women and children; it terrorizes everyone. These Jews ruin people's livelihoods, steal their money, and threaten their honor."[36] Ironically, the only time the true enormity of the Holocaust tends to be acknowledged is when it is compared to the plight of the Palestinians and it is argued they have suffered at the hands of Israel more than the Jews suffered during the Holocaust. Yet Hamas's anti-Semitism goes much farther than just denying the Holocaust and comparing the Jews to Nazis. Pervasive throughout the Arab world, anti-Semitism by way of degradation and calling for the murder of Jews is increasingly justified based on interpretations of Islam.[37]

Such indoctrination has led to a membership that is more organized and ideological than its rivals and thus somewhat less susceptible to infiltration by Palestinian, Israeli, and other intelligence agencies. Yet, showing again a high degree of political pragmatism, Hamas has recognized that its target population is not always interested or willing to have Islamist values forced upon it. Until recently, Islamic law in Gaza was imposed only in certain Hamas controlled areas, including the economy, education, and law and order. Although Hamas's rule still demonstrates a more pragmatic, gradual, and controlled way of imposing its will on a traditionally secular Palestinian society, it has been increasing the enforcement of Islamist laws and the targeting of what it views as non-Islamist values (such as UN-run camps, lingerie shops, and dress codes for women) in an effort to appease and compete with the rising power of Salafi-jihadist groups in the region.[38]

In conclusion, Hamas's unaltered official ideology has over time been coupled with a substantially more pragmatic political discourse that indicates a high potential for adaptation. This calculated moderation, which can be seen in everything from its policies toward Israel to its control over Palestinian lives, has led those who support a "purer" strain of Salafism—reminiscent of the al Qaeda ideology that manifested itself in Taliban-controlled Afghanistan—to begin to increasingly challenge the authority of Hamas in some of the areas under its control.[39] This even more radical version of Salafism has allegedly also been creeping into the militant leadership of Hamas in the Gaza Strip, as has been on display with the increasing number of radicals elected to Hamas's Shura Council, the main decision-making body.[40] It has also led to the creation of radical Salafi offshoots training in Gaza that do not take orders from Hamas or the PIJ. These groups are expanding their influence in the region as they attract members from Hamas and other groups that are not seen as radical enough.[41]

9 Structure

HAMAS'S STRUCTURE HAS CHANGED considerably since its founding. The organization was initially organized into three parts: (1) a political wing, (2) a military wing (known as the Izz ad-Din al-Qassam Brigade), and (3) an intelligence apparatus called the Organization of Jihad and Dawa (or Munazzamat al-Jihad wal-dawa—better known as al-Majd, or "Glory"). It was not long before al-Majd was incorporated into Hamas's military wing, which remained secretive and compartmentalized in comparison to its PLO rival.[1]

Political and Military Structure

Today, Hamas's entire organization is overseen by two main bodies: the Advisory Council (Majlis Shura or Shura Council) and the Political Bureau (al-Maktab al-Siyasi).[2] The Shura Council, considered the main decision-making body within the organization, issues binding directives on all significant political and strategic questions. This council comprises Hamas leadership both inside and outside of the Palestinian territories. Its exact composition and its members' identities have traditionally been kept secret. The Political Bureau, on the other hand, functions more as the group's executive organ, and is tasked with making sure Hamas's day-to-day operations and activities are carried out smoothly. The bureau achieves this objective through an administrative unit in both its West Bank and especially its Gaza offices, which oversees the group's *dawa* network and security activities.[3] In addition to monitoring the group's military wing, the bureau is also heavily involved in fundraising, making it an extremely powerful organ.[4]

At the moment, the Political Bureau is located in Damascus (although news reports in the spring of 2011 have been reporting that Hamas may be considering relocating to Qatar or elsewhere in light of the massive unrest occurring within Syria)[5] and is headed by Khaled Meshaal, together with its

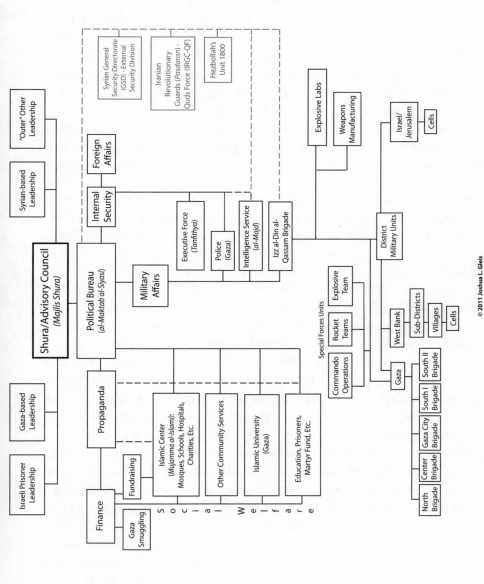

Hamas leadership structure. Based in part on Mishal and Sela, *The Palestinian Hamas: Vision, Violence and Coexistence, appendix 1.*

© 2011 Joshua L. Gleis

deputy head, the Gaza-based Mousa Abu Marzook.[6] Hamas's military wing is integrated into this structure, by being formally subordinated to the Political Bureau (which is in turn constrained in its decision-making process by the Shura Council). The military wing, however, retains a certain degree of autonomy and freedom of action and to this day is the organization's most flexible department, as it has gone through major structural reorganizations, primarily as a result of successful Israeli operations and changes in its theater of operations. In addition, the group's hierarchy in the aftermath of its electoral victory and armed takeover of Gaza has undergone a series of internal transformations. For instance, the group created additional internal special operations security forces, known as the Executive Force (Tanfithya). The Executive Force was created in Gaza in order to compete with the PA's own internal security forces that were loyal to Fatah.[7] Over time the Hamas forces have taken over the role of ensuring public order, administering justice and law enforcement, and repressing and isolating opposition to the Hamas government. Since its takeover of Gaza, Hamas's Executive Force has more than doubled in size to twelve thousand members and has also become an enforcer of Sharia law that includes ensuring women are veiled.[8] In total, it is believed that Hamas can yield up to approximately fifteen thousand fighters from its various units, capable of facing Israeli forces in any showdown in the Gaza Strip.[9]

In concert with its relatively sophisticated organizational structure, the internal leadership of Hamas also plays an important role in ensuring cohesion, creating alliances within different sectors of society, and enhancing the power of the organization. Hamas's historic leader, Sheikh Ahmed Yassin, founded the organization with the objective of "Fighting non-religious [Palestinian] factions in the territories and carrying out jihad operations against Israel."[10] Sheikh Yassin was a very popular figure, who represented Max Weber's "charismatic leader" and was able to draw wide support for the organization and cause. Moreover, under Yassin's leadership, order within the organization was maintained, as Yassin retained a large share of personal power and influence over the group's strategy at every level. Arrested twice by Israeli security forces, in 1984 and 1989, respectively, Yassin was finally killed in a security operation on March 22, 2004.[11] His death made him a martyr and even more powerful ideological figure in the eyes of his supporters, as well as a model for them to emulate. Yassin's assassination was hotly contested in Israeli circles and harshly criticized by many in the international community. Israel understood the psychological difficulty it would have in justifying the assassination of an elderly man and a paraplegic, whom Israel itself had medically treated in the past. However, as his direct involvement in terrorist attacks was clear, Israeli leadership decided his loss would be worth the repercussions. Avi Dichter, director of Israel's Shin Bet Security Service at the time, would later explain Israel's predicament: "We had intelligence confirming that Sheikh Yassin was behind the attempted [mega terror] attack at Ashdod. . . . His image as a disabled man caused us a lot of problems. After all, he was a paraplegic. He could barely speak. Everything about this man aroused pity. But the degree of evil he contained within himself was shocking."[12]

The internal shakeup did not end with the assassination of Yassin in March 2004. Dr. Abdel Aziz Rantissi immediately took over the top position in Hamas and was assassinated less than a month later. Internal control of Hamas would never be the same. After Rantissi, the organization at first kept a tight lid on who was his successor, but it soon became clear that the organization's Political Bureau would have an increasingly powerful role in Hamas's decision-making process, thus raising the internal power and status of its chair, the exiled leader Khaled Meshaal. Meshaal had himself survived a 1997 botched assassination attempt by the Mossad in Jordan. That operation helped catapult him to fame in Hamas and allowed him to operate from the organization's political headquarters in Damascus.[13] As an exiled leader, Meshaal at times has appeared out of touch with the Palestinians. In the past, he often took a harder line against Israel than did his counterparts in Gaza, such as the deputy of the Political Bureau Mousa Abu Marzook and Ismail Haniyeh, who was elected prime minister of the Palestinian Authority in 2006. Both of these Gaza-based leaders were seen as pragmatists with a better understanding of the situation on the ground than the Hamas leadership in Syria and elsewhere. However, in the months following the May 2011 Hamas-Fatah reconciliation, new divisions are allegedly emerging within Hamas, with Meshaal actually supporting an agreement with Fatah, and leaders from Gaza, headed by Mahmoud a-Zahar, rejecting it.[14]

Today, after Israel's withdrawal from the Gaza Strip and Hamas's June 2007 military takeover of that territory from the more secular Fatah, the organization has been seen as battling to preserve internal unity. Hamas's strict bureaucratic apparatus and its strong Shura-based decision-making role has helped to effectively maintain a degree of cohesion within the organization, avoiding some of the effects of disunity, such as the implementation of conflicting political policies or the undermining of external support. Yet, despite these accomplishments, divisions have become clear. These include temporary disagreements between Hamas's "inner" Gaza leadership and "outer" Damascus leadership, as well as within Hamas's Shura Council, where a more radical and militant group of leaders has begun to wrest control of the military branch. These ultra radicals are made up largely of younger members of the Izz ad-Din al Qassam Brigade who have proved their worth in the eyes of the Palestinian population not only by engaging in military and terrorist operations against Israelis but also through dealing with the consequences of such actions and sustaining long periods of time in prison or in hiding, risking assassinations, and evading arrest attempts.[15]

One telling story comes from the Izz ad-Din al-Qassam Brigade commander and famed Islamist leader Mohammed Deif, who, after being severely injured in an Israeli attack, was smuggled out of Gaza to receive treatment. While he was gone, the Salafi-aligned Ahmad Ja'abari took over his position. Ja'abari and his cohorts have been credited with some of Hamas's most important military and logistical achievements, including the development of Hamas's extensive tunneling network to bypass efforts to close the border of Gaza. Upon his return to the Gaza Strip, Deif reportedly complained that "Salafists had taken completely over."[16] Though perhaps an exaggeration, these episodes do seem to confirm that Hamas is experiencing a degree of internal division and that losing Yassin and Rantissi in such a short span of time left a vacuum in Hamas's leadership. However, unlike Hezbollah, Hamas was never under the strict leadership of one man. Therefore, given the more pluralist nature of Hamas's leadership, even the loss of a strong and beloved leader such as Yassin did not undermine the group in the same way that losing Nasrallah would likely affect Hezbollah. However, the fact that the group does not take direction well from states such as Iran or Syria, combined with the existence of internal disagreements and conflicts, has made Hamas's decision-making process much more divisive and not as strictly controlled as groups such as Hezbollah.

Social Activism and Grass-Roots Support

Passive support constitutes an important force multiplier for Hamas, and the organization implements numerous techniques to gain popular legitimacy and increase its constituency. These tactics include proselytism and indoctrination through the group's social networks, and in particular through

Hamas's extensive and well-organized educational programs and institutions. Furthermore, the group resorts to both ideological and esoteric factors, mostly rooted in the group's religious discourse, in order to attract support from within the Palestinian territories as well as from abroad.[17] In addition, Hamas's political leadership relied upon the group's honest reputation and its effective delivery of social services as additional tools to gain the support and vote of the Palestinian population.

In this sense, passive followers, sympathizers, and political supporters constitute a heterogeneous group within Palestinian society, and they represent a range of sociocultural indicators. In fact, Hamas's core constituents are generally the commoners, although the organization has increasingly expanded this support network to include all members of Palestinian society, from young to old, and farmers to university students, doctors, lawyers, and women.[18] Similarly, the Palestinian peoples' political alliance to Hamas has historically not been fixed but has been a variable of the perceived status of the conflict and effectiveness of the organization. For example, popular support for Hamas tended to decline sharply in times when the population perceived a potential breakthrough in the context of the negotiations with Israel, such as in the years following the 1993 Oslo agreements and immediately after the 1994 establishment of the Palestinian Authority.[19] In those years the Palestinian population largely backed Fatah and the ongoing negotiations with Israel—a trend that gradually began to reverse itself as both the peace process and the newly created Palestinian Authority proved incapable of substantially improving the reality on the ground for most Palestinians. Concurrently, with the decline in support for Fatah and for the "political solution" to the Palestinian problem in the late 1990s, support for Hamas and the armed struggle began to rise sharply, showing again the relationship between the degree of political backing for Hamas and the perceived status of the Arab-Israeli conflict.[20]

Aside from a large number of passive supporters in the Palestinian territories, Hamas also has a large number of supporters around the world, both in the Palestinian diaspora and among non-Palestinians. Although these supporters are not necessarily members of the organization, they play an important role in providing legitimacy and funding and may also partake in Hamas's social welfare networks. The organization enjoys considerable legitimacy in the Arab and Muslim worlds, which sympathize with the group's willingness to stand up to Israel through the use of force.

Recruitment for Hamas's active supporters is carried out, mainly through its web of social welfare activities. Palestinians with leadership skills are identified from a young age, and their indoctrination is nurtured through peers and mentors. Those deemed capable of meeting the physical and mental challenges of joining the group's military ranks are directed toward that part of the organization, while others participate in Hamas's plethora of other departments, including its Political Bureau and its offices of finance, propaganda, foreign affairs, and social welfare programs.

In the past, the group relied on a similar process to recruit members and train them to become suicide bombers, which they view as *shaheeds*, or "martyrs." Volunteers to carry out such operations were recruited through mosques, charities, universities, and student organizations such as the Kutla Islamiya (Hamas's Islamic block).[21] Other community institutions that are part of Hamas's military, political, and social network also played roles in recruitment. The group's own social network was a natural choice for Hamas recruiters. By maintaining a strong social apparatus, Hamas was able to foster a sense of community and inclusiveness, with strong social bonds between the organization and its members. These are all necessary elements in developing a code of shared meanings and values to shape identity, perceptions, and preferences.[22] In turn, this increased the chances of recruits to be loyal, reliable, and fully committed to their task. This was especially so in the case of suicide bombers: "An overarching sense of collectiveness consumes the individual. This fusion with group seems to provide the necessary justification for their actions with an attendant loss of felt responsibility . . . if the group says it is required and justified, and then it is required and justified."[23]

Communal bonds were thus as important as the religious and ideological appeals, and both factors were also integrated in a comprehensive framework to create a "culture of martyrdom" that promoted hate, glorified death, and generated a myth of honor and ethos around the martyr.[24] Simultaneously, the organization also boosted the role and status of the martyr in Palestinian society by establishing a number of social rituals, including public funerals and parades for the *shaheed*. These reinforced the perception of heroism and worthiness of the suicide bomber. In addition, appraisals from the media and religious authorities, such as Akhram Sabari, the mufti of Jerusalem, justified "self-martyrdom" operations by explaining their consistency with Islamic law.[25] Additional motives that led civilians to become Hamas recruits and specifically suicide operatives can be found in the economic deprivation under which most Palestinians live and in the perspective of gaining social status and economic retribution for their acts. For instance, a "martyr's family" received a cash payment of $1,000, plus additional donations.[26] Although these factors are insufficient by themselves to explain the motivations of suicide bombers, they should certainly be taken into account as contingent causes.

Finally, the cycle of suicide attacks was self-reinforcing, as the strength of the impact of the attacks generated a crop of volunteers to become the next *shaheed*.[27] Thus, the problem for Hamas was less about attracting and recruiting candidates and more of ensuring in the long term that it attracted only "fit" candidates.

Most of the suicide bombers and active militants of Hamas were unmarried males between the ages of nineteen and twenty-five. Their social class matched that of the average Palestinian, but their educational level tended in general to be above average. They also tended to have grown up in religious families.[28] However, Hamas was also able to draw support and active followers from Palestinian women and children. Female militants have been active in Hamas since at least the beginning of the second Intifada, both as facilitators in planning and organizing terrorist attacks and as suicide bombers. This was not seen as contradictory to the stricter Islamic mores that were advocated in the group's charter. In fact, Article 12 of Hamas's covenant states openly that resisting the enemy is a duty of every Muslim, including women: "A woman can go out to fight the enemy without her husband's permission, and so does the slave: without his master's permission." In addition, former Hamas chief Abdel Aziz Rantissi, during an interview with Abu Tibi Television at the end of August 2001, stated, "There is no reason that the perpetration of suicide attacks should be monopolized by men."[29] In order to ensure that this behavior was socially acceptable, the idea of the female martyr was constructed around consolidated gender norms and values, such as modesty, chastity, and honor, thus maintaining continuity with the collective identity and narrative while proposing a momentary deviation from the standard gender-defined roles in the name of "the cause."[30] This has led women—including young mothers—to carry out suicide attacks against Israelis on behalf of Hamas.[31] As part of their propaganda campaign one can find mothers of suicide bombers encouraging fellow Palestinians to become suicide bombers.[32]

Hamas has also recruited children into its ranks. Reports from the Coalition to Stop the Use of Child Soldiers stated that the group had recruited children below the age of fifteen, including children as young as twelve years

old to carry out military operations.[33] After the outbreak of the second Intifada, Israeli security forces apprehended teenagers between the ages of eleven
and eighteen who were trained and ready to perpetrate terrorist attacks, while
others successfully carried out their plans.[34] In the case of minors recruited
by Hamas, the incitement to violence came from Hamas's educational programs and institutions, as well as through television campaigns and Hamas-
run summer camps. All of these organs promoted the culture of martyrdom
and demonized both Israel and its cultural-religious identity.[35]

Fundraising

Since its founding in 1987, Hamas has developed a complex and integrated
financial model, combining logistic and financial support from states, corpo-
rations, charities, and nonprofit organizations, as well as funding from private
donors.[36] The group has also invested in self-generation of revenues and over
the years has diversified its financial activities, employing financial schemes
that range from legal procurement of funds, such as providing financial services, to illegal activities that included weapons smuggling and currency forg-
ery.[37] In addition, since its takeover of the Gaza Strip in June 2007, Hamas's
financial revenues and, of course, it financial needs have expanded as the
group has been involved in tax collections as well as in legitimate economic
activity and in the informal economy that surrounds the underground tunnels
built between Gaza and Egypt.

Currently, Hamas's financial structure and procurement strategy are based
on state sponsorship and third-party donations, as well as self-funding. Hamas
behaves as a global player when it comes to raising funds for its activities: the
group's revenues are raised worldwide, and the organization is increasingly
involved in transnational partnerships, including with criminal entities, to
finance its costly social, political, and military apparatus. An up-to-date estimate of the group's total annual budget appears difficult to obtain; however,
in 2003 the organization's annual revenues were estimated to be around $70
million,[38] although it is likely that this sum has risen steadily in the aftermath of the group's takeover of Gaza and its increased support from Iran.

With its roots in the Muslim Brotherhood, Hamas has always been adept at
collecting *zakat*, or charity, to carry out its missions and goals, including the
financing of its extensive social welfare network. The giving of alms is one of
the five pillars of Islam, and as such, private and public funding of religious

charitable organizations have throughout Islam's history been quite strong. In this sense, Hamas has developed an effective local and global network of charitable organizations dedicated to financing the group's extensive and costly social welfare programs.

Although most Hamas-affiliated charities officially do not explicitly raise money for the group's military apparatus—much of that is funded either directly through Hamas's Political Bureau or though Iranian injection—it is impossible to ascertain how much of the funds collected from their charities are diverted toward military activities. Hamas has gone to great lengths to show a separation between its military and social welfare "branches," seeking to highlight specifically to Western states that fundraising for its social welfare branch should be permitted, even if these governments disapprove of its militant activities. In actuality, as explained earlier, the line between Hamas's two activities is not always clear. Its social welfare programs can also serve its military activities by acting as front organizations that launder money and recruit new militants. When donated money does actually go to a given social welfare program, this funding is also significant as it only further legitimizes the group in its entirety and allows it to divert other funds for terrorist activities. Social welfare programs that the *dawa* support, including hospitals, universities, orphanages, schools, mosques, summer camps, sports clubs, and job training programs, all serve as critical channels for recruitment into militant activities. Furthermore, high numbers of Hamas members and supporters involved in legitimate social welfare programs allow the organization to launder money to fund militant activities.[39]

Maintaining and funding the group's wide social network are among Hamas's main priorities, and a substantial part of its budget is dedicated to ensuring the sustainability and effectiveness of its social programs. Hamas is deeply committed at an ideological level to operate as a social movement and preserve a network of social services. In fact, both of these tools are seen as essential to Islamize Palestinian society by employing a bottom-up approach, thus continuing the legacy of the Mujamma. Additionally, the organization's popularity and legitimacy is in large part derived from its grass-roots activities and social programs. For instance, the group's reputation of efficiency and lack of corruption—earned through its successful management of its welfare network—significantly contributed to Hamas's electoral success at the Palestinian municipal level in 2004 and 2005, as well as in its electoral victory in the January 2006 legislative elections.

The group's social network also directly contributes to preserving popular support for the organization by serving as an important source of employment for Palestinians.[40] This is particularly important, as the government continues to be the Palestinians' largest employer, and like other state-government counterparts in the Arab world, it demands personal loyalty in return for employment and financial benefits. This reality ultimately creates a client-type of relationship between the civilian population and the government. In this sense, support for a given Palestinian camp can mean the difference between whether you work, where you work, and how much money you earn. Hamas has adopted a similar approach within its own constituency, and it has been particularly adept at taking care of its own, thus gaining the loyalty of many Palestinians. For example, it established funds specially designated for families of Hamas "martyrs."[41] Moreover, in the aftermath of its takeover of Gaza in 2007, Hamas invested substantial efforts into developing a parallel client network of supporters within the Gaza Strip. In this sense, Hamas has focused on ensuring direct loyalty with respect to all public employees hired by the group to govern over Gaza, especially in the case of public order and security forces.

As mentioned previously, Hamas finances this massive social network through charity collection, personal donations, and local and global charities and foundations. In the last case, the organizations involved in channeling revenues to Hamas can be either directly affiliated with the group or part of larger organizations that divert part of their funds to Hamas's accounts. These organizations are located in the Middle East, Asia, North America, and Europe. Notably, some Hamas and PIJ financiers have been connected to fundraising activities for al Qaeda as well.[42]

In the years leading up to and immediately following 9/11, Hamas raised funds quite extensively in the United States, especially through the activities of the Holy Land Foundation, whose members were under investigation since the 1990s.[43] In November 2008 the leaders of the organization were convicted on 108 charges, including providing support to Hamas, money laundering, and tax fraud, while the courts found that the Holy Land Foundation had provided approximately $12 million to Hamas.[44] Following 9/11, the United States chose to respond not only by cracking down on organizations raising funds for terrorist organizations within its own borders but also by pressuring European states to shut them down as well. American and European-based "charitable" organizations that had funneled tens of millions of dollars to Hamas throughout the 1990s began to be investigated and closed following increased international attention.

An important milestone in this sense was the 2008 U.S. Treasury Department designation of the Saudi-based Union of Good (Etelaf al-Khair), an umbrella organization set up by Hamas on the eve of the second Intifada in 2000 to channel funds to the organization, as a global terrorist entity.[45] The Union of Good included more than twenty-four charitable organizations worldwide, such as the U.K.-based International Palestine Relief and Development Fund (Interpal), the international Al-Aqsa Foundation, the French Comité de Bienfaisance et de Secours aux Palestiniens (CBSP), the Association de Secours Palestiniens (ASP) of Switzerland, the Palestinian Association in Austria (PVOE), and the Sanabil Association for Relief and Development in Lebanon. Some of the groups associated with the Union of Good, such as the Al-Aqsa Foundation, had previously been designated as global terrorist entities (in 2003), and in the course of the following years the group's activities had been investigated and prohibited in European countries such as Germany, Denmark, and the Netherlands.[46] Interpal, one of the largest charitable groups in the United Kingdom and a founding member of the Union of Good, along with the now defunct Holy Land Foundation (another specially designated global terrorist entity under U.S. law), is still allowed to operate in the United Kingdom—this despite a 2009 inquiry into the group by the U.K. Charity Commission that criticized its lack of "due diligence" for participating in the Union of Good after being ordered to "dissociate" itself from the Saudi organization.[47] Despite these financial setbacks, Hamas continues to raise funds through its network of affiliated charities worldwide, while it supplements these revenues with private donations and contributions from states, such as Iran, Qatar, and Saudi Arabia.

The political and financial partnership between the Saudi government and Hamas started in the early 1990s. Following the 1991 Gulf War, aid that had been earmarked for the PLO began to find its way into Hamas's coffers in response to the PLO's public support for Saddam Hussein during that conflict. Even as relations between the PLO and Saudi Arabia improved, funding to Hamas continued, often to the dismay of Yasser Arafat, who wished to be in control of all money flowing into and out of Palestinian hands. Israeli raids on Palestinian Authority and Hamas locations outlined just how extensive Saudi funding had turned out to be.[48] In those years, Saudi Arabia financed Hamas mostly though banks, charities, and via individuals within the ruling class.[49]

From 2000 to 2006, most funds were delivered from Saudi Arabia to Hamas through the Committee for the Support of the Al Quds Intifadha.[50] According testimony of David D. Aufhauser to the U.S. House of Representatives, in the early 2000s, "As much as half of Hamas's income is derived from money raised in the Persian Gulf, including the Kingdom of Saudi Arabia— notwithstanding a May 2002 decree by Crown Prince Abdullah that ceased official Saudi support for the group."[51] Although the Saudis officially withdrew support for Hamas, funds continued to flow through families and donors within the crown's entourage as well as through the "special account ninety-eight," created ad hoc to fund Palestinian organizations, including Hamas.[52] In addition, Saudi funds were directed to Hamas through charitable organizations and events, such as an April 2002 Saudi Telethon that raised $150 million for the Palestinian population, including to Hamas.[53] More recently, as part of the U.S.-led crackdown against Hamas, that government increased political pressure on the Saudi regime to stop funding the organization, causing the amount of money channeled from that country to drastically diminish. However, even after 2006, the Saudis continue to provide financial assistance to Gaza through the Committee for the Relief of the Palestinian People, which operates in cooperation with UN agencies and invests in humanitarian relief programs for the Palestinian population at large.[54]

Although support from the governments of Saudi Arabia and some Gulf States has waned in the past few years, support from the Arab "street" continues because the organization's more militant stance in dealing with Israel is quite popular in that part of the world, including among Palestinians. Simultaneously, Hamas's financial and political relations with both Iran and Syria have grown in the aftermath of its January 2006 electoral victory. Iran in particular has significantly increased its funding to Hamas. U.S. officials have described Iran as "the central banker of terrorism," and its support for Hamas is no exception.[55] Iran has literally sent billions of dollars to terrorist groups around the world and is an open and proud supporter of Hamas.[56] Support from Iran has also meant increased political relations with Hezbollah, whose tactics were increasingly adopted by Hamas in the years following Israel's withdrawal from Gaza in 2005—often without the same results.[57] Although the two groups have at times been rivals, from an operational and logistical point of view Hezbollah and Hamas maintain political ties, and the Lebanese group has directly paid Palestinians to carry out attacks against Israel.[58] Notably, as ties between Iran and Venezuela have increased under presidents

Ahmadinejad and Hugo Chavez, there are now reports of Venezuelans also funding, training, and otherwise supporting Hamas.[59] In addition to fundraising through charities and state sponsorship, Hamas has also been investing in the self-generation of revenues, through direct involvement in money laundering and weapons smuggling in the Palestinian territories and worldwide, including such regions as the tri-border area of South America.[60]

Finally, Hamas's fundraising strategy has been shaped by the group's electoral victory in 2006 and its subsequent armed takeover of Gaza in 2007. In the past few years, Hamas has been able to raise funds by virtue of its position in Gaza, such as through tax collection on companies operating in Gaza and on numerous commodities imported into the area, mostly through the use of smuggling tunnels.[61] Additionally, the Hamas government in Gaza collects fees for carrying out public services, imposes fines, and collects customs duties on imported goods.[62] Hamas relies on these funds mostly to continue to administer the Gaza Strip and deliver social goods to the local population, a daunting task that has placed the organization under increased financial pressure since 2007. At the same time, taking control of the Gaza Strip has also allowed it to supplement its revenues, mostly by way of controlling part of the informal economy generated around the underground tunnels built between Gaza and Egypt, which includes the smuggling of weapons, cash, contraband goods, cigarettes, vehicles, cattle, and even people.[63]

10 Strategies and Tactics

WITHIN THE PALESTINIAN TERRITORIES, Hamas acquired its reputation and notoriety not only as a consequence of its combative nature vis-à-vis Israel but also as a result of its extensive political and social activities. Internationally, however, Hamas became a household name because of its suicide bombing campaigns against Israeli civilians and military targets during the period of peace negotiations between Israel and the Palestinian Authority under the framework of the Oslo Accords in the 1990s. This was further cemented during the second Intifada, where scenes of bloodied Israeli children in holiday costumes, young and elderly couples killed while sitting side by side on buses, and families blown apart while sharing a Passover Seder meal all helped earn Hamas notoriety from some and praise and admiration from others. Although the organization has claimed responsibility for everything from shootings and roadside bombs to the firing of rockets and conducting kidnappings, it was its suicide attacks that helped sear the organization's name into the consciousness of Israelis and Palestinians alike.

Military Operations

Hamas's suicide bombing campaigns on buses, in restaurants, and at holiday celebrations gripped Israel's citizenry with fear and worried counterterrorism officials worldwide. Suicide bombers were difficult to deter or arrest, and the terrorists knew it. Bombers were sometimes given narcotics before striking to ensure their nerves did not get the best of them. They would be disguised as everything from pregnant women to ultra-orthodox Jews or even IDF soldiers in order to elude authorities. Unlike Hezbollah, which had largely used suicide attacks against Israeli military targets, Hamas purposely used its human bombs to strike at the heart of Israeli cities teeming with civilians. As a Hamas training manual explained, "It is foolish to hunt the tiger when there are plenty of sheep around."[1]

Yet suicide bombings were just a small part of the tactics Hamas has employed to carry out its strategy of confronting and standing up to the Israelis, while gaining the upper hand in Palestinian domestic politics, as it redefined its people's national identity into a more Islamist nature. In addition to terrorism, Hamas used everything from propaganda to psychological warfare in order to carry out its missions, even using civilians to shield themselves from Israeli reprisals. For example, during the IDF incursions into the Gaza Strip in January 2009, Israel accused Hamas of hiding top operatives in hospitals to evade capture, bringing civilians to Hamas leaders' homes to deter Israel from conducting airstrikes, and both storing and firing weapons from mosques and schools and near UN facilities.[2] The IDF asserted that whole blocks of empty Palestinian homes were said to be rigged to explode—including a school—and suicide bombers were deployed to strike IDF patrols. The *Report of the United Nations Fact-Finding Mission on the Gaza Conflict* (aka the Goldstone Report), as well as additional investigations by human rights organizations, did not corroborate Israel's claims. In fact, the report made similar accusations against Israeli forces, charges the Israelis have vehemently denied.[3] Although Richard Goldstone, the lead author of the Goldstone Report, has since recanted and claimed he did not have all of the evidence when his report was produced, the IDF has nonetheless changed its military doctrine in order to better prepare for accusations of human rights violations in the future.[4] This development has occurred despite the fact that Israel and its allies continue to argue that the international community holds it to a double standard.[5]

Certainly, however, the 2009 incursion into Gaza posed for both parties the familiar problems of having to protect civilians while engaging in combat in an extremely densely populated urban area. It was particularly difficult for the IDF to differentiate between civilians and combatants, especially when considering that during combat Hamas members did not tend to wear uniforms and often hid among the civilian population.[6] This predicament led to high numbers of Palestinian civilian casualties, which quickly captured the attention of the media as footage of the carnage was broadcast worldwide—especially to the Arab and Muslim worlds. The 2009–10 Israel incursion into Gaza highlighted yet again the intense media war between Israelis and

Palestinians, in many respects providing another propaganda victory for the Islamist movement. If a picture is worth a thousand words, then television footage and front-page newspaper photos showing blocks of destroyed homes and mosques definitely contributed to shaping the international community's perception of the conflict, while raising international criticism toward Israeli actions.

Aside from the examples made evident in the 2009 war in Gaza between Hamas and Israel, the group confronted Israel through a variety of additional tactics as well. When taking more offensive measures, especially during the years leading up to the second Intifada, Hamas focused on more traditional terrorist tactics that targeted Israeli civilians by way of suicide bombers, active shooters, and even knife attacks that occurred within both Israel's "Green Line" borders and its West Bank and Gaza Strip settlements.[7] With a total operating budget that according to FBI testimony was estimated to be in excess of $70 million and an average attack ranging in cost from $600 to $50,000, Hamas had enough cash on hand to carry out hundreds of attacks against Israeli soft targets, achieving high-impact results with relatively little financial investment.[8] Many of the tactics were picked up by the more than 400 Palestinians who had been expelled by Israel in December 1992 to a no-man's land area on the Lebanese border. There they interacted with members of Hezbollah and acquired critical knowledge to conduct everything from car bombings to suicide attacks.[9]

In the years leading up to and immediately following Israel's withdrawal from the Gaza Strip in 2005, Hamas was forced to alter the way it fought as a result of Israeli countermeasures. Although it still threatened and attempted to carry out suicide attacks, fewer operatives were able to penetrate Israeli defenses, forcing a shift in Hamas tactics. The Islamist group consequently began to rely on the firing of both homemade and imported rockets and mortars to target Israeli population centers, mimicking Hezbollah's activities. In recent years, Hamas amassed and launched thousands of short-range rockets and mortars at Israeli cities, putting hundreds of thousands of Israeli citizens at risk. It has done so while also planting roadside bombs, burrowing extensive underground bunkers, digging tunnels used for carrying out attacks, and increasingly raising its targeting of Israeli settlers in the West Bank in order to demonstrate its continued efficacy in the face of Palestinian Authority and Israeli countermeasures. Yet Hamas has neither the freedom of operation nor the same access to support from Iran and Syria that Hezbollah has enjoyed.

As a result, Hamas's homemade "Qassam" rockets and other projectiles smuggled into Gaza such as the Russian-made Grad have caused relatively few Israeli casualties, despite the difficulties they create for much of Israel's civilian population.[10] Hamas has been working hard to smuggle in more advanced rockets and missiles with the help of the Iranians, but it has not yet shown an ability to either use them effectively or amass a more advanced arsenal on a significant scale.

As Hamas focused increasing attention on securing the Gaza Strip from its fellow Palestinian rivals, it continued to bolster its defenses against future Israeli incursions, occasionally attacking Israeli military personnel and civilians. It has done so through a range of tactics, including deployment of roadside IEDs, kidnappings, hit-and-runs, ambushes of Israeli police and civilians, and the launching of rockets, missiles, and mortars. Although these tactics have not proved as successful as its previous suicide bombing campaigns, Hamas has been determined to show that it is still capable of striking out against adversaries, despite the best efforts to put a stop to them.[11] After Israel's 2009 Gaza incursion—dubbed Operation Cast Lead by the IDF—Hamas almost immediately began to reassess its military strategy, demonstrating its ability to evolve, while noting that the Hezbollah and Iranian strategy and training it had adopted were insufficient. Consequently, it began to incorporate a more diverse doctrine that is based on experiences of North African states as well, calling for improvements in antiarmor arsenals, supply lines, and communications networks.[12]

One area in which Hamas has been particularly effective has been in its ability to Islamize the conflict between the Israelis and the Palestinians. Thanks to Hamas and other Islamist groups, the Palestinian-Israeli and Arab-Israeli conflicts are increasingly seen not just as a conflict between two competing nationalist camps but rather as a greater conflict between Islam and the West. Islamist groups have managed to reprogram the conflict into a battle of religions: one in which Islam is fighting for its survival, and ultimately its supremacy, against what it views as an invasion by Jews and Christians.[13] This narrative has only increased in recent years with the rising religious sentiment piercing Israeli settler and military ranks, which have also increasingly bought into that argument. Islamist claims of a clash of civilizations between Muslim and *kufr*, or nonbeliever, is one that is increasingly spreading to Israel's Arab citizenry as well, who today comprise approximately 20 percent of the Israeli population.[14] As a Jewish state, Israel is viewed as a religious Jewish country that needs to be destroyed and turned into a religious Islamist state instead.[15]

Terrorism

Because it almost always acts in a calculating and rational way, Hamas uses terrorism to achieve its goals and not as a means in and of itself. The Islamist group recognizes that terrorism has its limits and thus uses it strategically and when it will be most beneficial. While the increasingly pervasive role of Salafi influence in the Gaza Strip has made its willingness to forgo violence more difficult, Hamas has shown its ability to negotiate and keep to unofficial cease-fires with Israel, demonstrating it can make more moderate moves when such activities are in the group's best interests. With that said, terrorism and other uses of violence consistently prove to be one of Hamas's greatest weapons available in its arsenal. In the past, Hamas has relied on both blind terrorism and selective terrorism. Blind terrorism targets Israelis in general, with the only goal being to achieve maximum casualties. Selective terrorism targets specific people in order to achieve a particular objective or to send an explicit message.[16] At times, Hamas has also demonstrated its ability to put differences aside with its adversaries in order to take on its greater enemy, Israel. For instance, at the onset of the second Intifada Hamas's leadership agreed to work with the Palestinian Authority and other competing groups in order to more effectively combat the Israelis.[17]

Strategically speaking, Hamas in many ways has pioneered the concept of spoiling negotiations and the outcome of elections through the use of violence. Its increasing attacks in the run-up to both Palestinian and Israeli elections have proved successful in ushering in parties less amenable to an Israeli-Palestinian peace agreement, which would seriously hamper Hamas activities if ever reached. This strategy has become so successful that it may have influenced al Qaeda to attempt similar attacks before significant U.S. and allied elections around the world.[18]

During the years of the second Intifada, Hamas also showed an interest in attempting unsophisticated chemical-biological-radiological (CBR) suicide attacks, showing the group's desire to upgrade its operations and capacities to inflict greater damage upon its enemy. As early as August 2001, Hezbollah's Al-Manar produced a report published by the Hamas-affiliated Palestinian Center for Information Sources—Gaza, stating: "Serious thinking has begun a while ago about developing a Palestinian weapon of deterrence. This weapon terrifies the Israeli security apparatuses . . . mainly because obtaining its primary components, whether biological or chemical, is possible without too much effort, let alone that there are hundreds of experts who are capable of handling them. . . . A few bombs or death-carrying devices will be enough, once they are deployed in the secluded areas and directed at the Israeli water resources or the Israeli beaches, let alone the markets and the residential centers."[19] Following up on this plan, Hamas is reported to have first tried to conduct a biological attack against Israel through the spread of hepatitis. The May–June 2001 attacks at both the Netanya mall and the Tel Aviv Dolphinarium dance club were allegedly conducted with infected suicide bombers, requiring the Israeli Ministry of Health to immunize all the victims of the attacks against Hepatitis B.[20] The following year, in August 2002, in the course of the trial of Hamas military leader Abbas Sayyid, it emerged that he had intended to dispatch terrorists with a bottle of cyanide to spread the chemical agent.[21] Sayyid's nephew, Tarek Zaidan, allegedly acquired and smuggled 350 grams of cyanide from Jordan, "to murder hundreds of people, if not more."[22] This evidence also confirmed a January 2002 Israeli intelligence report that claimed Hamas had an interest since 1997 in chemical homemade bombs using pesticides and poisons.[23] Finally, in June 2006 a *Haaretz* report claimed that Hamas was attempting to stockpile explosives for the next attacks against Israel, and that it was planning to add chemicals to its bombs, upgrading to "mega-terrorism" operations.[24] This information had been obtained through the interrogation of a Hamas military commander in the West Bank, who was captured by the IDF in May 2006.[25] Although these comments appear at least in part to be wishful thinking and an attempt to instill fear into the Israeli population, their efforts still serve to indicate the group's intention during and after the second Intifada to rely even more prominently on more lethal suicide operations.

To develop and conduct these plans, as well as its "regular" suicide campaigns, Hamas focused on building its operational headquarters in Gaza. The Gaza Strip, in fact, has always been Hamas's primary base of support, much more so than the more secular and open West Bank. In both territories, however, the group has used the densely populated civilian areas much to its advantage. This means, for example, that weapons and explosives have been found hidden in mosques, schools, and hospitals, and Palestinian Red Crescent ambulances have at times been used to transport suicide bombers, weapons, and known Hamas fighters wanted by the Israelis. At the same time, the group invested in massive public campaigns to increase the legitimacy and popularity of its suicide campaign and thus ensure the backing of the Palestinian population.[26] Hamas continues to take a page out of Iranian and Hezbollah playbooks by setting up its operational headquarters in bunkers beneath some of the largest hospitals and schools.[27]

As Israeli countermeasures have increased and become more effective, Hamas has consistently proved its ability to think outside the box. In the case of conducting kidnappings of Israelis—an act that often both yields a psychological victory and results in lopsided prisoner exchanges—Hamas has shown some savage ingenuity. In 1994 Hamas terrorists disguised themselves as Orthodox Jews in order to kidnap an Israeli-American corporal in the IDF named Nachshon Wachsman. Wachsman was later murdered by his captives in a failed rescue attempt by Israeli special forces.[28]

In June 2006 Hamas tunneled past Israeli security barriers and underneath an IDF military outpost inside Israel in order to conduct another kidnapping operation. In that attack, two Israeli soldiers were killed and an IDF corporal named Gilad Shalit was kidnapped. Shalit had been held for more than five years by Hamas and its affiliates in the Palestinian Resistance Committees (PRC), before being released in 2011.[29]

In addition to being used to conduct attacks and kidnapping operations, Hamas uses tunnels quite extensively in a fashion similar to Hezbollah. The tunnels move fighters and weaponry while bypassing Israeli efforts to restrict the Islamist organization from collecting outside support in the form of arms, money, and training.[30]

Apart from kidnappings, Hamas has shown cunning through the use of other tactics, including many that have since been incorporated by other insurgency and terrorist groups. For instance, information gleaned from interrogations of prisoners indicates that encoded messages directing terrorist operations have been released by Hamas spokespeople during televised statements.[31] U.S. intelligence officials fear that this tactic is now being used by groups such as al Qaeda to pass on operational information and activate sleeper cells. This is one reason why past speeches by al Qaeda leaders were not fully broadcast in the United States. Another tactic of Hamas that was later adopted by other groups is the recruitment of terrorists from countries friendly with Israel in order to gain access to the Jewish state and target sites they would otherwise be barred from visiting. For instance, in 2003 Hamas introduced the first non-Palestinian suicide attackers to be launched against Israel. In an attack on a Tel Aviv bar known as Mike's Place, a British bomber of Pakistani origin blew himself up, killing three civilians and wounding sixty more. A second intended bomber's explosive vest failed to detonate.[32] All of these tactics indicate that Hamas is a shrewd adversary that has learned to adapt and grow in response to increasingly advanced counter-terrorism and counterinsurgency tactics.

Propaganda and Psychological Warfare

Hamas has come a long way from its modest roots in the sphere of propaganda. In its earlier years, propaganda was little more than fiery speeches in mosques and some locally distributed pamphlets. Today the organization has an entire propaganda division at its disposal, including television stations such as Al Aqsa TV, multiple radio bands, newspapers, and Internet sites.[33] Pictures of its suicide bombers are plastered in streets and on school walls, and messages of indoctrination are spread throughout its vast social welfare networks. Taking a page out of Hezbollah's playbook, Hamas has also begun recording attacks so they may be studied, viewed on air or online, and distributed or sold for propaganda purposes to those interested in spreading their messages of resistance and jihad.[34] As is the case for many sophisticated Islamist groups today, the use of media has become an important tool of war, and it is one that Hamas has devoted substantial time and funding to nurture and develop. The group has been able to conduct its media campaigns both through its own propaganda and media divisions and by relying on mainstream media to convey its message.

In particular, in the Israeli-Palestinian conflict, arguably more so than in any other conflict elsewhere in the world, including Lebanon, the sheer number of reporters in such a small land provides the Palestinians with an incredible opportunity to relay and tailor their messages to the world, and they have done a very effective job at doing so. "Unequal political conflicts" are said to be where the media is most likely to have the largest impact, and the Israeli-Palestinian conflict has become the best example of such a battleground.[35] Hamas's media campaigns have focused on spreading a particular narrative of the conflict, which portrays Israel as the Goliath and the main aggressor in the conflict. Similarly, Hamas seeks to paint the conflict in black-and-white terms according to which Israeli occupiers overreact to Palestinian peaceful demands for self-determination and lash out with little regard for Palestinian lives. This framing of the conflict could not have been possible without the unintended assistance of Israeli misstatements and actions. Comments such as Yitzhak Rabin's now infamous orders for his soldiers to "break their [Palestinians'] bones" back when he was defense minister during the first Intifada did little to help Israel's image.[36]

Using passionate arguments, and often mixing accurate facts with misinformation and distorted statistics, Hamas and its supporters in the pro-Palestinian camp have managed to promote their understanding and framing of the conflict with respect to large sectors of the international community, aligning themselves with members of the far Left from around the world as well. The cause of Palestine has become *the* issue so many seem to be concerned with, and it is generally accepted that for the past thirty or so years the Palestinians have been winning the media war with Israel.[37] This is all too evident at the plethora of rallies that take place around the world: from anarchists' rallies, to pro-Tibetan concerts, or even at events held by the Independence for Puerto Rico movement, signs of "Free Palestine" can be seen front and center, even when it is not the main focus of an event.[38] One analysis on the media and the war on terrorism explained Israel's dilemma this way:

> Even though Arab governments and sources tended to inflate figures and distort reality . . . the thrust of Middle East coverage portrayed Israel as the conquering Goliath and the Palestinians as the embattled but tough David. There is no escape from the journalists who, with a laptop and satellite phone, are helping to shape policy and diplomacy.[39]

Well aware of the predicament Israel finds itself in, Hamas has been very effective at taking advantage of it. Israelis, of course, view themselves as the David in this bitter conflict, fighting on the front lines of a war against Islamist extremists and other nationalist movements. The Israeli government and pro-Israel NGOs have been taking part in the media war by promoting their opposite vision of the conflict, pointing out the size of the Israeli state relative to the nearly two dozen Arab states.

At times, Hamas has also been known to provide inflated or false data to the world's news media—information that consequently has been reported by outlets worldwide, contributing to the promotion of the group's understanding of the conflict. For example, Hamas has falsely blamed Israel for everything from power outages to massacres.[40] These stories often become front-page news reports beamed into homes around the world. When an error in the report is pointed out, more often than not there is little more than a small correction somewhere on a newspaper back page.[41] By that time, the damage has been done.

Journalists are only human, of course, and in high-profile conflicts such as the Israeli-Palestinian one, both sides are always vying for their attention. As Glenn Frankel, Pulitzer Prize–winning correspondent for the *Washington Post* once explained, "We [journalists] are in a war. Each side is attempting to use us, to enlist us if you will, to convince us, to cajole us into accepting their version of reality, and their version of reality is based on their strategic needs."[42] Yet there are cases when members of the media have been found to be actively and knowingly engaged in assisting the Palestinian cause. For example, a fourteen-year veteran correspondent of the BBC named Fayad Abu Shamala was found speaking at a Hamas rally in Gaza, where she said, "Journalists and media organizations [are] waging the campaign shoulder-to-shoulder together with the Palestinian people."[43] For years before that speech Shamala had been accused of anti-Israel bias but had been defended by the news agency. The BBC eventually let the reporter go once news of that speech broke. The opposite is also true when it comes to "pro-Israeli" activists and media—thus, in this sense, both parties of the conflict can count on a number of "loyal" reporters and news outlets.

When media outlets have not been as forthcoming in spreading Hamas's message, the organization has found other ways of getting its point across to a larger audience. For example, when journalists work overseas assignments, they require local translators, guides, and other "fixers" to help them maneuver through that particular area of the world. Hamas and other Palestinian groups have thus developed a network of fixers who are politically aligned with them and can help steer journalists toward the stories they wish to be told and stage photo shoots that will make great accompaniments to those stories.[44] Similarly, Palestinian groups in the past have ensured that the reported numbers of Palestinian civilian casualties were inflated through the cooperation and sometimes coercion of groups that are identified by their neutrality, such as the Palestinian Red Crescent.[45]

At the same time, in addition to having developed a massive presence in global, regional, and local news media, Hamas has also spread its message by relying on its channels and the venues owned by sympathetic groups. Hamas's rhetoric and storyline is frequently broadcast by Hezbollah's Al-Manar satellite television and the Qatari-based Al Jazeera. Through these popular stations, Hamas has been able to communicate its ideological and operational agenda to wider audiences in the region and worldwide. In this sense, these stations have become a powerful weapon in its psychological warfare campaign, providing continuous support to groups like Hamas. At the same time, since January 2006 Hamas has also developed its very own satellite television channel, Al Aqsa TV, which together with Al Aqsa Radio greatly enhances the organization's outreach and media capabilities.[46] Both the television channel and the radio station are now core tools that Hamas employs to spread its worldview and values to the Palestinian population and outside world. The stations broadcast programs that share Hamas's framing of the conflict and its role within Palestinian society, not just via news reports but through entertainment programs and children's shows as well.

The Internet also plays a major role in Hamas's strategy, as the group has one of the greatest presences on the Web of any terrorist group, thanks in kind to both affiliated Web sites and Web pages created by sympathizers.[47] While some of Hamas's Web sites use secret codes, passwords, and private mailing lists to communicate internally among followers, most sites are dedicated to reaching out and promoting its cause to a broader public. Particularly in the case of Western-oriented Web sites, Hamas tends to avoid details of its more violent operations, while justifying the use of violence by delegitimizing Israel and emphasizing Hamas's role as the "weaker side," which has no choice but to defend its people against Israeli aggression. They accomplish this by employing graphic visuals of dead or wounded women and children, lacing reports with words such as "genocide" and "slaughter" when referring to Israeli actions, and focusing on language such as "freedom fighters" and "resistance" when referring to Hamas operatives.[48]

The group's main information Web site is the Palestinian Information Center,[49] which is available for viewing in English, French, Arabic, Russian, Farsi, Urdu, and Indonesian. But the group also runs other sites, including islamic-block,[50] which coordinates Hamas-affiliated student associations, and Hamas's Al-Qassam military wing Web site.[51] Hamas also publishes sev-

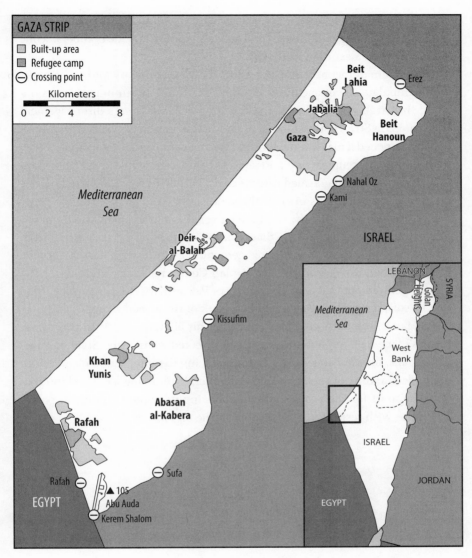

Gaza Strip with Egypt and Israel border areas. The World Factbook, 2009 *(Washington, DC: Central Intelligence Agency, 2009), www.cia.gov/library/publications/the-world -factbook/index.html.*

eral Web-based publications, including *Filasteen Al-Muslima* (Muslim Pales-tine),[52] which is based in London and actively glorifies suicide bombers, while criticizing the Palestinian Authority.[53]

Hamas simultaneously employs all of these instruments to draw support and manipulate the image of the conflict. For example, an important example of this strategy was Hamas's campaign preceding Israel's disengagement from the Gaza Strip. In the summer of 2005 following Israel's Gaza withdrawal, Hamas launched a massive media and Internet campaign to proclaim its "victory" over the "occupier" and portrayed the unilateral withdrawal from Gaza as a direct result of its "armed resistance."[54] This drive was conducted on several levels: on the streets of Gaza through parades and posters, on the Internet and through Hamas-affiliated media venues, and via mainstream newspapers and television channels that released interviews and statements from Hamas's leaders before the disengagement. The campaign was a success. Khalil Shikaki, director of the Palestinian Center for Policy and Survey Research, pointed out that a large majority of Palestinians (84 percent) believed that the disengagement was the direct result of the armed struggle, and they given Hamas the most credit for reaching this achievement.[55] In this sense, Hamas's "media war" has not only been directed against the State of Israel but has also focused on shaping and influencing the international community's understanding of the Arab-Israeli conflict, by drawing local and international support for the group and by enhancing its domestic political power and status with respect to other groups in the region.

PART III COUNTERING HEZBOLLAH AND HAMAS

11 Israeli Counterinsurgency and Counterterrorism

NO STUDY OF HEZBOLLAH and Hamas would be complete without a basic understanding of the efforts to combat them, and no country is more involved in that effort than Israel. Israeli difficulties in effectively conducting counterinsurgency and counterterrorism campaigns against Hamas forces in the Palestinian territories—and particularly in its stronghold of the Gaza Strip—has traditionally been quite different from its experiences against Hezbollah in southern Lebanon. At only 360 square miles and with a population of approximately 1.3 million, the Gaza Strip is a far more heavily populated area than other theaters of combat Israel has had to deal with in the past. Within the territory are numerous refugee camps, narrow alleyways, and extensive tunnel systems.[1] As a result, engaging in combat in this highly populated area makes it more difficult for the IDF to operate without causing heavy civilian casualties. Similarly, Palestinian groups fighting Israel—particularly Hamas and the Palestinian Islamic Jihad—have been very effective at using this dense civilian population both to protect themselves and to make it more difficult for the IDF to operate effectively. Israel, Hamas, and Hezbollah are all well aware of the Israeli "democratic dilemma" that comes as a result of negative political backlash when IDF actions result in the killing of innocent civilians in the course of counterinsurgency and counterterrorism operations.[2] Many have come to argue that the IDF has come a long way since its more destructive days during the first Intifada and that, through an extensive learning curve, it developed a counterinsurgency doctrine that helped minimize civilian casualties during operations, often at a higher cost to Israeli soldiers.[3] At the same time, the international community continues to accuse Israel of not showing enough military restraint and proportionality in conducting its military operations. These criticisms were in evidence yet again in the aftermath of Israel's large-scale military campaign into Gaza, dubbed Operation Cast

Lead by Israel, in 2009–10. That mission led international human rights organization to once again point the finger at Israel's counterinsurgency doctrine.[4]

From an operational perspective, Israel's military operations against Hezbollah and Hamas have evolved substantially in the past few decades. Since the second Intifada, when Israel implemented its Operation Field of Thorns— the initial operation designed to deal with the Palestinian uprising—the IDF increasingly transformed its military doctrine from one that focused on short conventional wars to ones that confronted low-intensity conflicts such as those found in earlier years of combat against Hezbollah and Hamas.[5] This was highly evident during Israel's March 2002 Operation Defensive Shield— the largest military operation of the second Intifada—as well as during Israel's "second Lebanon war" in 2006 and Operation Cast Lead in 2009.

Operation Defensive Shield was carried out in response to a campaign of seven suicide bombings against Israelis in a two-week period, which included an attack that killed 30 civilians in the city of Netanya, where families had gathered to celebrate the traditional Passover Seder meal. It was the first time that Israel reconquered areas that had been previously handed over to the Palestinian Authority as a result of the Oslo Accords. The principle Israeli objective was to put an end to the terrorist attacks that were being carried out by Palestinian groups, and it was very effective at meeting that goal. It did not, however, put an end to the second Intifada as a whole. Politically, Operation Defensive Shield further contributed to the weakening of the Palestinian Authority, which it viewed as complicit in many of the attacks. These actions consequently enhanced the ongoing political decay of the Fatah party, which in turn unintentionally benefited Hamas, which was able to fill the political and security vacuum left by the destroyed PA institutions, including the distribution of social goods. Operation Defensive Shield received strong international criticism because of not only its "collateral damage" in terms of civilian casualties but also the temporary restrictions of basic freedoms placed on Palestinian civilians and the destroyed infrastructure of the community.[6]

In the course of the operation, Israel confronted an increasingly challenging battlefield that required it to adopt new counterinsurgency tactics. One particularly hard-fought campaign occurred in a terrorist nest in the city of Jenin, where twenty-three suicide bombers had come from in the eighteen months before the Israeli operation.[7] The IDF went house to house in the city's refugee camps, routing out insurgent forces. In an interview with an Egyptian newspaper, a member of the Palestinian Islamic Jihad who helped booby trap a refugee camp explained what type of fight Israel was up against: "We had more than 50 houses booby-trapped," the bomb-maker explained. "We chose old and empty buildings and the houses of men who were wanted by Israel because we knew the soldiers would search for them. . . . We cut off lengths of main water pipes and packed them with explosives and nails. Then we placed them about four meters apart . . . in cupboards, under sinks, in sofas."[8]

In later years, these tactics increased considerably by Hamas. In response to such measures, Israel used a number of inventive tactics to overcome these difficulties, some of which were later incorporated by Western forces, including Americans operating in Iraq. For instance, after warning civilians to leave a given area, some homes were bulldozed by IDF forces in order to lower the risk to soldiers' lives. It is a controversial measure that also resulted in massive destruction of civilian infrastructure within the city. In the narrow alleyways where armored vehicles could not enter, IDF troops often moved house to house by blowing holes through walls to protect themselves from snipers and explosives that had been planted at the entrances of buildings.[9] Additionally, many IDF units use dogs mounted with cameras to help identify targets, explosives, tunnels, suspects, and booby traps.[10] Whereas dogs used to be operated almost exclusively by IDF Special Forces and an elite dog-training combat unit known as Oketz, infantry units of all kinds now make use of them along with UAVs, in an effort to get a better understanding of the previously unknown battlefield both inside homes and outside on the street.

During Operation Defensive Shield, the IDF did not make full use of its powerful air force or its extensive artillery corps, because of the risk of heavy civilian casualties. Rather, it used its infantry for house-to-house combat, in what it argued was an effort to save civilian lives. In total, the exact number of casualties has not been universally agreed upon; however, estimates point to approximately fifty-two Palestinians and twenty-three Israeli soldiers killed.[11] Despite this reality, Palestinian sources originally reported that more than five hundred civilians were killed and dubbed the operation a "massacre." News of this apparent slaughter spread to media stations around the world with breaking news interrupting other programs and initially reporting the Palestinian claims of a massacre. The IDF had prevented foreign press from entering the area while the operation was underway, making it even more difficult for media outlets to get the facts. After investigations by the United Nations and independent human rights groups, it was eventually confirmed that no massacre had taken place, although the report still harshly criticized Israel for its military conduct, stressing the IDF's massive destruction of local infrastructure. To this day many speak of an Israeli massacre at Jenin as if it were a factual event.

Israel's difficulties in effectively dealing with terrorists and insurgents while maintaining that its activities are acts of self-defense and permissible under international law has been a constant battle. The Jewish state is often accused of using "disproportionate force," as evidenced following Hamas's decision not to extend a six-month truce with Israel that had begun in June 2008.[12] Instead, the Islamist group chose to fire hundreds of crude rockets, mortars, and missiles into Israeli territory.[13] Israel responded with the heaviest pounding of the Gaza Strip since the 1967 war, in an effort to end the rocket attacks and reach another, more amenable, cease-fire arrangement. Just a few days into the operation known as Cast Lead, the United Nations along with multiple states and NGOs all called for an end to Israel's "disproportionate" use of force, noting again the civilian toll of the military endeavor. In response to these claims, Israel asserted that the IDF went out of its way to protect civilians and that, as a result, its hands remained severely tied when trying to achieve its military objectives. The IDF cited examples of its forces risking the success of their missions by placing telephone calls to thousands of Palestinians before operations commenced in order to warn civilians to leave their homes if they were located near Hamas infrastructure or personnel.[14]

On the other hand, those within the international community who criticized Israel's military conduct in the course of Operation Cast Lead pointed out several examples to counter Israeli claims. These included aerial attacks and shelling of Hamas government facilities not directly affiliated with the combatants, along with attacks on police forces, hospitals, and civilian homes.[15]

Similar discrepancies also existed in terms of agreeing on a final number of casualties, which has ranged from 1,100 to approximately 1,500, differing especially with regard to the reported civilian-military casualty ratio. According to reports by Italian and Israeli newspapers that cited Palestinian physicians upon conclusion of the January 2009 Gaza incursion, the number of casualties—and particularly those of Palestinian civilian casualties—was significantly lower than what local and international NGOs as well as human rights organizations had claimed. One Palestinian physician was quoted as saying, "It was strange that the nongovernmental organizations, including Western ones, repeated the number without checking, but the truth will come to light in the end."[16] However, even relying exclusively on IDF official data, the number of casualties in the "Gaza War" remained at 1,166 Palestinians.[17] Challenges such as those cited in the preceding examples have left Israeli military officials with quite the challenge in finding effective means to combat and deter Hamas forces. In the past, Israel has struggled when seeking to find tactics that prevent and deter suicide bombings within Israel. On this matter, as Dr. Chuck Freilich, a former Israeli deputy national security adviser explained, the "Palestinians have developed a threshold for punishment so high, that you can't deter them anymore."[18] The many times that Israel tried to deter Palestinians from carrying out attacks, its tactics either proved ineffective or were subject to international criticism. Because death itself does not constitute a deterrent for suicide bombers—these human bombs were promised not only a paradise in heaven but that their families would be taken care of once they die—for many years Israel carried out a controversial policy of demolishing the homes of suicide bombers in an effort to deter them. The effectiveness of house demolitions has been highly questionable, however, and it raised the issue of whether such acts create more suicide bombers than they prevent. Moreover, house demolitions have been criticized by international human rights organization as well as by the United Nations and the International Committee of the Red Cross for constituting a form of "collective punishment": a measure prohibited under international humanitarian law. Pictures and videos of house destructions became great propaganda for Hamas and other groups seeking to demonize Israeli actions. Over time, international law and Israeli legal rulings curbed demolitions of the homes of suicide bombers and their families.

More recently, since Hamas assumed control of the government in Gaza, Israel has struck out against all Hamas infrastructure in the hope that these assaults would pressure the Palestinian people to rise up against the Hamas government. It is a tactic Israel to a lesser extent attempted and was unsuccessful in achieving against Hezbollah in the summer of 2006, as Hezbollah at the time was not a major party in the ruling Lebanese government. Arguably, this strategy could have proved more effective in the Gaza Strip than in Lebanon, but at the moment Hamas is still solidly in control of Gaza, and the overall benefits of this strategy are still being debated.

One of Israel's most effective but controversial counterterrorism measures has been the building of its security barrier in the West Bank, which has political overtones in addition to just counterterrorism ones. In 1994 Israel began building a security barrier around the Gaza Strip, when it withdrew from approximately 80 percent of that territory under the Oslo Accords. Since that barrier's completion, it has helped prevent hundreds if not thousands of infiltrations into Israel by Palestinian terrorists and illegal workers. From just 2000–3, there were more than four hundred failed attempts to carry out attacks in Israel from the Gaza Strip.[19] In fact, since its creation, only a handful of successful suicide attacks has come from Gaza. During the second Intifada, Israel realized the need for a similar barrier for the West Bank as well, considering that some Palestinian cities are less than fifteen kilometers from Israel's densely populated coastal area.[20] Even with good intelligence, the short walk or drive by suicide bombers and other terrorists from Palestinian areas into Israeli population centers drove the Jewish state to search for a way to slow or stop potential attacks. As a result, in 2002 the Israeli government began construction of a security barrier in the West Bank.[21]

Made up largely of trenches and fences with a little under 10 percent consisting of high cement walls in areas where sniper fire is a major risk or Palestinian and Israeli villages are very close to one another, the West Bank barrier has become highly controversial as it was not built along the 1967 "Green Line" border. Palestinians argued that building the barrier was an effort to carry out another "fact on the ground" that resulted in both a land grab and a violation of international law. Israelis countered that the government was required to build within the West Bank territory to better protect its citizens both inside and outside the Green Line—a border that had until recently not been recognized as the legitimate boundary by any members of the international community. Only once a political agreement was reached, the Israeli government contended, could the barrier than be adjusted.

Since its construction began, the barrier has been condemned by much of the international community, including human rights organizations, the UN General Assembly, officials from the European Union, and the International Court of Justice (ICJ).[22] Among the criticisms advanced against this barrier is the claim that it represents Israel's attempt to annex territory in violation of international law, as well as the claim that it directly and substantially affects the basic freedoms of Palestinians in the West Bank; especially restricting their freedom of movement. It has also been considered more harmful than

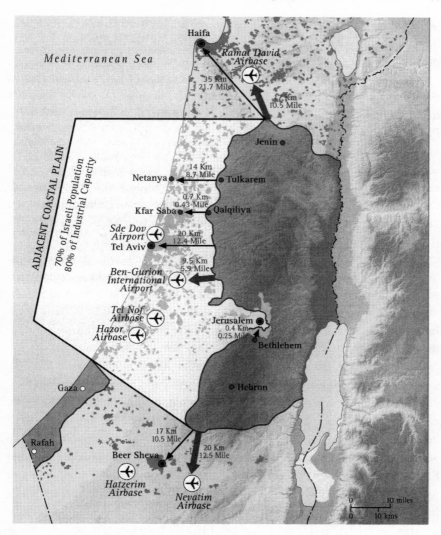

Threat to Israeli population centers from West Bank terrain. Defensible Borders for a Lasting Peace (Jerusalem Center for Public Affairs, 2008), www. jcpa.org.

beneficial by a number of former heads of Israel's Shin Bet security service.[23] While the Israeli Supreme Court has forced the Israeli government to move the barrier in certain areas where it was deemed to have caused unnecessary harm to Palestinian civilians, it has also ruled that the barrier in general is acceptable. The barrier has been called everything from an "apartheid" or a "separation" wall by pro-Palestinian groups to an "antiterrorism security fence" by pro-Israelis, with pictures of the walled parts of the barrier making great propaganda pieces for groups arguing against the barrier's construction.

Irrespective of the legitimacy of each side's claims, what is clear is that in the areas where the barrier has been built, the number of suicide bombers has sharply decreased, and it has become an admittedly effective obstacle for Palestinian groups seeking to carry out attacks inside Israel proper.[24] At the same time, it has also led Palestinian groups to focus their energies on penetrating or attacking the border checkpoints into Israel in order to carry out successful attacks. In the past, one popular technique had been to take advantage of Israel's humanitarian policies toward Palestinians, especially women and children. For instance, Hamas and other groups have used ambulances to transport suicide belts under stretchers of genuinely ill patients and recruited those who have received permission for medical treatment in Israel in order to carry out suicide attacks.[25] These facts have led Israeli security personnel to at times further limit the number of humanitarian passes it distributes and to more severely scrutinize those seeking entry into the country for humanitarian purposes. This in turn has led to increased criticism from human rights organizations and members of the international community.

More generally, from a military perspective, the barrier is one major reason that Palestinians are developing new techniques for attacking Israeli civilians, using everything from rocket fire to bulldozers in an effort to inflict casualties. Israel is not, however, alone in the use of barriers. Similar ones have been adopted for security purposes around the world—including in the Arab world—at locations such as Sharm el-Sheikh in Egypt and on the contested Saudi-Yemeni border.[26] More famously, the United States erected miles of wall in Baghdad—not without controversy itself—to help lower sectarian violence and protect its own forces.[27]

Another controversial tactic has been Israel's policy of targeted assassinations, which it used to kill both Hezbollah and Hamas leaders.[28] Israel has argued that targeted assassinations of terrorist and insurgent leaders saves lives on both sides of the border as it negates the need to send in IDF soldiers to arrest or kill a given target. Some critics of Israel's assassinations take issue with the concept of the killings themselves, arguing that they are extrajudicial and contrary to international humanitarian and human rights law, while others object when civilians are caught in the crossfire.[29] In the narrow streets and dense villages of Gaza, where Hamas infrastructure is often intertwined with the civilian population, Israel's assassinations and assassination attempts have more often than not killed Palestinian civilians along with the given targets. Most assassinations are carried out by Apache or Cobra helicopter gunships, although other aircraft such as F-16s and unmanned aerial vehicles (UAVs) are occasionally used for heavier payloads or greater operational surprise. Over time and as a result of internal and external pressures, Israel has become more efficient in its targeted assassinations, lowering the number of civilian casualties but not ending them completely. This has not, however, lowered the amount of international criticism against this measure, as many within the international community hold the view that targeted assassinations are illegal under international law.

Though rare, Israel has also carried out assassinations and assassination attempts overseas as well. In 1997 a Mossad hit team attempted to assassinate Hamas political leader Khaled Meshaal in Jordan, using a poisonous liquid sprayed in his ear.[30] The plot was uncovered and after great embarrassment, Israel handed over an antidote and released Hamas leader Sheikh Ahmed Yassin, who had been in an Israeli prison up until that time. In January 2010, Israel again got caught under the international spotlight for allegedly orchestrating and carrying out the assassination of Hamas military commander and liaison Mahmoud al-Mabhouh in Dubai.[31] Relying on forged British and Irish passports, a team of twenty-seven agents allegedly working for the Israeli Mossad entered Dubai and killed the Hamas commander and liaison, generating an intense wave of international criticism and diplomatic repercussions.[32]

Israeli-Palestinian warfare continues to mimic the cat-and-mouse games of the past, only with new and inventive tactics. For instance, in response to the placement of Palestinian civilians on the rooftops of Hamas infrastructure and leaders' homes in the course of the 2009 military operations in Gaza, the Israeli Air Force began using dummy nonexplosive missiles that land on rooftops and scare away the civilians, before explosive missiles are then fired.[33] Similarly, when targeted assassinations by air are not feasible, or when arrests need to be made, the IDF uses Special Forces units that concentrate on the type of urban warfare environment found in the Palestinian territories. One such unit, known as Sayeret Duvdevan, is made up of small undercover teams that wear Arab clothing and specialize in assassinations and arrests.[34] Other hunting and assassination teams over the years have included Shimshon (also very effective at targeting rocket and mortar launching units) and Rimon.[35] These units operate in conjunction with and often at the direction of Israel's extensive intelligence gathering network, which incorporates signals intelligence (SIGINT) and human intelligence (HUMINT) forms of collection through the use of everything from UAVs to informers. Israeli Military Intelligence (Agaf HaModiin, or AMAN) and the General Security Service (GSS) or Israeli Security Agency (ISA) (also commonly known as the Shin Bet or Shabak) are Israel's main intelligence arms operating in the West Bank and Gaza Strip. Many IDF forces train for urban warfare combat and special counterinsurgency operations in extensive mock Arab "villages" that Israeli security forces have at their disposal. Since the outbreak of the second Intifada, Israel has been very effective at hindering the operational capabilities of Hamas and other Palestinian groups. Unlike the situation vis-à-vis Hezbollah, Israeli tactics and strategy against the Palestinians instead have weakened and limited the organization's abilities to act.[36] Although suicide bombing and other terrorist attacks are still carried out, most Palestinian assaults fail to materialize, which has led to less effective tactics, such as firing of mortars and rockets over the Gaza border. Recent fighting between Israel and Hamas has demonstrated the difficulties of low-intensity conflict in such densely populated areas such as the Gaza Strip and the obstacles to what the Israeli military machine is trying to accomplish in its mission of combating Hamas and other adversaries while still trying to reduce civilian "collateral damage" and protect the lives of its own soldiers and civilians. Despite its many operational successes through the development of anti-missile and anti-rocket technology, such as the Iron Dome, David's Sling, and Green Pine Radar, none have brought complete quiet to Israel's towns and cities.[37] It is generally recognized today that only a political solution and a peace agreement with the Palestinians might bring about genuine quiet for both the Israeli and Palestinian people. The major question today is whether a solution to the conflict could be found, and then whether there is a Palestinian or Israeli partner willing, or more importantly able, to enforce it.

In the meantime, Israel has learned that it is facing an adversary much more complicated than those more straightforward conflicts of the Cold War.[38] In addition, the recent and rapid pace of social and political change in the Middle East also complicates matters from an Israeli perspective, as the level on instability and volatility in the region carries a series of potential risks for the Jewish state, as the old regional balance of power is redefined and new, still unknown, regimes begin to rise. Hezbollah and Hamas are likely to find themselves in additional wars with Israel—in the case of Hezbollah, perhaps one more severe than anything seen in the region since 1973. The question is not only how these two groups will manage but also what role their allies such as Iran will play in shaping their futures.

Conclusions

TOLSTOY FAMOUSLY WROTE that "all happy families resemble one another, but each unhappy family is unhappy in its own way," a contention that can be equally applied to the two politico-military organizations analyzed in this book. A first impression of Hezbollah and Hamas could in fact lead to the perception that these groups are virtually identical. However, we hope that the analytical description of the birth and evolution of the two organizations will allow the reader to better grasp each group's uniqueness, while still being able to recognize the common organizational, ideological, and (to a lesser degree) operational threads that are shared by these two powerful actors.

First and foremost, one of the main striking commonalities in analyzing the two groups is how much their identity and raison d'être is embedded in the context of the Arab-Israeli conflict. More specifically, both Hezbollah and Hamas were created in the midst of—and in response to—an ongoing Israeli territorial occupation of southern Lebanon and the Gaza Strip, respectively, thus highlighting how these groups' "resistance" agenda is a core theme in shaping outlook and strategy against the Israeli state. However, at a deeper level, both of these groups not only were a popular and organized response to a foreign territorial occupation but were also the culmination of an internal trend of growing Islamization and radicalization of Palestinian and Lebanese societies. In the case of Hezbollah, the creation of the Lebanese Shiite militia corresponded to an internal process of political mobilization of the historically marginalized and impoverished Shiites in Lebanon, together with an ongoing Islamization of that same community, spurred by the ideology produced by the Iranian revolution. Hamas too—as an offshoot of the Palestinian Muslim Brotherhood—was created in the context of the ongoing Islamization of the Palestinian population, especially in the Gaza Strip, and it served the need of creating a religious and indigenous alternative to the secular and diaspora-based PLO and Fatah. In other words, while both Hezbollah and

Hamas were founded with the stated purpose of fighting Israel outwardly, inwardly both groups came into being to create an alternative Islamist discourse of national liberation and to shift the local population away from the mainstream and secular political organizations of Fatah and Amal, respectively.

Because of this common military and political purpose, Hezbollah and Hamas share another core organizational similarity: they are highly complex organizations. Again defying one of the main clichés of the literature depicting terrorist organizations as unsophisticated, clandestine, and alienated from society, both Hezbollah and Hamas are sophisticated military and political machines. These groups are simultaneously operating as large military organizations, organized political parties with institutional power and representation, broad media apparatuses, welfare and charity organizations, and grass-roots movements. The book repeatedly highlights this organizational complexity, for example, by presenting an-depth picture of the vast arrays of social services organized by the two groups, as well as by highlighting these organizations' complex fundraising structures and their direct involvement in both legitimate and illegitimate businesses.

Why is it important to stress this point? First, from a scholarly perspective, in order to truly understand how Hezbollah and Hamas operate it is important to move beyond reductionist portrayals of these organizations as merely terrorist groups and to provide a more solid description of these sophisticated politico-military groups. Second, when it comes to devising a strategy to counter the spread of these groups, it is crucial to grasp their complex and diverse nature in order to avoid focusing only on the security and military dimensions of the conflict.

Aside from this common organizational complexity, Hezbollah and Hamas also share another key characteristic: they are both organized as bureaucratic hierarchies, both formally headed by a central legislative body, a Majlis al-Shura. However, at a more substantive level, the two organizations are quite different organizationally, having different levels of vertical and horizontal integration, internal cohesion, and centralization.

On the one hand, Hezbollah has always been characterized by an extremely high level of internal integration and unity. In turn, this depends on three main factors, as previously highlighted in the book: the role and impact of the secretary-general, the tight organizational structure, and the group's ideological background and connection to Iran. Since 1992, the group has been headed by the same charismatic leader, Hassan Nasrallah. Because of this continuity of leadership, the current secretary-general has been able to maximize his power and authority within the organization in order to provide organizational continuity and marginalize internal dissent. In addition to the role of the group's leader in providing cohesion and structure, Hezbollah's organizational structure is perfectly hierarchical, avoiding overlap in power and maximizing the degree of command and control. The group's ideology is powerfully shaped by that of Ayatollah Khomeini's formulation of the *wilayat al-faqih*, and, as such, the organization and its members recognize Iran's "Supreme Leader" as their maximum authority and, when necessary, the ultimate judge of internal dissent. In other words, because of the internally accepted role of Iran's supreme leader as ultimate arbiter and judge, the organization has a powerful internal system to deal with dissent and divisions.

In contrast, the internal level of integration and cohesion of Hamas is not nearly as high. The group has never benefited from the same degree of internal centralization and leadership continuity, partly thanks to the success of Israeli counterterrorism operations in arresting or killing the group's leaders, and partly because of the ongoing internal competition at the leadership level. Before his death in 2004, Ahmed Yassin was certainly the most prominent and influential leader within Hamas, but, even so, his role in the organization was never as vital as Nasrallah's. In addition, Hamas's internal organizational structure is much less cohesive than its Lebanese-Shiite counterpart, with the organizational power geographically split between Gaza, Damascus, Doha, and the West Bank, and between the Legislative Council, the Political Bureau, and the semi-independent military units. Finally, Hamas lacks an internally accepted ultimate judge and arbiter who would serve as the equivalent of Iran's supreme leader for Hezbollah and, in cases of internal conflicts could resolve internal disputes. In a sense, this deliberative process provided by its Legislative Council allows Hamas a higher degree of internal democracy, but it also has the effect of increasing the risk of internal clashes and disunity.

Differing in their organizational structure, the two groups also present significant divergences in terms of their political and military partnerships. Again, even if the conventional wisdom on the groups would highlight that both Hezbollah and Hamas share the same regional allies—Syria and Iran in particular—the depth of the relationships of the two groups with these countries is substantially different. The partnership between Iran and Hezbollah is much deeper and substantial than the convenience-based alliance with

Hamas. Hezbollah's ideological inspiration is rooted in the Iranian Revolution, and since its beginnings Iran was instrumental in creating the organization. The ideological proximity between the two actors is also strengthened by Hezbollah's deference to Iran's supreme leader. In contrast, the Sunni Islamist group Hamas does not have a strong ideological affinity with Iran, nor is the partnership as deep and long-standing. However, this is not to deny that in the past decade—and especially in the aftermath of Hamas's electoral victory in 2006—the group and the Islamic Republic have grown closer. In turn, this has also led to Hezbollah and Hamas being part of the very same "Resistance Axis" that includes the two groups with Syria and Iran. At the moment, Hezbollah and Hamas have certainly grown to be strong supporters of each other's agendas as well as two solid regional political allies, but this has not transcended into a direct military alliance. For example, in the 2009–10 Gaza War Hezbollah did not join Hamas in confronting Israel, although the group did show ideological and, to a minor degree, logistical support. Additionally, since the beginning of the anti-Assad protest in 2011, Hamas has somewhat distanced itself from Iran, Syria, and Hezbollah.

Another important theme of the book worth highlighting is the importance of grasping the multifaceted ideological belief system of both Hezbollah and Hamas. At their core, both organizations draw on Islam to shape their identity and goals. Hezbollah's ideology is grounded in its adherence to Shiite Islam and, more specifically, to the teachings of Ayatollah Khomeini and the Iranian Revolution, whereas Hamas's belief system is equally founded upon its Islamist orientation and values. However, since its foundation, Hamas has combined this Islamist background and agenda with a strong nationalist dimension, defining itself simultaneously as a nationalist and Islamist group. In contrast, at the time of its birth in 1982, Hezbollah downplayed its Lebanese and Arab dimensions and emphasized instead its transnational and revolutionary links with the Shiite communities outside of Lebanon and with Iran. Hezbollah changed its discourse and developed a stronger nationalist identity only in the aftermath of the civil war, when the organization transitioned from being a revolutionary and antisystemic militia to a nationally recognized political and military group.

In addition to combining Islamist and nationalist elements into their discourse, both groups have also adopted a broad political and military agenda that is both outwardly and inwardly focused. With respect to their own constituencies and societies, Hezbollah and Hamas have since their foundings shared a common objective: the taking of power and the creation of an Islamic state. However, although these initial objectives have not been formally repealed or modified, both organizations have in the past decades developed a more nuanced political discourse, downplaying their stated goal of establishing an Islamic state and asserting that such a political outcome would not be imposed on the population against its own will. Clearly, this remarkably similar conversation in both groups is essential to strengthen their political constituency and operate within the existing Palestinian and Lebanese political systems. It is an argument increasingly uttered by Islamist parties across the Middle East—from Turkey to Egypt—when attempting to allay the fears of secularists. Although the original stated Islamist goals are still very much part of these groups' ideologies, the fact that in practice both organizations have chosen to develop alternative political discourses does show their capacity to adapt to shifting political and security environments.

However, despite a certain degree of adaptation with regard to their inwardly focused political goals, the same cannot be said when analyzing their outwardly focused policies. In this respect, there is a substantial level of continuity and ideological rigidity in both of the groups. Their raison d'être was always to wage war against the State of Israel, with the ultimate goal of bringing about its destruction. Both groups show a similar level of ideological continuity in rejecting the notion of recognition and peace with the Jewish state and emphasizing the importance of their "resistance." At a practical level, however, Hezbollah's and Hamas's approaches to Israel have been quite different. On the one hand, Hezbollah's stance has remained unaltered in terms of both rejecting Israel's existence and recognizing no political solution to the Arab-Israeli conflict short of Israel's destruction; Hamas, on the other hand, has developed in the past decades a more nuanced political discourse based on the notion of accepting temporary and phased agreements (the *hudna* analysis in the book) and on the creation of a Palestinian state on the 1967 borders. The reason behind this more pragmatic approach is evident: unlike Hezbollah, Hamas is deeply involved in local Palestinian politics and, as such, has a much more direct stake in the evolution of the conflict. In the event of the creation of a Palestinian state, the group does not want to shut itself out of power by a priori rejecting such political outcome. It thus finds Quranic passages and religiously feasible legal arguments to justify a temporary peace with Israel.

In line with both organizations' complex organizational structures and multifaceted belief systems, Hezbollah and Hamas have also shown a high-level capacity to evolve and adapt to their changing local and regional environments. In the case of Hezbollah, the group has definitely shown a huge learning curve, moving from a locally marginalized armed militia in the early 1980s into a powerful armed group and prominent political party. Some have pointed to Hezbollah's increased involvement in politics and to its policy of *infitah* as evidence that it is not just adapting but also moderating itself.[1] Indeed, it seems true that Hezbollah has shown through the past decades a formidable capacity to learn and adapt to shifting political and security environments, along with a high dose of pragmatism. However, as the analytical description in the book has pointed out, it appears that rather than moderating its stance, Hezbollah has evolved and adapted without ever relinquishing its revolutionary ethos and its main objective to wage jihad against Israel.

For these reasons and more, the group has become a leading insurgency organization whose activities and tactics are mimicked around the world. In particular, the fact that Hezbollah has developed into a mainstream political party and massive social movement in parallel to maintaining its armed activities demonstrates an additional level of complexity that makes it stand out from other armed groups. Today, Hezbollah's military transition has been equally impressive, with the group now able to act as a hybrid army and to rely simultaneously on nonconventional as well as conventional tactics.

Within the Palestinian territories, Hamas has also demonstrated a similar multifaceted and complex nature, developing simultaneously as a religious and social movement, a political organization, and an armed group. Over the past decades, Hamas has evolved into the most lethal and sophisticated armed group operating from within the Palestinian territories, and it has risen to confront and end the political monopoly of Fatah over Palestinian politics. Even today, Hamas continues to operate at the social, political, and military level. In addition, since 2006 the Islamist group has become an institutional player within Palestinian politics by winning the legislative elections, while since 2007 it has operated as the de facto government in the Gaza Strip and engaged in numerous attempts at national unity governments with Fatah.

Yet, while firmly in control of Gaza, Hamas has not risen to the same level of power and organizational strength as its Lebanese counterpart. Encircled by Israel and Egypt, Hamas never had the freedom to arm and develop as Hezbollah has, nor did it ever enjoy the same level of funding. As the director of the Palestinian TV and Radio Authority said in an interview with the Palestinian Authority's *Al-Hayat Al-Jadida* newspaper, with respect to Hamas's campaign against Israel in 2009, "Hamas behaved like a superpower, as if they have weapons and means like Hizbullah in Lebanon, and as if they can conduct a war like the July war [of 2006]. Hamas' people thought they have a number of missiles that can enable them to prevail in a war of such size."[2] However, the aftermath of the 2009 Gaza War showed that the group still falls short of matching Hezbollah's military capabilities and apparatuses. Similarly, Hamas's military machine has also grown to be more "conventional," especially since taking over the Gaza Strip and conducting internal security and policing operations in such capacity. Yet it still falls short of matching Hezbollah's hybrid-army status.

Despite the undeniable difference in power and military strength between the two organizations, it is important to emphasize the shared organizational evolution of both groups, transitioning from outside players into groups highly entrenched in local politics, and from loosely organized militias into highly sophisticated military organizations.

The chapter on counterterrorism and counterinsurgency measures helped identify how Israel—one of the leading unifiers of the Hezbollah and Hamas ideologies—has tried to combat both of these groups, at times successfully and at times badly. It is a permanent yet ever-changing threat that Israel faces with respect to these groups. As a result of Hezbollah's and Hamas's continued aggressive posture toward Israel and the denial of its right to exist, the Jewish state will continue to face low- and medium-intensity conflicts against Hezbollah on its northern border and Hamas along the Gaza Strip and perhaps the West Bank as well. With each conflagration, the costs are likely to rise higher as the loss of innocent life is increasingly used to achieve political and military objectives.

Irregular warfare has proved to be the only type that has shown promise of wearing thin Israeli resolve and providing at least some positive military achievements for the Arab world. As a result, these wars of attrition are likely to continue as they enable weaker parties to affect and demoralize large portions of Israeli society, while not providing Israel with any easy solutions in turn to resolve these crises, as emphasized in the chapter on Israeli counterinsurgency strategy.[3]

At the same time, the rules of the game between Hamas, Hezbollah, and the State of Israel are not set in stone, as the modus operandi and tactics adopted by these groups are continuously evolving. In the case of Hezbollah, the group has been moving in the aftermath of the July 2006 war toward a more aggressive buildup with respect to its main foe Israel. This new approach is centered on notions of strategic parity and proportional retaliation in the context of a renewed conflict with the Jewish state, marking the group's desire to take any future armed confrontation against Israel to the next level of warfare. This paradigm was recently reiterated by the group's secretary-general, Hassan Nasrallah, who stated that in the course of the next round of confrontation with Israel, Hezbollah would respond to any territorial invasion of the IDF with its own territorial invasion into Israel by sending its units to occupy the Galilee region.[4] This concept was further reiterated by Hezbollah MP Hasan Fadlallah, who said that the organization was planning on "taking control of land in return for taking control of land," confirming the group's self-perception of power.[5]

Given this continuous shifting of tactics and the ongoing military evolutions of both groups, the IDF's military response to both Hezbollah and Hamas also needs to show a similar degree of flexibility, along with an appreciation of these groups' desires to combine low- and medium-intensity warfare and to intermix irregular and conventional warfighting tactics along with strong psychological and media campaigns to more effectively engage their adversaries. Along with these military lessons is an important policy implication—that is, how focusing solely on how to counter these groups militarily can lead to an insufficiently nuanced approach. In fact, as is increasingly the case in insurgencies, both Hezbollah and Hamas are much more than just armed groups, and as such they should be understood and engaged at all levels, including the political and social ones.

Likewise, these groups' strengths lay well beyond the military theater of operations. As political parties, they have real leverage and influence on local political processes within both Lebanon and the Palestinian territories, and as such they have the opportunity to directly shape the political course of their countries as well as the progress of the Arab-Israeli conflict. Of course, this does not mean that their roles are necessarily identical. On the one hand, Hezbollah's ideological stance with respect to Israel, its reliance on the Arab-Israeli conflict as a strong raison d'être, and its position as outsider in the context of the Palestinian-Israeli political process allow it to act as a classic spoiler in the conflict. Hamas, on the other hand, is in a radically different position, and as such the group has developed a comparatively more nuanced role.

In addition, the strength of Hezbollah and Hamas is also a function of their position as social movements and direct providers of goods and services to their populations. In turn, this contributes to maintaining their constituency as well as diversifying their bases of legitimacy and support. Finally, these groups' ideologies have an important role in shaping both Palestinian and Lebanese attitudes toward the Arab-Israeli conflict and are also a main factor behind the ongoing process of Islamization of the Palestinian and the Lebanese Shiite populations.

Within the broader Middle East, Hezbollah and Hamas have an impact that transcends the borders of the Palestinian territories and Lebanon, contributing to the shape of the regional narrative and inspiring people with their Islamist and violent ideologies. In addition, both groups are also very much part of a broader Iranian-Syrian "Axis of Resistance," attempting to shift the existing balance of power and regional dynamics in their favor, to the detriment of Israel's security and with broader implications for regional stability.

This existing alliance has acquired a particularly important role in the context of the political turmoil in the region initiated in early 2011 and known as the "Arab Spring." Although the protest movements that led to regime changes in Tunisia and Egypt and that are shaking the political foundations of other regional actors that include Yemen, Syria, Bahrain, Jordan, and Libya, have no direct ideological or operational ties with Hezbollah or Hamas, both groups have been adamant supporters of all but the Syrian revolutions (in the case of Hezbollah)—as the Assad regime is a key ally to both groups. In particular, the fall of the Egyptian regime has been especially welcomed by both organizations, which saw in the demise of Hosni Mubarak the decline of one of the groups' main regional opponents. In his February 16, 2011, speech, Nasrallah eloquently explained this paradigm by stating: "The major blow to the resistance . . . was the participation of the Egyptian regime in [the] Camp David Agreement and consequently the emergence of Egypt from the Arab-Israeli struggle."[6] The fall of Mubarak is then seen as marking the end of the Israeli-Egyptian détente, which will in turn change the balance of power in the Arab-Israeli conflict in favor of the "resistance."

In this sense, both Hezbollah and Hamas have praised the revolutionary movements within the Middle East, also attempting to portray the ongoing revolutions as part of a regional realignment away from the West and toward the "Resistance Axis." In the same speech, Nasrallah also claimed that the ongoing protests in the Arab world represented "the revolution of the poor, the free, the freedom seekers and the rejecters of humiliation and disgrace which this [Egypt] nation was subject to due to giving up to the will of America and Israel. . . . It is the revolution [against] the regime's policy in the Arab-Israeli struggle."[7] In addition to trying to portray the focus for the revolution as being about Egypt's relationship with Israel, he compared the protest movements to "the Lebanese resistance in [the] July War [of] 2006 and the historic steadfastness of the Palestinian resistance during Gaza War in 2008 [sic],"[8] again riding the wave of regional turmoil to boost the "resistance" cause. Contrary to the gusto with which Hezbollah in particular supported other revolutionaries across the Arab world, when it came to protests in Syria and Iran and their subsequent bloody crackdowns, Hezbollah remained outspoken in its support of those regimes.

As the ink dries on the writing of this book, the "Arab Spring" of 2011 continues to change the setting of the Middle East, like molten lava spewing from the earth to create unknown new lands. Rather than being the final word on these two critical organizations, this book should serve as an anchor for what clearly remains one of the most volatile and significant corners of the earth. It remains to be seen whether Hezbollah and Hamas will fall or flourish in this ever-changing landscape.

Notes

Introduction

1. "In the Party of God: Are Terrorists in Lebanon Preparing for a Larger War?," *New Yorker*, October 14, 2002, 180.

2. "The Al-Qaeda–Hezbollah Relationship" (accessed June 28, 2010), available from www.cfr.org/publication/11275/alqaedahezbollah_relationship.html.

3. See "Exclusive: Hezbollah Poised to Strike? Officials Say 'Sleeper Cells' Activated in Canada" (accessed November 9, 2008), available from www.abcnews.go.com/Blotter /Story?id=5203570&page=1; "In the Party of God: Are Terrorists in Lebanon Preparing for a Larger War?," 180.

4. Naim Qassem, *Hizbullah: The Story from Within* (London: Saqi, 2005), 178–83.

5. Qassem, 260–61.

Chapter 1. The Lebanese Players: A Background

1. "Lebanon" (accessed May 19, 2011), available from www.cia.gov/library/publica tions/the-world-factbook/geos/le.html.

2. Febe Armanios, "Islam: Sunnis and Shiites," *Congressional Research Service Report*, February 23, 2004, 6.

3. Alawites are also known as Nusayri. There is also still a tiny official Jewish popula- tion in Lebanon of some 300 citizens. See "Beirut's Jewish Community Faces Slow De- cline" (accessed June 25, 2010), available from http://afp.google.com/article/ALeqM5g SU4RDnqvZrcgPP9GfhOoAcTiDRA.

4. Hala Jaber, *Hezbollah: Born with a Vengeance* (New York: Columbia University Press, 1997), 9.

5. Ibid.

6. Augustus Richard Norton, *Hezbollah: A Short History* (Princeton: Princeton Uni- versity Press, 2007), 49.

7. Ahmad Nizar Hamzeh, *In the Path of Hizbullah* (Syracuse: Syracuse University Press, 2004), 9.

8. Joseph Olmert, "The Shi'is and the Lebanese State," in *Shi'ism, Resistance and Rev- olution*, ed. Martin Kramer (Boulder, CO: Westview Press, 1987), 190.

9. Hamzeh. The majority of Lebanese Shiites are Twelver Shiites.

10. Hamzeh, 10.

11. Richard M. Wrona Jr., "Lebanon, Hizbollah, and the Patrons of Terrorism," in *Countering Terrorism and Insurgency in the 21st Century: International Perspectives*, ed. James J. F. Forest (Westport, CT: Praeger Security International, 2007), 367–68.

12. Jaber, 9.

13. Hamzeh, 11–12.

14. Hamzeh, 19.

15. Martin Kramer, "The Moral Logic of Hizballah," *Occasional Papers*, no. 101 (Tel Aviv: Dayan Center for Middle Eastern and African Studies, 1987), 4.

16. Olmert.

17. Jaber, 11.

18. Hamzeh, 15.

19. Steps have since been taken by the Lebanese to arrest Qaddafi as a result of what they see as his complicity in Sadr's disappearance. See "Lebanon Seeking Arrest of Gaddafi over Missing Shi'ite Leader" (accessed June 25, 2010), available from www.haaretz.com/hasen/spages/1016073.html.

20. Jaber, 13.

21. Augustus R. Norton, *AMAL and the Shiʿa: Struggle for the Soul of Lebanon* (Austin: University of Texas Press, 1987), 86.

22. Norton, *Hezbollah: A Short History*, 32.

23. Norton, *AMAL and the Shiʿa*, 86.

24. Jaber, 14.

25. Augustus Richard Norton, "The Origins and Resurgence of AMAL," in *Shiʿism, Resistance and Revolution*, ed. Martin Kramer (Boulder, CO: Westview Press, 1987), 230.

26. Norton, *Hezbollah: A Short History*, 17.

27. Norton, *AMAL and the Shiʿa*, 86.

28. Norton, *Hezbollah: A Short History*, 32.

29. Husain Mussawi should not to be confused with the late Hezbollah leader, Sayyid Abbas al-Musawi.

30. Norton, *AMAL and the Shiʿa*, 88.

31. Norton, "The Origins and Resurgence of AMAL," 233.

32. Ibid.

33. Ibid.

34. Norton, *Hezbollah: A Short History*, 23.

35. Norton, *Hezbollah: A Short History*, 16.

36. Judith Palmer Harik, *Hezbollah: The Changing Face of Terrorism* (London: I. B. Tauris, 2004), 51.

37. Qassem, 102.

38. Norton, *Hezbollah: A Short History*, 31.

39. Qassem, 101.

40. Lebanon (accessed June 25, 2010).

41. Jaber, 9.

42. Jaber, 10.

43. The United States and Lebanon: A Meddlesome History (accessed June 25, 2010), available from www.fpif.org/fpiftxt/3237.

44. Jaber, 10.

45. Ze'ev Schiff and Ehud Ya'ari, *Israel's Lebanon War* (New York: Simon and Schuster, 1984), 18.

46. Augustus Richard Norton and Jillian Schwedler, "(In)security Zones in South Lebanon," *Journal of Palestine Studies* 23, no. 1 (Autumn, 1993): 63. For perspective, the PLO received an estimated $300 million during the civil war, and the rest of the groups together received another $400 million from outside actors.

47. Schiff and Ya'ari, 25.

48. Schiff and Ya'ari, 23.

49. Schiff and Ya'ari, 24.

50. Ibid.

51. Norton and Schwedler, 64–65.

52. "Interview with Hashem Akel—Thanks for Your Cooperation," *Haaretz*, October 29, 1999 (accessed June 25, 2010), available from http://outofkhiam.tripod.com/Hashem Akel.htm.

53. John A. Nagl, *Learning to Eat Soup with A Knife: Counterinsurgency Lessons from Malaya and Vietnam* (Chicago: University of Chicago Press, 2005), xiv.

54. Farid el Khazen, "Political Parties in Postwar Lebanon: Parties in Search of Partisans," *Middle East Journal* 57, no. 4 (2003): 605.

55. Sandra Mackey, *Lebanon: Death of a Nation* (New York: Congdon & Weed, 1989), 50–51.

56. Ibid.

57. Charles Winslow, *Lebanon: War and Politics in a Fragmented Society* (New York: Routledge, 1996), 198–99.

58. El Khazen, 615.

59. Ibid.

60. El Khazen, 615–67.

61. El Khazen, 622.

62. March 14–March 8 MPs (accessed June 25, 2010), available from http://nowlebanon .com/NewsArchiveDetails.aspx?ID=97943.

63. Winslow, 250–55.

64. "LF: Introduction" (accessed June 25, 2010), available from www.lebanese-forces .org/lfintroduction/index.shtml.

65. Oussama Safa, "Lebanon Springs Forward," *Journal of Democracy* 17, no. 1 (January 2006): 29.

66. March 14–March 8 MPs.

67. Pierre M. Atlas and Roy Licklider, "Conflict among Former Allies after Civil War Settlement: Sudan, Zimbabwe, Chad, and Lebanon," *Journal of Peace Research* 36, no. 1 (1999): 14.

68. Atlas and Licklider, 15.

69. Safa, 35–36.

70. David Schenker, "Lebanon Goes to the Polls: Last Minute Surprises and Long-term Implications," *Policy Watch*, no. 1526, Washington Institute for Near East Policy, 2009 (accessed June 25, 2010), available from www.washingtoninstitute.org/templateC05.php ?CID=3063.

71. Jaber, 12.

72. Sandra Mackey, *Lebanon: A House Divided* (New York: W. W. Norton, 2006), 129, 142.

73. Cairo Agreement, 1969 (accessed June 25, 2010), available from http://palestine facts.org/pf_1967to1991_lebanon_cairo_1969.php.

74. Robert B. Asprey, *War in the Shadows: Guerillas Past and Present* (New York: William Morrow and Company, 1994), 1156.

75. Richard A. Gabriel, *Operation Peace for Galilee* (New York: Hill and Wang, 1984), 51–52.

76. "The Palestinian Diaspora" (accessed June 25, 2010), available from www.global exchange.org/countries/mideast/palestine/refugeeFacts.html.

77. Before 1967, Jordan controlled both banks of the Jordan River and believed itself to be the legitimate ruler over the Palestinians.

78. R. D. McLaurin, "The PLO and the Arab Fertile Crescent," in *The International Relations of the Palestine Liberation Organization*, ed. Augustus Richard Norton and Martin H. Greenberg (Carbondale: Southern Illinois University Press, 1989), 26–27.

79. Asprey, 1156.

80. Asprey, 1159.

81. Norton and Schwedler, 64.

82. Asprey, 1156.

83. Jaber, 13.

84. AMAL stands for Afwaj al-Muqawama al-Lubnaniya. Jaber, 12.

85. Rashid Khalidi, *Under Siege: PLO Decision-Making during the 1982 War* (New York: Columbia University Press, 1986), 17.

86. Mackey, *Lebanon: A House Divided*, 142–43.

87. Norton and Schwedler, 61.

88. Mackey, *Lebanon: A House Divided*, 70.

89. Gary C. Gambill, "Islamist Groups in Lebanon," *Middle East Review of International Affairs (MERIA)* 11, no. 4 (2007) (accessed June 25, 2010), available from http://meria.idc.ac.il/journal/2007/issue4/jv11no4a3.asp.

90. Mackey, *Lebanon: A House Divided*, 70.

91. Mackey, *Lebanon: A House Divided*, 70–74.

92. Safa, 28.

93. Safa, 28–29.

94. "Parliamentary Elections: Lebanon 2005," *European Union Election Observation Mission—Final Report*, 2005, 20–21.

95. Ibid.

96. March 14–March 8 MPs.

97. Gambill.

98. Ibid.

99. Omayma Abdel-Latif, "Lebanon's Sunni Islamists—A Growing Force," Carnegie Endowment for International Peace, Middle East Center (Washington, DC: Carnegie Endowment for International Peace, 2008), 8.

100. Gambill.

101. March 14–March 8 MPs.

102. Abdel-Latif, 9–10.

103. Ibid.

104. Gambill.

105. Ibid.

106. Abdel-Latif, 10–11.

107. Bilal Y. Saab and Magnus Ranstorp, "Securing Lebanon from the Threat of Salafist Jihadism," *Studies in Conflict and Terrorism* 30 (2007): 829.

108. Abdel-Latif, 11–14.

109. Audrey Kurth Cronin, "The 'FTO List' and Congress: Sanctioning Designated Foreign Terrorist Organizations," *Congressional Research Services Report for Congress*, October 23, 2003 (accessed June 25, 2010), available from www.fas.org/irp/crs/RL32120.pdf.

110. In the Spotlight: Asbat al-Ansar (accessed June 25, 2010), available from www.cdi.org/terrorism/asbat.cfm.

111. Ibid.

112. Tine Gade, *Fatah al-Islam in Lebanon: Between Global and Local Jihad* (Kjeller: Norwegian Defence Research Establishment (FFI), 2007), 13.

113. Gade, 14.

114. "Jordan Helped Foil Attacks on Anti-terror Coalition, Embassies in Lebanon," Agence France Presse, October 16, 2001 (accessed March 1, 2010), available and translated by Foreign Broadcast Information Service (FBIS).

115. Ibid.

116. Saab and Ranstorp, 840.

117. Catherine Taylor, "Botched McDonald's Bomb Plot Exposed Global Chain," *Australian*, September 22, 2003, 13.

118. "Terror Suspect Rejects Charges in Beirut Military Tribunal" (accessed June 25, 2010), available from www.dailystar.com.lb/article.asp?edition_id=10&categ_id=1&article_id=11971#axzz0rtDGDLQb.

119. "Apparent Suicide Operation Thwarted" (accessed June 25, 2010), available from www.naharnet.com/domino/tn/NewsDesk.nsf/0/AADF0D9CB9E023DCC225745A00619DD2?OpenDocument.

120. Jund Al Sham Militants Disband in South Lebanon Camp (accessed June 25, 2010), available from http://yalibnan.com/site/archives/2007/07/jund_al_sham_mi.php.

121. "Apparent Suicide Operation Thwarted."

122. "Jund al-Sham Militant Shot Dead by Army at Ein al-Hilweh" (accessed June 25, 2010), available from www.naharnet.com/domino/tn/NewsDesk.nsf/0/DEE37E0B5ECB4BF1C225745A00549758?OpenDocument.

123. Saab and Ranstorp, 847–48.

124. Gade, 32.

125. One example of this is the freeing of the group's founder and leader, Shaker al Abssi, from Syrian jails and sending him to Lebanon. See Saab and Ranstorp, 842.

126. Saab and Ranstorp, 842–43.

127. Gade, 27.

128. Gade, 27–29.

129. "North Lebanon Reconciliation Struck through Joint Efforts" (accessed June 25, 2010), available from http://news.xinhuanet.com/english/2008-09/09/content_9880896.htm.

130. Janine Zacharia, "Calls to Stop Funding Lebanese Army Put Obama in Tight Spot," *Washington Post*, August 13, 2010, A7.

131. The Taif Agreement (accessed June 25, 2010), available from www.mideastinfo .com/documents/taif.htm.

132. Ibid.

133. See William Cleveland, *A History of the Modern Middle East*, 2nd ed. (Boulder, CO: Westview Press, 2000).

134. The Taif Agreement.

135. Ray Murphy, *UN Peacekeeping in Lebanon, Somalia and Kosovo* (New York: Cambridge University Press, 2007), 38.

136. "From the Minutes of the Council of Ministers Session Held at Grand Sérail on Monday 8/8/2005" (accessed June 25, 2010), available from www.elections-lebanon.org /elections/docs_1_1_A_1_e.aspx?lg=en.

137. "Parliamentary Electoral Draft Law" (accessed June 25, 2010), available from www.elections-lebanon.org/elections/docs_2_1_1_e.aspx?lg=en.

138. Ibid.

139. "The Lebanese Electoral System" (accessed June 25, 2010), available from www .scribd.com/doc/14792510/Lebanese-Electoral-System.

140. "Global Integrity Report—Lebanon: 2007" (accessed June 25, 2010), available from http://report.globalintegrity.org/Lebanon/2007.

141. Robert Worth, "Foreign Money Seeks to Buy Lebanese Votes," *New York Times*, April 22, 2009, www.nytimes.com/2009/04/23/world/middleeast/23lebanon.html?page wanted=all.

142. "Parliamentary Elections: Lebanon 2005," *European Union Election Observation Mission—Final Report*, 2005, 20–21.

143. "Assessment of the Election Framework" (accessed June 25, 2010), available from www.democracy-reporting.org/downloads/reports/report_lebanon_0902.pdf.

144. Ibid.

145. "From the Minutes of the Council of Ministers Session Held at Grand Sérail on Monday 8/8/2005."

Chapter 2. Hezbollah: History and Development

1. Telephone interview with Timur Goksel, August 8, 2008. Goksel was a spokes person for UNIFIL and in 1995 became its senior adviser.

2. Jaber, 19–20.

3. Barry Rubin and Judith Colp Rubin, *Anti-American Terrorism and the Middle East* (New York: Oxford University Press, 2002), 52.

4. Rubin and Rubin, 50–54.

5. Ibid.

6. Tom Diaz and Barbara Newman, *Lightning Out of Lebanon: Hezbollah Terrorists on American Soil* (New York: Presidio Press, 2006), 185.

7. Clinton Bailey, "Lebanon's Shi'is after the 1982 War," in *Shi'ism, Resistance and Revolution*, ed. Martin Kramer (Boulder, CO: Westview Press, 1987), 220.

8. Joseph Elie Alagha, *The Shifts in Hizbullah's Ideology: Religious Ideology, Political Ideology, and Political Program*, ISIM Dissertations (Amsterdam: Amsterdam University Press, 2006), 207.

9. Hezbollah's first secretary-general, Subhi al-Tufayli, was among the officials in Iran.

10. Jaber, 47.

11. Jaber, 53.

12. Hamzeh, 24.

13. Jaber, 54.

14. Jaber, 20.

15. Jaber, 19.

16. Hamzeh, 24.

17. Jaber, 20.

18. Jaber, 145.

19. Jaber, 20, 51.

20. Interview with Matthew Levitt, Washington, DC, April 30, 2007. Levitt served as deputy assistant secretary for intelligence and analysis at the U.S. Department of the Treasury from 2005 to 2007. From 2001 to 2005, he was founding director of its Terrorism Research Program (since renamed the Stein Program on Counterterrorism and Intelligence).

21. Jaber, 21.

22. Harik, 40.

23. Martin Kramer, "Hezbollah's Vision of the West," *Policy Papers*, no. 16 (Washington, DC: Washington Institute for Near East Policy, 1989), 1. Only under Iranian president Khatami's administration was funding to Hezbollah cut significantly, and that was later reinstated and increased considerably under Ahmadinejad.

24. Kramer, "Hezbollah's Vision of the West," 26.

25. Ibid.

26. Kramer, "Hezbollah's Vision of the West," 27–28.

27. Viewed in presentation by William Arkin at Harvard University, Cambridge, MA, March 2007. Arkin is a *Washington Post* online columnist and NBC News military analyst. He began his career as a U.S. Army Intelligence analyst and more recently conducted a study for the United Nations on Israel's 2006 war with Hezbollah.

28. Jaber, 30.

29. Ibid.

30. Alagha, 202.

31. Jaber, 31–32.

32. Hamzeh, 109.

33. "The Taif Accords," 1989 (accessed June 25, 2010), available from www.mideast web.org/taif.htm.

34. Alagha, 12.

35. "Lebanon Backs Hezbollah's Arms" (accessed June 25, 2010), available from http:// english.aljazeera.net/news/middleeast/2008/08/200881211335457856.html.

36. Daniel Sobelman, "Four Years after the Withdrawal from Lebanon: Redefining the Rules of the Game," *Jaffee Center for Security Studies Strategic Assessment* 7, no. 2 (August 2004): 52.

37. Qassem, 124–25.

38. Norton, *Hezbollah*, 105–7.

39. Krista E. Wiegand, "Reformation of a Terrorist Group: Hezbollah as a Lebanese Political Party," *Studies in Conflict and Terrorism* 32 (2009): 676.

40. Amal Saad-Ghorayeb, *Hizbu'llah: Politics and Religion* (London: Pluto Press, 2002), 82–87.

41. "Interview with Hassan Nasrallah," *As-Safir*, February 27, 1992, printed in *Voice of Hezbollah: The Statements of Sayyed Hassan Nasrallah*, ed. Nicholas Noe (London: Verso, 2007), 67.

42. Harik, 72–74.

43. Alagha, 12.

44. Richard Norton, "Hizballah and the Israeli Withdrawal from Lebanon," *Journal of Palestine Studies* 30, no. 1 (2000): 32–33.

45. "Hizballah's Christian Soldiers?," *Time Magazine*, August 6, 2007.

46. Harik, 77.

47. Saad-Ghorayeb, 54.

48. Hamzeh, 122–23.

49. Qassem, 196–200.

50. Ibid.

51. Norton, *Hezbollah*, 130–31.

52. "Hezbollah Takes Over West Beirut" (accessed June 25, 2010), available from http://news.bbc.co.uk/2/hi/7391600.stm.

53. Alagha, 204.

54. "The Speech Delivered by Hezbollah Secretary-General Sayyed Hassan Nasrallah on the Conduct and Performance of the International Investigation Committee and the International Investigators Delivered on Thursday October 28, 2010," Hezbollah Press Statement, October 28, 2010.

55. Arrest warrants issued in 2005 for the killing of former Lebanese prime minister (accessed July 12, 2011), available from www.dailystar.com.lb/News/Politics/2011/Jul-12/Jumblatt-says-opposes-severing-ties-with-STL.ashx#axzz1RuuhSIz4.

56. "Analysis: Nasrallah Comes to the Rescue of Assad" (accessed July 12, 2011), available from www.jpost.com/MiddleEast/Article.aspx?id=222390.

Chapter 3. Ideals and Belief System

1. "Nasrallah Announces Today the 'Rebirth' of Hezbollah," *As-Safir*, November 30, 2009 (translation by MidEast Wire).

2. Alagha, 13.

3. Hamzeh, 31–33.

4. Hamzeh, 35.

5. Jaber, 35.

6. Jaber, 70.

7. Harik, ix–2.

8. Hamzeh, 39.

9. Ibid.

10. See, for example, Hezbollah's operations in Lebanon, Iraq, and specifically Egypt. For more, see "Hezbollah Confirms Egypt Arrest" (accessed June 25, 2010), available

from http://news.bbc.co.uk/2/hi/7994304.stm. Sami Hani Shihab was the head of the Hezbollah cell in Egypt.

11. Saad-Ghorayeb, 113–14.

12. Daniel Sobelman, "Four Years after the Withdrawal from Lebanon: Redefining the Rules of the Game," *Jaffee Center for Security Studies Strategic Assessment* 7, no. 2 (August 2004): 16, 64–65.

13. Brenda Gazzar, "Lebanon Sunnis Freeze Hizbullah Deal," *Jerusalem Post*, August 21, 2008, 2.

14. Avi Jorisch, *Beacon of Hatred: Inside Hizballah's Al-Manar Television* (Washington, DC: Washington Institute for Near East Policy, 2004), 15.

15. See "Full Text of Hezbollah's New Political Document" (accessed June 25, 2010), available from www.hizb-australia.org/newsroom/global/1859-full-text-of-hezbollahs-new -political-document; Rubin and Rubin, 53.

16. "Lebanese Hezbollah Leader Outlines Party's Foreign, Domestic Policy," Al-Manar, December 1, 2009 (accessed March 1, 2010), available from LexisNexis (provided by BBC Worldwide Monitoring).

17. "Full Text of Hezbollah's New Political Document."

18. Ibid.

19. Ibid.

20. Ibid.

21. Ibid.

22. Jorisch.

23. Saad-Ghorayeb, 73.

24. Hamzeh, 39, 41.

25. Dean Godson, "The Outrage—and Then the Silence," *Times*, May 14, 2008, 17.

26. Saad-Ghorayeb, 170.

27. See, for example, "Hezbollah Leader Apologizes for Attack's Child Victims" (accessed May 28, 2010), available from www.cnn.com/2006/WORLD/meast/07/20/nasrallah.interview/index.html.

28. Ibid. See also "Report: Abbas Reiterates Refusal to Recognize Israel as 'Jewish State'" (accessed June 25, 2010), available from www.haaretz.com/news/report-abbas -reiterates-refusal-to-recognize-israel-as-jewish-state-1.234351.

29. Jorisch.

30. Norton, *Hezbollah*, 37–40.

31. Saad-Ghorayeb, 34–36.

32. Full Text of Hezbollah's New Political Document.

33. Mona Harb and Reinoud Leenders, "Know Thy Enemy: Hizbullah 'Terrorism' and the Polities of Perception," *Third World Quarterly* 6, no. 1 (2005): 179.

34. Rubin and Rubin, 50.

35. Press Conference with Secretary-General Hassan Nasrallah, November 30, 2009.

36. "Hezbollah's New Manifesto: The 'Rebirth'" (accessed June 25, 2010), available from http://palestinechronicle.com/view_article_details.php?id=15588.

37. Full Text of Hezbollah's New Political Document.

38. Ibid.

39. "Hezbollah's New System" (accessed June 25, 2010), available from www.daral hayat.com/portalarticlendah/82923.

40. "14 March Forces Criticize Hezbollah Political Document," Lebanese National News Agency, December 3, 2009 (accessed March 1, 2010), available from LexisNexis.

41. Press Conference with Secretary-General Hassan Nasrallah, November 30, 2009.

42. "Full Text of Hezbollah's New Political Document."

43. "14 March Forces Criticize Hezbollah Political Document."

44. Press Conference with Secretary-General Hassan Nasrallah, November 30, 2009.

Chapter 4. Structure

1. Hamzeh, 45.

2. Hamzeh, 45–46.

3. Hamzeh, 47–48.

4. Hamzeh, 48.

5. See "Profile: Hassan Nasrallah" (accessed June 28, 2010), available from www.cfr .org/publication/11132/; "Survey: Nasrallah Is the Most Admired Leader in the Arab World" (accessed June 28, 2010), available from www.haaretz.com/hasen/spages/975572 .html.

6. "Who Is Hasan Nasrallah?" (accessed June 28, 2010), available from www.lebanon -today.com/index2.php?option=com_content&do_pdf=1&id=1086.

7. See "What Iran Really Wants" (accessed June 28, 2010), available from www.ynet news.com/articles/0,7340,L-3565874,00.html; Lebanese Security and the Hezbollah (accessed June 28, 2010), available from www.csis.org/media/csis/pubs/060714_lebanese _security.pdf.

8. "Top IDF Officer: Iran Has Taken Over Hezbollah" (accessed May 21, 2011), available from www.haaretz.com/news/top-idf-officer-iran-has-taken-over-hezbollah-1.7700.

9. See Yaakov Katz, "IDF Names Top Iranian in Charge of Hizbullah," *Jerusalem Post*, July 8, 2010 (accessed July 11, 2010), available from LexisNexis; "Report: Nasrallah Replaced as Head of Hizbullah Military Wing" (accessed May 21, 2011), available from www.ynetnews.com/articles/0,7340,L-3482538,00.html.

10. Jaber, 51.

11. "Hezbollah's Lack of Structure Its Strength" (accessed June 28, 2010), available from www.atimes.com/atimes/Middle_East/HH11Ak03.html.

12. "Iran Appoints Successor to Mughniyeh" (accessed June 28, 2010), available from www.jpost.com/Home/Article.aspx?id=116874; "Iran Assuming Mughniyeh Role inside Hezbollah" (accessed June 28, 2010), available from www.haaretz.com/print-edi tion/news/iran-assuming-mughniyeh-role-inside-hezbollah-1.270945.

13. Qassem, 70.

14. Interview with a former high-ranking member of the Mossad, Tel Aviv area, Israel, July 3, 2006.

15. "Hezbollah's Lack of Structure Its Strength."

16. Chris Kraul and Sebastian Rotella, "Hezbollah Presence in Venezuela Feared," *Los Angeles Times*, August 27, 2008, 3.

17. It is worth noting that before Mughniyah's assassination, his ties to the organization and even his very existence were denied by Hezbollah. Only after his assassination

did Hezbollah recognize his position in the organization, exulting his leadership and even creating an impressive multimedia presentation to honor him and his life, replete with a "martyrs heaven" that is shown to wide-eyed schoolchildren who are bused to the location.

18. Interview with a former high-ranking member of the Mossad, Tel Aviv area, Israel, July 3, 2006.

19. "Hizballah External Security Organisation" (accessed May 21, 2011), available from www.ag.gov.au/agd/WWW/nationalsecurity.nsf/Page/What_Governments_are_doing _Listing_of_Terrorism_Organisations_Hizballah_External_Security_Organisation.

20. "The Next Mughniyah" (accessed July 10, 2011), available from www.haaretz .com/print-edition/features/the-next-mughniyah-1.239508.

21. "In the Party of God: Hezbollah Sets Up Operations in South America and the United States," *New Yorker*, October 28, 2002, 75. Hezbollah operatives have been discovered in Canada at an alarmingly high rate in recent years.

22. "Myrick Calls for Taskforce to Investigate Presence of Hezbollah on the US Southern Border" (accessed December 8, 2011), available from http://myrick.house.gov/index .cfm?sectionid=22&itemid=558.

23. Interview with William Arkin, Cambridge, MA, March 21, 2007. Arkin is a *Washington Post* online columnist and NBC News military analyst. He began his career as a U.S. Army Intelligence analyst and more recently conducted a study for the United Nations on Israel's 2006 war with Hezbollah.

24. Harik, 82.

25. Jaber, 147–49.

26. Harik, 82–83.

27. See U.S. Department of Treasury, "Fact Sheet: Designation of Iranian Entities and Individuals for Proliferation Activities and Support for Terrorism" (accessed June 25, 2010), available from www.treasury.gov/press/releases/hp644.htm; Hamzeh, 63.

28. Hamzeh, 63.

29. Ibid.

30. Hamzeh, 64.

31. Ibid.

32. "In the Party of God: Hezbollah Sets Up Operations in South America and the United States," 75.

33. For a small sample of some of Hezbollah's legal enterprises, see Jaber, 52.

34. See "Book, Video Show Hizballah Training Near Caracas" (accessed June 25, 2010), available from www.investigativeproject.org/blog/2010/05/book-video-show-hiz ballah-training-near-caracas.

35. U.S. Congress, House, Committee on International Relations, Subcommittee on International Terrorism and Nonproliferation, Subcommittee on the Middle East and Central Asia, *Hizbollah's Global Reach*, 109th Cong., 2nd sess., September 28, 2006.

36. Diaz and Newman, 79, 84–85.

37. Diaz and Newman, 205, 229–30.

38. "The Escalating Ties between Middle Eastern Terrorist Groups and Criminal Activity" (accessed June 25, 2010), available from www.washingtoninstitute.org/html/pdf /johnson-remarks20100119.pdf.

39. Foreign Terrorist Organizations (accessed June 25, 2010), available from www .state.gov/s/ct/rls/other/des/123085.htm.

40. Dr. Col. (Res.) Eitan Azani, Testimony on "Hezbollah's Global Reach," U.S. Congress, House, Committee on International Relations, Subcommittee on International Terrorism and Nonproliferation, Subcommittee on the Middle East and Central Asia, *Hizbollah's Global Reach*, 109th Cong., 2nd sess., September 26, 2006, 55.

41. For more information, see U.S. Congress, House, Committee on International Relations, Subcommittee on Europe and Emerging Threats, *Islamic Extremism in Europe Beyond al-Qaeda: Hezbollah and Hamas in Europe*, 109th Cong., 1st sess., April 27, 2005; Hezbollah's Terrorist Threat to the European Union (accessed June 25, 2010), available from www.heritage.org/Research/MiddleEast/hl1038.cfm; Glenn Kessler, "US Freezes Assets of Hezbollah Unit," *Washington Post*, August 30, 2006, A13.

42. Mariano César Bartolomé and Elsa Llenderrozas, "La Triple Frontera desde la Perspectiva Argentina: Principal Foco Terrorista en el Cono Sur Americano," *Center for Hemispheric Defense Studies, REDES* 2002.

43. Rex Hudson, "Terrorist and Organized Crime Groups in the Tri-Border Area (TBA) of South America," Federal Research Division, Library of Congress, July 2003.

44. "In the Party of God: Hezbollah Sets Up Operations in South America and the United States," 75.

45. Latin America Overview: Patterns of Global Terrorism, 2000 (accessed June 25, 2010), available from www.state.gov/s/ct/rls/crt/2000/2437.htm.

46. "Brasil Dice Que No Hay Pruebas De Celulas Terroristas En Triple Frontera," Agence France Presse, October 11, 2003; "Comando Sur De EEUU Advierte Sobre Potencial Terrorista En America Latina," Agence France Presse, March 3, 2004 (accessed March 1, 2010), available from LexisNexis.

47. "Ministro Israelí Dice Que Hezbollah Actúa En La Triple Fronter," UPI Reporte— Latin America, March 18, 2008 (accessed March 1, 2010), available from LexisNexis; América Latina: Una agenda de Libertad (accessed June 25, 2010), available from www .icpcolombia.org/archivos/publicaciones/Latinoamerica%20FAES.pdf.

48. See Benedetta Berti, "Assessing the Role of the *Hawala* System, Its Role in Financing Terrorism, and Devising a Normative Regulatory Framework," *MIT International Review* (Spring 2005): 15–17.

49. Hugo Alconada Mon, "La Triple Frontera Sigue En La Mira Por Lavado De Dinero," *La Nación*, March 1, 2008 (accessed March 1, 2010), available from LexisNexis.

50. "Paraguay-Terrorismo: US$ 20 Mm Desde La Triple Frontera," *ANSA Noticiero En Español*, July 18, 2005 (accessed March 1, 2010), available from LexisNexis.

51. See Carlos Fayt, *Criminalidad del Terrorismo Sagrado. El Atentado a la Embajada de Israel en Argentina* (Buenos Aires: Editorial Universitaria de La Plata, 2002).

52. "Sources: Terrorists Find Haven in South America" (accessed June 28, 2010), available from www.cnn.com/2001/WORLD/americas/11/07/inv.terror.south.

53. Bartolomé and Llenderrozas.

54. "Paraguay Jails US-Lebanese Man Tied to Hezbollah" (accessed June 21, 2010), available from www.google.com/hostednews/ap/article/ALeqM5iKi24Di06E5bsA806h1 UuPyZy6YwD9GCJVV81.

55. Harris Whitbeck and Ingrid Arneson, "Sources: Terrorists Find Haven in South America," *CNN*, November 8, 2001, http://articles.cnn.com/2001-11-08/world/inv.terror .south_1_paraguayan-prosecutors-assad-ahmad-barakat-intelligence-sources?_s=PM :WORLD.

56. Ibid.

57. See *Treasury Designates Islamic Extremist, Two Companies Supporting Hizballah in Tri-Border Area* (accessed June 28, 2010), available from www.treasury.gov/press/re leases/js1720.htm; and *Hizballah Fundraising Network in the Triple Frontier* (accessed June 28, 2010), available from http://paraguay.usembassy.gov/hizballah_fundraising_network _in_the_triple_frontier2.html.

58. "Controversia Con EE.UU. Por La Triple Frontera," UPI Reporte—Latin America, December 7, 2006 (accessed March 1, 2010), available from LexisNexis.

59. "Hizballah Fundraising Network in the Triple Frontier."

60. "Policia Paraguaya Detiene Primo De Lider Hizbullah," Deutsche Presse, May 11, 2003 (accessed March 1, 2010), available from LexisNexis.

61. "Caen Tres Paraguayos Y Un Argentino Con Gran Arsenal De Armas En Triple Frontera" Agence France Press, April 3, 2004 (accessed March 1, 2010), available from LexisNexis.

62. Spanish Newswire, June 3, 2004 (accessed March 1, 2010), available from LexisNexis.

63. "Narcotráfico En Frontera De Brasil Financia Terrorismo Islámico," Agence France Presse, March 4, 2007 (accessed June 28, 2010), available from LexisNexis; "Tri-Border Transfers 'Funding Terror' " (accessed June 28, 2010), available from http://news .bbc.co.uk/2/hi/americas/6179085.stm.

64. "Eeuu Preocupado Por Visas Otorgadas Por Hamed," UPI Reporte—Latin America, August 5, 2008 (accessed March 1, 2010), available from LexisNexis.

65. See Hezbollah Builds a Western Base (accessed June 28, 2010), available from www.msnbc.msn.com/id/17874369/; "Operation Syria" (accessed June 28, 2010), available from http://article.nationalreview.com/268719/operation-syria/rachel-ehrenfeld.

66. "Chavez Providing Aid to Hezbollah and Hamas, Says New Book" (accessed January 25, 2009), available from www.haaretz.com/hasen/spages/1058676.html.

67. See Kraul and Rotella, "Hezbollah Presence in Venezuela Feared"; "Narco-Terror Concerns in Latin America Amid New Concerns about a Possible Attack in Latin America" (accessed November 9, 2008), available from www.abcnews.go.com/Blotter/story ?id=5197261&page=1.

68. See, for example, "Antonio Salas es El Palestino" (accessed June 4, 2010), available from www.antena3.com/programas/espejo-publico/noticias/entrevistas/antonio-salas-pal estino_2010052500057.html.

69. "Venezuelan Ties to Hezbollah" (accessed June 4, 2010), available from www.ict.org .il/NewsCommentaries/Commentaries/tabid/69/Articlsid/477/currentpage/6/Default.aspx.

70. Martin Arostegui, "Venezuela Linked to Terror Groups," *Washington Times*, March 9, 2010, 9.

71. "World Briefing: Curacao: Hezbollah Connection in Drug Arrests," *New York Times*, April 30, 2009, 8.

72. "Blood Money: Hezbollah's Revenue Stream Flows through the Americas" (accessed June 4, 2010), available from www.steveemerson.com/4281/blood-money-hezbollahs-revenue-stream-flows. Reprinted from *American Legion Magazine*, March 2007.

73. Chris Kraul and Sebastian Rotella, "Investigators Link Colombian Drug Ring to Hizbullah," *Irish Times*, October, 23, 2008, 14.

74. See "Congresswoman Raises Red Flag on Hezbollah-Cartel Nexus on U.S. Border" (accessed June 27, 2010), available from www.foxnews.com/politics/2010/06/25/congresswoman-raises-red-flag-hezbollah-cartel-nexus-border/; "Bolivia's Tri-border Zone a Haven for Terror Funding (accessed July 10, 2011), available from www.washingtontimes.com/news/2010/jul/13/bolivias-triborder-zone-a-haven-for-terror-funding/.

75. Editorial, "Close to Home: Hezbollah Terrorists Are Plotting Right on the U.S. Border," *New York Daily News*, July 11, 2010.

Chapter 5. Strategies and Tactics

1. Edward Cody, "Hizballah Threatens Tel Aviv; Chief's Statement Clarifies Strategy," *Washington Post*, August 4, 2006, A13.

2. Qassem, 70–71.

3. See Harik, 17; Joshua L. Gleis, "A Disproportionate Response? The Case of Israel and Hizballah," *Jerusalem Viewpoints*, Policy Brief 549 (Jerusalem: Jerusalem Center for Public Affairs, December 1, 2006).

4. "Hezbollah's Lack of Structure Its Strength" (accessed June 28, 2010), available from www.atimes.com/atimes/Middle_East/HH11Ak03.html.

5. Harik, 132.

6. U.S. Congress, House, Committee on International Relations, Subcommittee on International Terrorism and Nonproliferation, Subcommittee on the Middle East and Central Asia, *Hizbollah's Global Reach*, 109th Cong., 2nd sess., September 28, 2006, 5; "In the Party of God: Are Terrorists in Lebanon Preparing for a Larger War?," *New Yorker*, October 14, 2002, 180.

7. Yaakov Amidror, "The Risks of Foreign Peacekeeping Forces in the West Bank," *Jerusalem Center for Public Affairs* (accessed June 28, 2010), available from www.jcpa.org/text/security/amidror.pdf.

8. Gleis, "A Disproportionate Response? The Case of Israel and Hizballah."

9. "Israel Sees Battlefield Hidden in Southern Lebanon" (accessed May 21, 2011), available from www.google.com/search?sourceid=chrome&ie=UTF 8&q=israel+sees-+battlefield+hidden+in+southern+Lebanon; "Stronger Hezbollah Emboldened for Fights Ahead" (accessed July 11, 2011), available from www.nytimes.com/2010/10/07/world/middleeast/07hezbollah.html.

10. See Hamzeh, 87; "Hezbollah Riding on a Wave of Confidence" (accessed May 21, 2011), available from www.spiegel.de/international/world/0,1518,723870,00.html; "Resistance Land" (accessed May 21, 2011), available from www.foreignpolicy.com/articles/2010/07/08/resistance_land.

11. "Listening to Iran" (accessed June 28, 2010), available from www.cbc.ca/world/story/2008/08/27/f-rfa-milewski.html.

12. "IDF Spokesman: Hizbullah Attack on Northern Border and IDF Response" (accessed June 28, 2010), available from www.mfa.gov.il/MFA/Terrorism-+Obstacle+to

+Peace/Terrorism+from+Lebanon-+Hizbullah/Hizbullah+attack+on+northern+border +and+IDF+response+12-Jul-2006.htm. The "Blue Line" refers to the border line demarcated by the United Nations recognizing Israel's complete withdrawal from southern Lebanon in May of 2000.

13. Qassem, 109.

14. "Photos Show Hezbollah Has Missiles, Report Claims" (accessed June 22, 2010), available from www.globalsecuritynewswire.org/gsn/nw_20100601_7682.php.

15. "Gates: Hezbollah More Armed than Most Gov'ts; Resistance Vows to Continue Arming" (accessed June 24, 2010), available from www.almanar.com.lb/newssite/News Details.aspx?id=135312&language=en.

16. See Daniel Sobelman, "Four Years after the Withdrawal from Lebanon: Redefining the Rules of the Game," *Jaffee Center for Security Studies Strategic Assessment* 7, no. 2 (August 2004): 8.

17. "Text of Cease-Fire Understanding" (accessed June 28, 2010), available from www .mfa.gov.il/MFA/Terrorism-+Obstacle+to+Peace/Terrorism+from+Lebanon-+Hizbullah /TEXT%20OF%20CEASE-FIRE%20UNDERSTANDING%20-%2026-Apr-96.

18. Sobelman, 70–78.

19. Sobelman, 78.

20. Patrick Moser, "Israel Images Show Hezbollah Hiding Arms," Agence France Presse, July 8, 2010 (accessed June 24, 2010), available from www.google.com/hosted news/afp/article/ALeqM5h9HSk3U8306wTB10fC51coXFGjWg.

21. Jonathan Randal, *Osama: The Making of a Terrorist* (New York: Alfred A. Knopf, 2004), 155.

22. Jaber, 39.

23. Interview with Giora Inbar, Tel Aviv, Israel, July 4, 2006. Brigadier General (ret.) Inbar was commander of the Lebanon Division during the withdrawal from Lebanon in 2000 and in charge of southern Lebanon in the period leading up to the 2000 withdrawal. His responsibilities have also included areas of the Gaza Strip.

24. Harik, 132.

25. See "Iranian Strategy in Iraq, Politics and 'Other Means,'" Combating Terrorism Center at West Point, Occasional Papers Series (accessed June 28, 2010), available from http://ctc.usma.edu/Iran_Iraq/CTC_Iran_Iraq_Final.pdf; Michael R. Gordon and Dexter Filkins, "Hezbollah Helps Iraq Shiite Army, U.S. Official Says," *New York Times*, November 27, 2008, 1; "US: Quds, Hezbollah Training Hit Squads in Iran" (accessed August 28, 2008), available from www.huffingtonpost.com/2008/08/15/ap-iran-train ing-iraqi-hi_n_119104.html?page=13&show_comment_id=14712350#comment _14712350.

26. Jaber, 40.

27. Tom Vanden Brook, "U.S. Learns from Israel-Hezbollah War; Pentagon Uses Study to Retool Combat Tactics," *USA Today*, February 14, 2008, 11A.

28. Nicholas Blanford, "Hezbollah Phone Network Spat Sparks Beirut Street War," *Christian Science Monitor*, May 9, 2008, 5.

29. Yoram Schweitzer, "Divine Victory and Earthly Failures: Was the War Really a Victory for Hizbollah," in *The Second Lebanon War: Strategic Perspectives*, ed. Shlomo Brom and Meir Elran (Tel Aviv: Institute for National Security Studies, 2007), 132.

30. Stephen Biddle and Jeffrey A. Friedman, "The 2006 Lebanon Campaign and the Future of Warfare: Implications for Army and Defense Policy," Strategic Studies Institute, U.S Army War College, September 2008, 52.

31. Biddle and Friedman, xii.

32. Ibid.

33. Vanden Brook, "U.S. Learns from Israel-Hezbollah War; Pentagon Uses Study to Retool Combat Tactics," 11A.

34. Ibid.

35. This Islamic Jihad referenced above is not connected to the Palestinian Islamic Jihad (PIJ).

36. U.S. Congress, House, *Hizbollah's Global Reach*.

37. "Hezbollah Retribution: Beware the Ides of March" (accessed June 28, 2010), available from www.stratfor.com/weekly/hezbollah_retribution_beware_ides_march.

38. According to information from a former Israeli intelligence officer who requested not to be named.

39. "Turkish Forces Foil Hezbollah Attack on Israeli Target" (accessed June 24, 2010), available from www.haaretz.com/print-edition/news/turkish-forces-foil-hezbollah-attack -on-israeli-target-1.2529.

40. See "Hezbollah Activating Sleeper Cells in Canada: Report" (accessed June 24, 2010), available from www.cbc.ca/world/story/2008/06/19/hezbollah-canada.html; "Shin Bet Warns El Al about Terror Abroad" (accessed June 24, 2010), available from www.jpost .com/Home/Article.aspx?id=113251.

41. Sobelman, 60–61.

42. "Will Hizbullah Intervene in the Gaza Conflict?" (accessed July 11, 2011), available from http://electronicintifada.net/content/will-hizballah-intervene-gaza-conflict/7957.

43. See "MP Raad: Resistance in Gaza Will Surprise Israel," Al-Manar, January 2, 2009 (accessed March 7, 2010), available from LexisNexis.

44. "Hezbollah 'Conveyed' Hamas Method to Destroy Israeli Tank—Iran Film Maker," *Hemayat*, January 5, 2009 (accessed March 3, 2010), available from LexisNexis.

45. Xinhua General News Service, December 27, 2008 (accessed March 7, 2010), available from LexisNexis.

46. "Nasrallah Commemorates Al-Quds Day," speech transcript, September 18, 2009 (accessed March 7, 2010), available from LexisNexis (translation by MidEast Wire).

47. "Hezbollah Calls for Urgent Steps on Gaza among Arab Leaders" (accessed June 28, 2010), available from http://news.xinhuanet.com/english/2008-12/27/content_1056 8613.htm.

48. "Lebanon: Hezbollah Leader Criticizes Egyptian Stand on Gaza," Al-Manar, January 14, 2009 (accessed March 7, 2010), available from LexisNexis (available through BBC Monitoring Middle East).

49. "Speech Delivered by Hezballah Secretary General Sayyed Hassan Nasrallah during a Ceremony Marking the Anniversary of the Martyr Leaders Held in Sayyed Ashuhada Compound on Wednesday, February 16, 2011." Available through Hezbollah press office.

50. Interview with former high-ranking member of the Mossad, Tel Aviv area, Israel, July 3, 2006.

51. "Iran's Involvement in Somalia, with al Qaeda" (accessed June 28, 2010), available from www.longwarjournal.org/archives/2006/11/irans_involvement_in.php.

52. "Egypt Arrests 50 for Alleged Extremist Ties" (accessed June 28, 2010), available from www.ynetnews.com/articles/0,7340,L-3699106,00.html.

53. "Egypt Refers 26 Hezbollah Suspects to Trial" (accessed June 28, 2010), available from http://abcnews.go.com/International/wireStory?id=8177279.

54. "Egypt: Hezbollah Cell Plotted against Israelis" (accessed June 28, 2010), available from www.ynetnews.com/articles/0,7340,L-3700695,00.html.

55. "Egypt Refers 26 Hezbollah Suspects to Trial."

56. "Egypt and the Aggressive Claims against Hezbollah" (accessed June 28, 2010), available from www.almanar.com.lb/newssite/NewsDetails.aspx?id=81051&language=en.

57. Abdullah al-Najjar, "Hezbollah And the Incursion into Kuwait," *Al-Watan*, October 9, 2009 (accessed March 7, 2010) (translation by MidEast Wire).

58. "Three Explosives Experts from Hezbollah Killed in Saada," *Al-Ittihad*, October 17, 2009 (accessed March 7, 2010), available from LexisNexis (translation by MidEast Wire).

59. Joseph, Nye, "How to Counter Terrorism's Online Generation," *Financial Times*, October 13, 2005 (accessed July 11, 2011), available from http://belfercenter.ksg.harvard.edu/publication/1470/how_to_counter_terrorisms_online_generation.html.

60. Yael Shahar, "Information Warfare," February 26, 1997 (accessed June 28, 2010), available from www.iwar.org.uk/cyberterror/resources/CIT.htm.

61. John Arquilla and David Ronfeldt, "Cyberwar Is coming!," *Comparative Strategy* 2, no. 2 (Spring 1993) (accessed December 5, 2006), available from www.rand.org/publications/MR/MR880/MR880.ch2.pdf.

62. "In the Party of God: Are Terrorists in Lebanon Preparing for a Larger War?," 180.

63. See Stephen Hess and Marvin Kalb, eds., *The Media and the War on Terrorism* (Washington, DC: Brookings Institution Press, 2003), 187–88; Gleis, "A Disproportionate Response? The Case of Israel and Hizballah."

64. Hess and Kalb, 185.

65. See Ariel Cohen, "Knowing the Enemy," *Policy Review*, no. 145 (Washington DC: Hoover Institution, Stanford University, October and November 2007); Jorisch, xiii, 26.

66. See, for example, "A Bibliography of Anti-Arab Discrimination, Stereotyping, and Media Bias" (accessed June 28, 2010), available from www.adc.org/index.php?id=505; CAMERA: Committee for Accuracy in Middle East Reporting in America (accessed August 31, 2008), available from www.camera.org/; Saad-Ghorayeb, 93; Palestine Media Watch (accessed August 31, 2008), available from www.palwatch.org/.

67. Hess and Kalb, 183, 185.

68. Jorisch, 26.

69. Jaber, 42.

70. Jorisch, 15, 26.

71. Jorisch, 26–27, 29.

72. See, for example, "Hezbollah Sinks Australian Ship" (accessed June 28, 2010), available from http://blogs.news.com.au/heraldsun/andrewbolt/index.php/heraldsun

/hezbollah_sinks_australian_warship/; Gleis, "A Disproportionate Response? The Case of Israel and Hizballah"; "The Red Cross Ambulance Incident" (accessed June 28, 2010), available from www.zombietime.com/fraud/ambulance/.

73. "Time Is Not in Israel's Favour—Lebanese Hezbollah Leader Nasrallah," Al-Manar, December 31, 2008 (accessed March 8, 2010), available from LexisNexis (translation by BBC Monitoring Middle East).

74. "Hezbollah Chief Congratulates Islamic Jihad's Shallah on 'Divine Victory,'" Al-Manar, January 20, 2009 (accessed March 8, 2010), available from LexisNexis (translation by BBC Monitoring Middle East).

75. Jorisch, 29, 52–53.

76. For example, see Bruce Riedel, "The Elections Are Coming. Is Al Qaeda?," *Washington Post*, August 10, 2008, B03.

77. U.S. Congress, House, *Hizbollah's Global Reach*.

Chapter 6. The Palestinian Players: A Background

1. "World War I Creation of Jordan" (accessed December 15, 2008), available from http://palestinefacts.org/pf_ww1_british_mandate_jordan.php.

2. Efraim Karsh, *The Arab-Israeli Conflict: The Palestine War 1948* (Oxford: Osprey Publishing, 2002), 88; "The Palestinian Refugees" (accessed December 15, 2008), available from www.mideastweb.org/refugees1.htm.

3. "Jewish Refugees from Arab Countries" (accessed December 15, 2008), available from www.americansephardifederation.org/sub/sources/jewish_refugees.asp.

4. Benny Morris, *1948: A History of the First Arab-Israeli War* (New Haven: Yale University Press, 2008), 415.

5. Karsh, 92.

6. Shaul Mishal and Avraham Sela, *The Palestinian Hamas: Vision, Violence and Coexistence* (New York: Columbia University Press, 2000), 17.

7. Ibid.

8. Mishal and Sela, 16–17.

9. Mishal and Sela, 78.

10. Mishal and Sela, 16–17.

11. Dan Diker, "The Expulsion of the Palestinian Authority from Jerusalem and the Temple Mount," *Jerusalem Issue Brief* 3, no. 31 (Jerusalem: Jerusalem Center for Public Affairs, August 5, 2004).

12. "United Nations Security Council Resolution 252 (1968)," May 21, 1968 (accessed March 31, 2010) available from http://unispal.un.org/UNISPAL.NSF/0/46F2803D78A04 88E852560C3006023A8.

13. Ibid.

14. Howard M. Sachar, *The Course of Modern Jewish History* (New York: Random House, 1990), 780.

15. Michael Oren, *Six Days of War: June 1967 and the Making of the Modern Middle East* (New York: Oxford University Press, 2002), 253.

16. "United Nations Security Council Resolution 242 (1967)" (accessed March 31, 2010), available from http://daccess-ods.un.org/TMP/8596911.43035889.html.

17. Sachar, 780–81.

18. The Israeli government argues that since the Golan Heights was captured in defensive wars (in 1967 and again in 1973) and that land was later incorporated in 1981 with all inhabitants offered Israeli citizenship in accordance with international law, the cities and towns of the Golan Heights should no longer be called settlements as the land is no longer occupied. Rather, the government argues, it is today a part of Israel. The annexation will make it more complicated to hand over the Golan Heights to Syrian control if a peace agreement is ever reached.

19. "A Brief History of the Gaza Settlements" (accessed December 16, 2008), available from www.jewishvirtuallibrary.org/jsource/Peace/gaza_settlements.html; "Israeli Settlements in Gaza and West Bank Evacuated under the Disengagement Plan 2005 with Approximate Population of Settlements" (accessed December 16, 2008), available from www.mideastweb.org/israel_disengagement_map_2005.htm.

20. "Settlements in the Gaza Strip" (accessed December 4, 2008), available from www.fmep.org/settlement_info/settlement-info-and-tables/stats-data/settlements-in-the-gaza-strip-1.

21. Oren, 253.

22. Beverley Milton-Edwards, *Islamic Politics in Palestine* (New York: I. B. Tauris, 1999), 78–79.

23. Matthew Levitt, *HAMAS: Politics, Charity and Terrorism in the Service of Jihad* (New Haven: Yale University Press, 2006), 24.

24. J. Millard Burr and Robert J. Collins, *Alms for Jihad* (Cambridge: Cambridge University Press, 2006), 214.

25. Ibid.

26. Mishal and Sela, 27.

27. While the Palestinian territories do have a sizable (though increasingly shrinking) Christian population, they reside, namely, in the West Bank. The Gaza Strip is 99 percent Muslim. See "Gaza Strip" (accessed December 16, 2008), available from www.cia.gov/library/publications/the-world-factbook/geos/gz.html; "West Bank" (accessed December 16, 2008), available from www.cia.gov/library/publications/the-world-factbook/geos/we.html.

28. Mishal and Sela, 33.

29. For an interesting poll on Palestinian feelings toward both an Islamic and secular state in 1986, see Rashid Khalidi, "The PLO as Representative of the Palestinian People," in *The International Relations of the Palestine Liberation Organization*, ed. Augustus Richard Norton and Martin H. Greenberg (Carbondale: Southern Illinois University Press, 1989), 65–66.

30. Milton-Edwards, 78–79.

31. Milton-Edwards, 4; "Palestinian National Authority" (accessed December 16, 2008), available from www.worldstatesmen.org/Palestinian_National_Authority.htm.

32. "Constitution of the State of Palestine" (accessed December 16, 2008), available from www.jmcc.org/documents/palestineconstitution-eng.pdf. See Article 5.

33. David Galula, *Counterinsurgency Warfare: Theory and Practice* (Westport, CT: Praeger Security International, 2006), 39.

34. Bard E. O'Neill, *Insurgency and Terrorism: From Revolution to Apocalypse*, 2nd ed., rev. (Dulles: Potomac Books, 2005), 8.

35. "Seventh Arab League Summit Conference Resolution on Palestine" (accessed December 16, 2008), available from http://domino.un.org/UNISPAL.NSF/dcb71e2bf9f2d ca585256cef0073ed5d/63d9a930e2b428df852572c0006d06b8!OpenDocument; Mishal and Sela, 43.

36. "Hamas: The Organizations, Goals and Tactics of a Militant Palestinian Organization" (accessed December 8, 2008), available from www.fas.org/irp/crs/931014-Hamas .htm; Mishal and Sela, 13–14.

37. "The Mitchell Report" (accessed June 29, 2010), available from www.jewishvirtu allibrary.org/jsource/Peace/Mitchellrep.html.

38. John Kifner, "Israel Surrounds Arafat Compound in a Predawn Raid," *New York Times*, June 10, 2002, 1.

39. Khalidi, "The PLO as Representative of the Palestinian People," 66.

40. Mishal and Sela, 33.

41. Mishal and Sela, xviii.

42. Dore Gold, *Hatred's Kingdom: How Saudi Arabia Supports the New Global Terrorism* (Washington, DC: Regnery Publishers, 2003), 204; Burr and Collins, 226–27.

43. Burr and Collins, 225–26; "Hamas, Arafat Discussed Ways to Step Up Uprising: Hamas Leader" (accessed December 8, 2008), available from http://english.peopledaily .com.cn/english/200010/09/eng20001009_52120.html.

44. Andrea Nüsse, *Muslim Palestine: The Ideology of Hamas* (Amsterdam: Harwood Academic Publishers, 1998), 159, 165; Milton-Edwards, 159.

45. Stephen Hess and Marvin Kalb, eds., *The Media and the War on Terrorism* (Washington, DC: Brookings Institution Press, 2003), 186.

46. "Gaza Bomb Hits US Convoy" (accessed December 16, 2008), available from http://news.bbc.co.uk/2/hi/middle_east/3194432.stm.

47. "IDF Seizes PA Weapons Ship: The Karine A Affair" (accessed December 16, 2008), available from www.jewishvirtuallibrary.org/jsource/Peace/paship.html; Joshua Muravchik, *Covering the Intifada: How the Media Reported the Palestinian Uprising* (Washington, DC: Washington Institute for Near East Policy, 2003), 79.

48. Mishal and Sela, xvi.

49. "And a Thief, Too: Yasser Arafat Takes What He Likes," *National Review*, July 29, 2002; Burr and Collins, 223.

50. Burr and Collins, 223–24.

51. "Fatah-Hamas Unity Talks; Fayyad to Step Down" (accessed July 10, 2011), available from www.carnegieendowment.org/publications/?fa=view&id=22798.

52. "Foreign Terrorist Organizations," Office of Counterterrorism, Department of State, January 19, 2010 (accessed April 6, 2010), available from www.state.gov/s/ct/rls /other/des/123085.htm.

53. Milton-Edwards, 116.

54. Mishal and Sela, 32.

55. Levitt, 25.

56. Ibid. The PIJ did attempt to develop a social welfare network, but this was rather short-lived.

57. Chris P. Ioannides, "The PLO and the Islamic Revolution in Iran," in *The International Relations of the Palestine Liberation Organization*, ed. Augustus Richard Norton and Martin H. Greenberg (Carbondale: Southern Illinois University Press, 1989), 100.

58. Charles Enderlin, *The Lost Years: Radical Islam, Intifada, and Wars in the Middle East, 2001–2006* (New York: Other Press, 2007), 253–54.

59. Burr and Collins, 217.

60. Levitt, 26; Gold, 260.

61. Milton-Edwards, 163.

62. Levitt, 27.

63. Burr and Collins, 217; Levitt, 27.

64. "Islamic Jihad Voices Support for Hamas Positions," BBC Monitoring Middle East, March 23, 2006 (accessed April 2, 2010), available from LexisNexis.

65. "Ruling Palestine I: Gaza under Hamas," International Crisis Group, Middle East Report, no. 73, March 19, 2008, 29.

66. Ibid.

67. Ibid.

68. Daniel Williams, "Salafism: A New Threat to Hamas," *New York Times*, October 29, 2009 (accessed April 7, 2010), available from LexisNexis.

69. Jonathan Spyer, "Al-Qaida-Style Islamism Comes to Gaza. Millions of Petrodollars Are Flowing in Every Month to Fund Islamist Extremists," *Jerusalem Post*, August 20, 2009 (accessed April 7, 2010), available from LexisNexis.

70. "Terrorists Who Fought U.S. in Iraq Make Way to Gaza" (accessed April 7, 2010), available from www.haaretz.com/hasen/spages/1106689.html.

71. Hasan Jabr, "Al-Ayyam Opens File on Salafi Groups in the Gaza Strip," *Al-Ayyam*, May 17, 2007 (accessed April 6, 2010), available from LexisNexis.

72. Ibid.

73. Reuven Paz, "Salafi-Jihadi Responses to Hamas' Electoral Victory," *Current Trends in Islamist Ideology* 4 (November 1, 2006) (accessed April 7, 2010), available from http://currenttrends.org/research/detail/salafi-jihadi-responses-to-hamas-electoral-victory.

74. For some of the first reports, see Khaled Abu Toameh, "Al-Qaida-linked Terrorists in Gaza," *Jerusalem Post*, February 6, 2005 (accessed April 6, 2010), available from LexisNexis; "Al-Qa'idah Claims Attack on Palestinian Official," *Al-Arabiya*, May 21, 2006; Khaled Abu Toameh, "'Al-Qaida in Palestine' Issues Death Threat against Abbas. PA Foils Attempt to Kill Fatah Security Chief," *Jerusalem Post*, May 22, 2006 (accessed April 7, 2010), all available from LexisNexis.

75. "The Danger of an Islamized Gaza" (accessed July 10, 2011), available from www.latimes.com/news/opinion/commentary/la-oe-vanesveld-gaza-20100627,0,5317748.story.

76. Yoram Cohen, Matthew Levitt, and Becca Wasser, "Deterred but Determined: Salafi-Jihadi Groups in the Palestinian Arena," *Policy Focus*, no. 99, Washington Institute for Near East Policy, January 2010, 2.

77. Abu Toameh, "Al-Qaida-Linked Terrorists in Gaza."

78. Ibid.

79. "Ruling Palestine I: Gaza under Hamas," 25.

80. Hasan Jabr, "Al-Ayyam Opens File on Salafi Groups in the Gaza Strip," *Al-Ayyam* (accessed April 7, 2010), available from LexisNexis.

81. "Islamist Group Claims Attack on Gaza Al-Arabiya Office," Maan News Agency, January 25, 2007 (accessed April 7, 2010), available from LexisNexis.

82. "Salafi Group Threatens Internet Cafes in Gaza Strip," *Al-Ayyam*, September 2, 2006 (accessed April 6, 2010), available from LexisNexis.

83. "Islamist Group Claims Attack on Gaza Al-Arabiya Office," Maan News Agency.

84. Michael Slackman and Souad Mekhennet, "A New Group That Seems to Share Al Qaeda's Agenda," *New York Times*, July 8, 2006 (accessed April 6, 2010), available from LexisNexis.

85. Ibid.

86. Kifah Zibun, "The Salafi Groups in Gaza Are Close to Al-Qa'idah, and Have Split from Factions Including Hamas," *Al-Sharq al-Awsat*, August 16, 2009 (accessed April 6, 2010), available from LexisNexis.

87. Ibid.

88. Donald Macintyre, "Tape Provides First Evidence That BBC Reporter Was Taken," *Independent*, May 10, 2007 (accessed April 6, 2010), available from LexisNexis.

89. "Ruling Palestine I: Gaza under Hamas," 25–27.

90. Cohen, Levitt, and Wasser, 21.

91. "New Organization Dubbed 'Army of the Nation' Claims Firing 3 Rockets at Sederot," Ramattan News Agency, June 9, 2007 (accessed April 6, 2010), available from LexisNexis.

92. See, for example, "IDF Troops Kill Palestinian Youth In West Bank, Two New Militant Groups Emerge," Maan News Agency, September 17, 2007; "Jaysh al-Ummah Claims Responsibility for Sniping Two Israeli Farmers East of Al-Qararah," Ramattan News Agency, April 4, 2008 (accessed April 6, 2010), all available from LexisNexis.

93. "Al-Ayyam Interviews One of Its Leading Figures in the Gaza Strip: Is Jaysh Al-Ummah the Palestinian Version of Al-Qa'idah Organization?," *Al-Ayyam*, January 12, 2008 (accessed April 6, 2010), all available from LexisNexis.

94. Ibid.

95. "Palestinian Group Threatens to Kill US President—Details," Maan News Agency, January 8, 2008 (accessed April 6, 2010), available from LexisNexis.

96. "Al-Ayyam Interviews One of Its Leading Figures in The Gaza Strip: Is Jaysh Al-Ummah the Palestinian Version of Al-Qa'idah Organization?"

97. "Al-Arabiya TV Airs Footage of Al-Qa'idah-Affiliated Jaysh Al-Ummah in Gaza," BBC Monitoring Middle East, September 3, 2008 (accessed April 6, 2010), available from LexisNexis.

98. News of the Terrorism and Israeli-Palestinian Conflict (accessed April 6, 2010), available from www.terrorism-info.org.il/malam_multimedia/English/eng_n/html/nov_e003.htm.

99. "Gaza Armed Group Says Hamas Arrested Seven Fighters," Maan News Agency, May 26, 2009 (accessed April 6, 2010), available from LexisNexis.

100. Fathi Sabbah, "Gaza, a 'Suitable Greenhouse' for the 'Takfiri Groups,'" *Al-Hayat*, August 16, 2009 (accessed April 6, 2010), available from LexisNexis.

101. Khaled Abu Toameh, "Jund Ansar Allah Group Was Armed by Fatah Operatives, Hamas Claims. Radicals Were Latest in Gaza to Seek Imposition of Islamic Law," *Jerusalem Post*, August 16, 2009 (accessed April 6, 2010), available from LexisNexis.

102. Zibun, "The Salafi Groups in Gaza Are Close to Al-Qa'idah, and Have Split from Factions Including Hamas."

103. "Rafah Clashes between Hamas Police, Salafi Group," *Al-Arabiya*, August 14, 2009 (accessed April 6, 2010), available from LexisNexis.

104. "Mideast: Hamas Declares Salafi Group Leader Dead; Rafah Calm," Al-Arabiya Television, August 15, 2009 (accessed April 6, 2010), available from LexisNexis.

105. "Gaza Salafi Groups Claim Firing Two 'Projectiles' at Israel Agency," Maan News Agency, October 2, 2009; Fares Akram and Isabel Kershner, "Friday Rocket from Gaza Kills Thai Worker in Israel; Attack by Jihadist Group Comes as E.U. Foreign Policy Chief Visits Region," *International Herald Tribune*, March 19, 2010 (accessed April 6, 2010), all available from LexisNexis.

106. Hasan Jabr, " 'Jaljalat' Is Waiting to Carry Out a Big Operation in Order to Dedicate It to Bin-Ladin," *Al-Ayyam*, July 11, 2009 (accessed April 6, 2010), available from LexisNexis.

107. Jonathan Spyer, "New Fundamentalist Movements on the Rise in Gaza. Salafi Groups Find Support among Hamas Militants," *Jerusalem Post*, October 29, 2009 (accessed April 6, 2010), available from LexisNexis.

108. Ibid.

109. Zibun, "The Salafi Groups in Gaza Are Close to Al-Qa'idah, and Have Split from Factions Including Hamas."

110. Jabr, " 'Jaljalat' Is Waiting to Carry Out a Big Operation in Order to Dedicate it to Bin-Ladin."

111. Kifah Zibun, "Salafi Jihadi Movement Leader and Former Leading Member of Al-Qassam Brigades: We Will Take Revenge on Hamas; Islamic Emirate Will Be Achieved," *Al-Sharq al-Awsat*, September 25, 2009 (accessed April 6, 2010), available from LexisNexis.

112. "Jihadist Groups in Gaza Declare Hamas to Be Infidel. Their Loyalty Is to Bin Ladin and Their Bombings Reached the Home of Haniyah," *Al-Hayat*, March 3, 2010 (accessed April 6, 2010), available from LexisNexis.

113. Walid Phares, "Jihadist Games in Gaza; Western Media Must Be Careful," *Washington Times*, August 31, 2006 (accessed April 6, 2010), available from LexisNexis.

114. "Salafi Group Members Said Behind Killing of Italian Activist in Gaza," *Al-Hayat*, April 17, 2011 (accessed May 22, 2011), available from LexisNexis.

115. "Jihadist Groups in Gaza Declare Hamas to Be Infidel. Their Loyalty Is to Bin Ladin and Their Bombings Reached the Home of Haniyah."

116. Ibid.

Chapter 7. Hamas: History and Development

1. Mishal and Sela, 14.

2. Mishal and Sela, 34.

3. Burr and Collins, 216.

4. Mishal and Sela, 35.

5. Mishal and Sela, 46.

6. Adam Dolnik and Anjali Bhattacharjee, "Hamas: Suicide Bombings, Rockets, or WMD?," *Terrorism and Political Violence* 14, no. 6 (2002): 109.

7. Hamas Charter (accessed December 17, 2008), available from www.mideastweb .org/Hamas.htm.

8. Chris P. Ioannides, "The PLO and the Islamic Revolution in Iran," in *The International Relations of the Palestine Liberation Organization*, ed. Augustus Richard Norton and Martin H. Greenberg (Carbondale: Southern Illinois University Press, 1989), 102.

9. Milton-Edwards, 155.

10. Meyrav Wurmser, "The Iran-Hamas Alliance," *InFocus* 1, no. 2 (Fall 2007) (accessed July 10, 2011), available from www.jewishpolicycenter.org/57/the-iran-hamas-alliance.

11. Yonah Alexander, *Palestinian Religious Terrorism: Hamas and Islamic Jihad* (New York: Transnational, 2002), 1.

12. Hamas (Islamic Resistance Movement) Harakat al-Muqawama al-Islamiyya (accessed March 1, 2010), available from www.ict.org.il/.

13. Raphael Israeli, "A Manual of Islamic Fundamentalist Terrorism," *Studies in Conflict & Terrorism* 23, no. 3 (May–June 2002): 27–29.

14. Fatal Terrorist Attacks in Israel since the DOP (accessed March 1, 2010), available from www.mfa.gov.il/MFA/Terrorism-+Obstacle+to+Peace/Palestinian+terror +before+2000/Fatal+Terrorist+Attacks+in+Israel+Since+the+DOP+-S.htm.

15. James Piscatori, "Islam, Islamists, and the Electoral Principle in the Middle East," *ISIM Papers*, 2000, 35 (accessed March 15, 2010), available from www.scribd.com/doc /26446454/Islam-Islamists-and-the-Electoral-Principle-in-the-Middle-East-James -Piscatori.

16. Ibid.

17. Ibid.

18. Leonard Weinberg and Ami Pedahzur, *Political Parties and Terrorist Groups* (London: Routledge, 2003), 74–75.

19. Ibid.

20. Ibid.

21. Piscatori, 35–36.

22. Weinberg and Pedahzur, 76–77.

23. Anthony H. Cordesman, *Peace and War. The Arab-Israeli Balance Enters the 21st Century* (Westport, CT: Praeger, 2002), 241.

24. Ibid.

25. Khalil Shikaki, "Palestinian Politics after Disengagement and the Upcoming Parliamentary Elections," Middle East Seminar, Weatherhead Center for International Affairs, Harvard University, November 3, 2005.

26. Mishal and Sela, 123–33.

27. Hamas (accessed March 15, 2010), available from www4.janes.com/K2/doc.jsp ?K2DocKey=/content1/janesdata/binder/jwit/jwito132.htm@current&QueryText=null &Prod_Name=JWIT&image=browse&#toclink-j0010490021266.

28. Herb Keinon and Nathan Guttman, "Mofaz to Rice: We Won't Meddle in PA Elections," *Jerusalem Post*, November 3, 2005 (accessed March 15, 2010), available from LexisNexis.

29. "Performance-based and goal-driven roadmap, with clear phases, timelines, target dates, and benchmarks aiming at progress through reciprocal steps by the two parties in the political, security, economic, humanitarian, and institution-building fields,

under the auspices of the Quartet [the United States, European Union, United Nations, and Russia]. The destination is a final and comprehensive settlement of the Israel-Palestinian conflict by 2005, as presented in President Bush's speech of 24 June, and welcomed by the EU, Russia and the UN in the 16 July and 17 September Quartet Ministerial statements." U.S. Department of State, "A Performance-Based Roadmap to a Permanent Two-State Solution to the Israeli-Palestinian Conflict" (accessed March 15, 2010), available from: http://2001-2009.state.gov/r/pa/prs/ps/2003/20062.htm.

30. *Behind the Headlines: The Hamas Democracy Hypocrisy* (accessed March 15, 2010), available from www.mfa.gov.il/MFA/Terrorism+Obstacle+to+Peace/Terror+Groups/Ha mas+kidnaps+and+slays+Jerusalem+businessman+28-Sep-2005.htm.

31. "Abbas Backs Hamas Election Participation" (accessed December 5, 2006), available from www.jpost.com/servlet/Satellite?cid=1129540652080&pagename=JPost%2FJP Article%2FShowFul.

32. "How Do You Like Your Democracy Now, Mr. Bush?" (accessed June 29, 2010), available from www.salon.com/news/opinion/feature/2006/01/27/hamas.

33. "2005 Presidential Elections" (accessed November 23, 2005), available from www .elections.ps/template.aspx?id=55.

34. "The Final Results of the Second PLC Elections" (accessed March 17, 2010), available from available from www.elections.ps/template.aspx?id=291. "The list of Change and Reform obtained 74 seats; the Fatah Movement obtained 45 seats; the list of the Martyr Abu Ali Mustapha obtained 3 seats; the Alternative received 2 seats; Independent Palestine received 2 seats; the Third Way received 2 seats; and the Independents list obtained 4 seats."

35. Mishal and Sela, xxvii.

36. "Severe Crisis of Palestinian Representation," Reut Institute, October 18, 2006 (accessed March 17, 2010), available from http://reut-institute.org/Publication.aspx?Pub licationId=1036.

37. "Hamas-Led Cabinet Is Approved" (accessed March 17, 2010), available from http://pqasb.pqarchiver.com/washingtonpost/access/1011516501.html?dids=1011516501 :1011516501&FMT=ABS&FMTS=ABS:FT&fmac=&date=Mar+29%2C+2006&author =Scott+Wilson&desc=Hamas-Led+Cabinet+Is+Approved.

38. "Fatah MPs Boycott Parliament," *Al Jazeera News*, March 16, 2006 (accessed March 17, 2010), available from LexisNexis.

39. "In Gaza, Politics at the End of a Gun. Foot Soldiers Carry Power Struggle of Hamas and Fatah into the Streets" (accessed March 17, 2010), available from www.wash ingtonpost.com/wp-dyn/content/article/2006/05/19/AR2006051901713.html.

40. "U.S. and Europe Halt Aid to Palestinian Government" (accessed March 15, 2010), available from www.nytimes.com/2006/04/08/world/middleeast/08hamas.html ?_r=1&scp=4&sq=aid&st=nyt.

41. Ibid.

42. "Prolonged Crisis in the Occupied Palestinian Territory: Recent Socio-economic Impacts," UNRWA, November 2006 (accessed March 16, 2010), available from www .unrwa.org/userfiles/20100118135754.pdf.

43. Associated Press Worldstream, September 1, 2006; Associated Press Worldstream, September 25, 2006 (accessed March 15, 2010), available from LexisNexis.

44. "Chronology: Key Events since Hamas Came to Power" (accessed March 15, 2010), available from www.reuters.com/article/idUSL09597423.

45. "Israel Says Hamas Leaders Arrested on Suspicion of Terror Links" (accessed March 15, 2010), available from LexisNexis. See also Donald Macintyre, "Israel Arrests 64 Hamas Officials in Gaza Raids," *Independent*, June 30, 2006 (accessed December 16, 2011). Available from LexisNexis.

46. Conal Urquhart, "Hopes for Peace as Hamas Agrees to Truce: Agreement with Israel Could Lead to Release of Captured Soldier, a New Palestinian Government and an End to Gaza Incursions," *Observer*, November 26, 2006 (accessed March 15, 2010), available from LexisNexis.

47. "After Mecca: Engaging Hamas," International Crisis Group, Middle East Report, no. 62, February 28, 2007, 16.

48. Ibid.

49. Sarah El Deeb, "Abbas Dissolves Palestinian Government after Hamas Vanquishes Fatah and Takes Control of Gaza," Associated Press, June 15, 2007 (accessed March 15, 2010), available from LexisNexis.

50. Ellen Knickmeyer, "Israel Blocks Supplies, Steps Up Gaza Airstrikes; Actions a Response to Continuing Rocket Fire," *Washington Post*, January 19, 2008 (accessed March 15, 2010), available from LexisNexis.

51. Jihan al-Husayni and Muhammad Yunus, "Egypt Contacts Palestinians on New Government; Rafah Crossing to Be Opened," *Al-Hayat*, May 13, 2011 (accessed May 22, 2011), available from LexisNexis.

52. "Occupied Palestinian Territories: Torn Apart by Factional Strife," Amnesty International, October 24, 2007 (accessed March 15, 2010), available from www.amnesty.org/en/library/info/MDE21/020/2007/en.

53. Ibid.

54. Ibid.

55. "Hamas' Stand" (accessed March 15, 2010), available from www.latimes.com/news/opinion/la-oe-marzook10jul10,0,1675308.story?coll=la-opinion-rightrail.

56. Ibid.

57. "Fatah and Hamas Sign Reconciliation Deal" (accessed March 15, 2010), available from http://uk.reuters.com/article/idUKL23831120080323?pageNumber=1&virtualBrandChannel=0.

58. Shlomo Brom, "The Fatah-Hamas Reconciliation Agreement," *INSS Insight*, no. 253, Institute for National Security Studies (INSS), May 3, 2011 (accessed Amy 23, 2011), available from www.inss.org.il/publications.php?cat=21&incat=&read=5127.

59. Ibid.

60. Peter Hirschberg, "Israel Lends Support to Egyptian Plan for Truce with Hamas," *Irish Times*, June 12, 2008 (accessed March 15, 2010), available from LexisNexis.

61. "Ahmadinejad: Iran Will Support Hamas until Collapse of Israel" (accessed December 8, 2008), available from www.haaretz.co.il/hasen/spages/1020630.html.

62. "Iran's Ahmadinejad Congratulates Hamas Leader," Agence France Presse, January 30, 2006 (accessed March 12, 2010), available from LexisNexis.

63. "Hamas Chief Seeks Iran Support, Vows Resistance," Agence France Presse, February 21, 2006 (accessed March 12, 2010), available from LexisNexis.

64. "Palestinian Hamas MPs to Visit Iran," Agence France Presse, April 11, 2006 (accessed March 12, 2010), available from LexisNexis.

65. "Iran to Give 50 Mln Dollars Aid to Hamas Government," Agence France Presse, April 16, 2006 (accessed March 12, 2010), available from LexisNexis.

66. "Haniya: We Will Never Recognize Israel" (accessed March 30, 2010), available from www.palpress.ps/english/index.php?maa=ReadStory&ChannelID=13159.

67. "KSA Refuses to Host Haniya, Calls on Him to Cut Ties with Iran" (accessed March 30, 2010), available from www.palpress.ps/english/index.php?maa=ReadStory&ChannelID=13199.

Chapter 8. Ideals and Belief System

1. See Ziad Abu-Amr, "Hamas: A Historical and Political Background," *Journal of Palestine Studies* 22, no. 4 (1993): 6; Milton-Edwards, 12.

2. Milton-Edwards, 17.

3. Milton-Edwards, 19.

4. Muhammad Maqdsi, "Charter of the Islamic Resistance Movement (Hamas) of Palestine," *Journal of Palestine Studies* 22, no. 4 (1993): 122–34.

5. Shultz, Richard, "State Disintegration and Ethnic Conflict: A Framework for Analysis," *Annals of the American Academy of Political and Social Science* 541, no. 1 (1995): 78.

6. Jonathan Fox and Shmuel Sandler. "The Question of Religion and World Politics," *Terrorism and Political Violence* 17, no. 3 (2005): 293–300.

7. David Cook, *Understanding Jihad* (Berkeley: University of California Press, 2005), 97–99.

8. Paul Berman, "The Philosophy of Islamic Terrorism," *New York Times*, March 23, 2003 (accessed November 16, 200), available from LexisNexis.

9. Hatina Meir, *Islam and Salvation in Palestine: The Islamic Jihad Movement* (Tel Aviv: Moshe Dayan Center for Middle Eastern and African Studies, Tel Aviv University, 2001), 17.

10. John L. Esposito, *Islam the Straight Path* (New York: Oxford University Press, 1991), 16.

11. Berman.

12. Bruce Hoffman, *Inside Terrorism* (New York: Columbia University Press, 1998), 100.

13. Bernard Lewis, *The Crisis of Islam: Holy War and Unholy Terror* (New York: Modern Library, 2003), 153.

14. Levitt, 204–5, 208.

15. Levitt, 37.

16. See "Mashaal: Bin Laden Assassination an Atrocity" (accessed July 10, 2011), available from www.ynetnews.com/articles/0,7340,L-4065265,00.html; "Hamas Praises Osama bin Laden as Holy Warrior" (accessed July 10, 2011), available from www.guardian.co.uk/world/2011/may/02/hamas-osama-bin-laden; "Among the Palestinians, Some Sympathy for Bin Laden" (accessed July 10, 2011), available from www.time.com/time/world/article/0,8599,2069293,00.html.

17. Rohan Gunaratna, *Inside Al Qaeda* (New York: Berkley Publishing Group, 2002), 28; Jonathan Randal, *Osama: The Making of a Terrorist* (New York: Alfred A. Knopf, 2004), 63.

18. "Shalom, Hamas" (accessed December 25, 2008), available from www.motherjones.com/news/outfront/2008/07/outfront-shalom-Hamas.html?welcome=true.

19. Rashid Khalidi, *Palestinian Identity: The Construction of Modern National Consciousness* (New York: Columbia University Press, 1998), 148.

20. Mary Habeck, "Al-Qaʿida and Hamas: The Limits of Salafi-Jihadi Pragmatism," *Sentinel* 3, no. 2 (2010): 5.

21. See "Al Qaeda: Al-Zawahiri's Latest Message Reveals Little" (accessed December 25, 2008), available from www.stratfor.com/al_qaeda_al_zawahiris_latest_message _reveals_little; "Analysis: Al-Qaida-Style Extremism Gains Real Power within Hamas" (accessed December 3, 2008), available from www.jpost.com/servlet/Satellite?cid =1227702404879&pagename=JPost%2FJPArticle%2FShowFull.

22. "Among the Palestinians, Some Sympathy for Bin Laden" (accessed July 10, 2011), available from www.time.com/time/world/article/0,8599,2069293,00.html.

23. Muhammad Maqdsi, "Charter of the Islamic Resistance Movement (Hamas) of Palestine," *Journal of Palestine Studies* 22, no. 4 (1993): 126.

24. Mishal and Sela, 190.

25. Richard Beeston, "Hamas Leader Accepts the 'Reality' of Israel," *Times*, January 11, 2007 (accessed March 22, 2010), available from LexisNexis.

26. "Hamas Accepts 1967 Borders, but Will Never Recognize Israel, Top Official Say" (accessed July 10, 2011), available from www.haaretz.com/news/diplomacy-defense /hamas-accepts-1967-borders-but-will-never-recognize-israel-top-official-says-1.361072.

27. Paul Scham and Osama Abu-Irshaid, "Hamas: Ideological Rigidity and Political Flexibility," United States Institute for Peace, June 2009, 8.

28. Orly Halpern, "Exiled Hamas Leader Gives Interview," *Jerusalem Post*, February 21, 2006 (accessed March 20, 2010), available from LexisNexis.

29. "Cites: Hamas Movement Following the Elections," Reut Institute, February 23, 2006 (accessed March 21, 2010), available from http://reut-institute.org/Publication.aspx ?PublicationId=402.

30. Ibid.

31. Efraim Halevy, *Man in the Shadows: Inside the Middle East Crisis with a Man Who Led the Mossad* (New York: St. Martin's Press, 2006), 165–66.

32. Mishal and Sela, 186.

33. "Summer Camps in the Gaza Strip" (accessed December 27, 2008), available from www.terrorism-info.org.il/malam_multimedia/English/eng_n/html/Hamas_e004.htm; Arnon Groiss, *Palestinian Textbooks: From Arafat to Abbas and Hamas* (New York: Center for Monitoring the Impact of Peace, 2008); Gold, 266.

34. Levitt, 84.

35. "Hamas: 'Jewish Lobby' in U.S. to Blame for Global Financial Crisis'" (accessed October 7, 2008), available from www.haaretz.com/hasen/spages/1027306.html.

36. Mishal and Sela, 188.

37. Mudar Zahran, "Anti-Semitism: The New Necessity for Arab Regimes," January 24, 2011 (accessed July 10, 2011), available from www.hudson-ny.org/1821/anti-semitism -arab-regimes.

38. See "The Danger of an Islamized Gaza, 2011" (accessed July 10, 2011), available from www.latimes.com/news/opinion/commentary/la-oe-vanesveld-gaza-20100627,0 ,5317748.story.

39. "Analysis: Al-Qaida-Style Extremism Gains Real Power within Hamas."

40. "Hamas Reportedly Ups Ante for Schalit" (accessed February 27, 2009), available from www.jpost.com/servlet/Satellite?cid=1219913192489&pagename=JPost%2FJPArticle %2FShowFull.

41. Yoram Cohen, "Jihadist Groups in Gaza: A Developing Threat," *Policy Watch*, no. 1449, Washington Institute for Near East Policy, January 5, 2009.

Chapter 9. Structure

1. See Milton-Edwards, 149; Mishal and Sela, 173.

2. Mishal and Sela, 147–72.

3. Ibid.

4. Ibid.

5. "Hamas Leadership to Relocate from Syria to Qatar, Al-Hayat Says," *Al-Hayat* (accessed May 21, 2011), available from www.bloomberg.com/news/2011-04-30/hamas-leadership-to-relocate-from-syria-to-qatar-al-hayat-says.html.

6. Matthew Levitt, *Hamas: Politics, Charity, and Terrorism in the Service of Jihad* (New Haven: Yale University Press, 2006), 43–47.

7. The Executive Force today operates openly only in the Gaza Strip.

8. See "Hamas-Led PA Expands Executive Force" (accessed December 27, 2008), available from www.janes.com/security/law_enforcement/news/jdw/jdw070115_1_n .shtml; "Analysis: Al-Qaida-Style Extremism Gains Real Power within Hamas" (accessed December 3, 2008), available from www.jpost.com/servlet/Satellite?cid=1227702404879 &pagename=JPost%2FJPArticle%2FShowFull.

9. Experience has shown that during Israeli incursions the bulk of these forces usually stand down. For more, see "Meet the Hamas Military Leadership" (accessed December 28, 2008), available from www.jpost.com/servlet/Satellite?pagename=JPost/JPArticle /ShowFull&cid=1229868807023.

10. Quoted by Matthew Levitt, "Sheikh Yassin and Hamas Terror," *Peace Watch*, no. 448, Washington Institute for Near East Policy, March 23, 2004 (accessed December 5, 2006), available from www.washingtoninstitute.org/templateC05.php?CID=2139.

11. Israel Ministry of Foreign Affairs, Ahmed Yassin, Leader of Hamas Terrorist Organization (accessed December 5, 2006), available from www.mfa.gov.il/MFA/Terrorism +Obstacle+to+Peace/Terror+Groups/Ahmed%20Yassin.

12. Enderlin, 230.

13. "Profile: Khaled Meshaal of Hamas" (accessed December 27, 2008), available from http://news.bbc.co.uk/2/hi/middle_east/3563635.stm.

14. Shlomo Brom, "The Storm within Hamas," *INSS Insight*, no. 316, February 28, 2012.

15. "Analysis: Al-Qaida-Style Extremism Gains Real Power within Hamas." Mishal and Sela, 159.

16. "Analysis: Al-Qaida-Style Extremism Gains Real Power within Hamas."

17. Bard E. O'Neil, *Insurgency and Terrorism* (Washington, DC: Brassey's, 1990), 74–85.

18. Mishal and Sela, viii.

19. Khalil Shikaki, "Peace Now or Hamas Later," *Foreign Affairs* 77, no. 7 (1998): 30–33.

20. Ibid.

21. Jamie Chosak and Julie Sawyer, "Hamas' Tactics: Lessons from Recent Attacks," *Peace Watch*, no. 522, Washington Institute for Near East Policy, October 19, 2005 (accessed March 23, 2010), available from www.washingtoninstitute.org/templateC05.php ?CID=2382.

22. Marc Sageman, *Understanding Terror Networks* (Philadelphia: University of Pennsylvania Press, 2004), 158.

23. Jerold M. Post, Ehud Sprinzak, and Laurita M. Denny, "The Terrorists in Their Own Words: Interviews with 35 Incarcerated Middle Eastern Terrorists," *Terrorism and Political Violence* 13, no. 1 (Spring 2003): 176.

24. Shaul Kimhi and Shemuel Even, "Who Are the Palestinian Bombers?," *Terrorism and Political Violence* 16, no. 4 (Winter 2004): 828–30.

25. Kimhi and Even, 821.

26. Assaf Moghadam, "Palestinian Suicide in the Second Intifada: Motivations and Organizational Aspects," *Studies in Conflict and Terrorism* 26, no. 2 (2003): 72.

27. Bruce Hoffman and Gordon H. McCormick, "Terrorism, Signaling, and Suicide Attack," *Studies in Conflict and Terrorism* 27, no. 4 (July–August 2004): 255.

28. David Lester, Bijuou Yang, and Mark Lindsay, "Suicide Bombers: Are Psychological Profiles Possible?," *Studies in Conflict and Terrorism* 27, no. 4 (2004): 284–85.

29. Ibid.

30. Cindy D. Ness, "In the Name of the Cause: Women's Work in Secular and Religious Terrorism," *Studies in Conflict and Terrorism* 28, no. 5 (September–October 2005): 362.

31. "Mother of Two Becomes First Female Suicide Bomber for Hamas" (accessed December 28, 2008), available from www.haaretz.com/hasen/pages/ShArt.jhtml?itemNo =383183&contrassID=1&subContrassID=5&sbSubContrassID=0&listSrc=Y.

32. See "Female Bomber's Mother Speaks Out" (accessed December 29, 2008), available from http://news.bbc.co.uk/2/hi/middle_east/1791800.stm; Jaber, 90–92.

33. "Child Soldier Global Report," in *Coalition to Stop the Use of Child Soldiers* (London: Coalition to Stop the Use of Child Soldiers, 2001), 288, available from www.child-soldiers .org/library/global-reports?root_id=159&directory_id=215.

34. Israel Ministry of Foreign Affairs, "Participation of Children and Teenagers in Terrorist Activity during the Al-Aqsa Intifada," January 30, 2003 (accessed March 24, 2010), available from www.mfa.gov.il/MFA/MFAArchive/2000_2009/2003/1/Particip ation+of+Children+and+Teenagers+in+Terrori.htm.

35. Daphne Burdman, "Education, Indoctrination, and Incitement: Palestinian Children on Their Way to Martyrdom," *Terrorism and Political Violence* 15, no. 1 (Spring 2003): 96–105.

36. Dean C. Alexander, *Business Confronts Terrorism: Risks and Responses* (Madison: University of Wisconsin Press / Terrace Books, 2004), 50.

37. Alexander, 69.

38. Loretta Napoleoni, *Modern Jihad: Tracing the Dollars behind the Terror Networks* (London: Pluto Press, 2003), 71.

39. Levitt, *Hamas*, 91. Ironically, now that Hamas has a political monopoly in the Gaza Strip, its reputation is being tarnished as it increasingly favors those directly affiliated with the organization.

40. Levitt, *Hamas*, 84–85.

41. Levitt, *Hamas*, 57.

42. Levitt, *Hamas*, 167.

43. Gretel C. Kovach, "U.S. Wins Convictions in Retrial of Terrorism-Financing Case," *New York Times*, November 25, 2008, 16.

44. "US-Based Muslim Charity Convicted of Funding Terrorism" (accessed March 25, 2010), available from www.google.com/hostednews/afp/article/ALeqM5jQhamE6J-SM -obuNztsdmJD9imHQ.

45. United States Department of Treasury, "Treasury Designates the Union of Good" (accessed March 22, 2010), available from www.treas.gov/press/releases/hp1267.htm.

46. United States Department of Treasury, "Treasury Designates Al-Aqsa International Foundation as Financier of Terror Charity Linked to Funding of the Hamas Terrorist Organization" (accessed March 22, 2010), available from www.ustreas.gov/press /releases/js439.htm.

47. "Response to Interpal Inquiry by Charity Commission" (accessed March 20, 2010), available from http://news.bbc.co.uk/panorama/hi/front_page/newsid_7915000 /7915916.stm.

48. See, for example, Gold, 261–67.

49. Matthew Levitt, "A Hamas Headquarters in Saudi Arabia?," *Peace Watch*, no. 521, Washington Institute for Near East Policy (accessed December 5, 2006), available from www.washingtoninstitute.org/templateC05.php?CID=2378.

50. Sherifa Zuhur, "Hamas and Israel: Conflicting Strategies of Group-Based Politics," Strategic Studies Institute, U.S. Army War College, December 2008, 51.

51. United States Department of Treasury, "Written Testimony of David D. Aufhauser, General Counsel before the House Financial Services Committee" (accessed March 22, 2010), available from https://www.treasury.gov/press/releases/js758.htm.

52. Levitt, "A Hamas Headquarters in Saudi Arabia?"

53. Napoleoni, 71.

54. Zuhur, 51.

55. Matthew Levitt and Michael Jacobson, "The Money Trail: Finding, Following and Freezing Terrorist Finances," *Policy Focus*, no. 89, Washington Institute for Near East Policy, November 2008, 14.

56. See ibid.; "Iranian Official: Tehran Proud of Its Support for Hezbollah, Hamas" (accessed December 7, 2008), available from www.haaretz.com/hasen/spages/1030525 .html.

57. Interview with Yonatan Fighel, Herzliya, Israel, December 31, 2006. Colonel (ret.) Yonatan Fighel is a senior researcher and professor at the Interdisciplinary Center, Herzliya, Israel, and former military governor of Ramallah. He is an expert on Palestinian and military affairs.

58. See "How Hamas-Hezbollah Rivalry Is Terrorizing Israel," *Time Magazine*, April 23, 2001; "Hizbullah Pays Palestinians to Attack" (accessed December 8, 2008), available from www.jpost.com/servlet/Satellite?cid=1226404820137&pagename=JPost%2FJP Article%2FShowFull.

59. "Chavez Providing Aid to Hezbollah and Hamas, Says New Book" (accessed January 25, 2009), available from www.haaretz.com/hasen/spages/1058676.html. In fact, there are reports that al Qaeda, Hezbollah, IRA, and FARC members are all operating in

Venezuela. For more, see "Venezuela Linked to Terror Groups" (accessed July 11, 2011), available from www.washingtontimes.com/news/2010/mar/09/venezuela-linked-to-terror-groups/.

60. Diaz and Newman, 110.

61. Matthew Levitt, "Financial Setbacks for Hamas," *Policy Watch*, no. 1436, Washington Institute for Near East Policy, December 3, 2008 (accessed March 22, 2010), available from www.washingtoninstitute.org/templateC05.php?CID=2969.

62. Ibid.

63. Ibid.

Chapter 10. Strategies and Tactics

1. "Suicide Bombing: No Warning, and No Total Solution" (accessed December 9, 2008), available from www.janes.com/security/international_security/news/jtsm/jtsm010917_1_n.shtml.

2. Hamas is known to hide personnel and weaponry among civilians. For a small sample of stories, see Yossi Klein Halevi and Michael B. Oren, "Defeat Hamas to Defeat Iran," *Los Angeles Times*, January 4, 2009, A22; "Diskin: Hamas Dealt a 'Serious Blow' " (accessed January 4, 2009), available from www.jpost.com/servlet/Satellite?cid=1230456543368&pagename=JPost%2FJPArticle%2FShowFull; "Israel Targets Gaza Mosques Used by Hamas" (accessed January 4, 2009), available from www.google.com/hostednews/ap/article/ALeqM5i76F_YBU1eqSSoDoIAG_5vtJCzaAD95E75Too; "Israeli Airstrike Kills a Top Hamas Leader" (accessed January 4, 2009), available from http://news.yahoo.com/s/ap/20090101/ap_on_re_mi_ea/ml_israel_palestinians. For a video of a Hamas fighter firing from behind a white flag, see "Hamas Terrorist Hides behind White Flag Gaza 8 January 2009" (accessed May 21, 2011), available from www.youtube.com/watch?v=YJgfZ9_6miE.

3. UN General Assembly, *Report of the United Nations Fact-Finding Mission on the Gaza Conflict*, A/HRC/12/48 (accessed March 25, 2009), available from www2.ohchr.org/english/bodies/hrcouncil/docs/12session/A-HRC-12-48.pdf.

4. "Pushed by Goldstone, Israeli Army Embraces New 'Smart' Warfare" (accessed May 21, 2011), available www.jta.org/news/article/2011/04/11/3086821/pushed-by-goldstone-idf-embraces-new-smart-warfare.

5. Joshua Mitnick, "Why Israel Sees Double Standard in Response to Wikileaks' Iraq Files" (accessed November 29, 2011), www.csmonitor.com/World/Middle-East/2010/1025/Why-Israel-sees-double-standard-in-response-to-Wikileaks-Iraq-files. It should be noted that the other authors of the Goldstone Report continue to stand by the report's content.

6. For more on how Hamas fires from civilian neighborhoods and uses civilian cooperation to its advantage, see "Hamas and Its Discontents" (accessed January 22, 2009), available from www.newsweek.com/id/180691.

7. Interview with Israeli's former deputy national security adviser Chuck Freilich, Cambridge, MA, November 21, 2006.

8. Suicide belts were estimated to cost anywhere from $1,500 to $4,300. Levitt, 54–55.

9. Mishal and Sela, 65–66.

10. Marie Colvin and Uzi Mahnaimi, "Gaza's Missile Maze," *Sunday Times* (London), January 4, 2009 (2nd ed.), 18.

11. Interview with IDF colonel (res.) Itamar Ya'ar, former deputy head of Israel's National Security Council, Jerusalem, Israel, January 14, 2007.

12. "Hamas to Change Strategy and Expand Arsenal after Gaza Lessons" (accessed March 30, 2009), available from www4.janes.com.ezproxy.library.tufts.edu/subscribe /jdw/doc_view.jsp?K2DocKey=/content1/janesdata/mags/jdw/history/jdw2009/ jdw39378.htm@current&Prod_Name=JDW&QueryText=.

13. Interview with Matthew Levitt, Washington, DC, April 30, 2007.

14. Levitt, 115.

15. Nüsse, 30.

16. Galula, 39–40.

17. Interview with IDF colonel (ret.) Yonatan Fighel, Herzliya, Israel, December 31, 2006; Gold, 204.

18. Bruce Riedel, "The Elections Are Coming. Is Al-Qaeda?," *Washington Post*, August 10, 2008, B03.

19. "Special Dispatch No. 255: A Palestinian Information Center: There Is Serious Thinking about Obtaining Biological Weapons,"Middle East Media and Research Institute, August 15, 2001.

20. Haim Shadmi, "Suicide Bombers May Have Had Hepatitis," *Haaretz*, June 21, 2001 (accessed March 25, 2010), available from LexisNexis.

21. "Israel: Hamas Leader Charged with Planning Mass Cyanide," *BBC Monitoring International Reports*, August 1, 2002 (accessed March 25, 2010), available from LexisNexis.

22. Dorit Gabai, "Foiled Plan: Cyanide Attack with Hundreds of Casualties," *Ma'ariv*, November 2, 2005 (accessed March 25, 2010), available from LexisNexis.

23. Daniel McGrory, "Israel Fears Chemical Attack by Hamas Suicide Bombers," *Times*, January 2, 2002 (accessed March 25, 2010), available from LexisNexis.

24. "Hamas Operatives Working on Adding Toxic Chemicals to Bombs" (accessed March 25, 2010), available from www.haaretz.com/hasen/pages/ShArt.jhtml?itemNo=723309.

25. Ibid.

26. For information on hiding weaponry in schools (particularly kindergartens), see Levitt, 36. For hospitals and ambulances, see Palestinian Misuse of Medical Services and Ambulances for Terrorist Activities (accessed December 28, 2008), available from www.mfa.gov.il/MFA/Government/Law/Legal+Issues+and+Rulings/Palestinian+ Misuse+of+Medical+Services+and+Ambulances+for+Terrorist+Activities+13-Oct-2004 .htm; Levitt, 99. For information on children being encouraged to participate in attacks, see Justus Weiner, "The Recruitment of Children in Current Palestinian Strategy," *Jerusalem Issue Brief* 2, no. 8 (October 1, 2002) (Jerusalem: Jerusalem Center for Public Affairs).

27. Steven Erlanger, "A Gaza War Full of Traps and Trickery," *New York Times*, January 11, 2009, A1.

28. "His Name Was Nachshon Wachsman" (accessed December 28, 2008), available from www.aish.com/jewishissues/israeldiary/His_Name_Was_Nachshon_Wachsman.asp.

29. "Kerem Shalom Attack and Kidnapping of Cpl. Gilad Shalit" (accessed December 28, 2009), available from www.mfa.gov.il/MFA/MFAArchive/2000_2009/2006/Gaza+kidnapping+25-Jun-2006.htm.

30. Khaled Abu Toameh, "Perfume, Viagra, Lions and Fuel—Smuggling Is Gaza's Growth Industry. With Nearly 1,000 Tunnels Operating, Israel's Blockade Is Hardly Hurting Hamas," *Jerusalem Post*, November 14, 2008, 1.

31. Levitt, 38.

32. Chris McGreal et al., "The British Suicide Bombers: Officials Say Passports of Attacker Who Died and Accomplice on Run Show They Travelled to Kill," *Guardian*, May 1, 2003, 1.

33. Al-Quds, Hamas' Second Satellite TV Channel (accessed December 8, 2008), available from www.terrorism-info.org.il/malam_multimedia/English/eng_n/html/Hamas_e010.htm.

34. Interview with Yonatan Fighel, Herzliya, Israel, December 31, 2006.

35. Gadi Wolfsfeld, *Media and Political Conflict: News from the Middle East* (New York: Cambridge University Press, 1997), 2.

36. "Yitzhak Rabin and Yasser Arafat" (accessed July 11, 2011), available from www.time.com/time/magazine/article/0,9171,1125850,00.html.

37. Wolfsfeld, 167–68.

38. For more, see "Freedom House's Country Report," available at www.freedomhouse.org/template.cfm?page=363&year=2008.

39. Hess and Kalb, 184.

40. For more on the "Jenin Massacre," see Stephanie Guttman, *The Other War: Israelis, Palestinians, and the Struggle for Media Supremacy* (San Francisco: Encounter Books, 2005), 145. For more on the blackouts, see Khaled Abu Toameh, "Hamas Staged Some 'Blackouts' Palestinian Journalists Admit," *Jerusalem Post*, January 24, 2008, 2.

41. For example, during Operation Cast Lead newspapers and television stations around the world reported that the IDF bombed an UNWRA school and killed civilians who were seeking shelter there. After about a month, the United Nations released a statement that said mortar fire and all casualties occurred outside of the school; however, the story never became widespread, as the operation had ended weeks earlier. For more, see "UN Backtracks on Claim That Deadly IDF Strike Hit Gaza School" (accessed February 3, 2009), available from www.haaretz.com/hasen/spages/1061189.html.

42. Hess and Kalb, 187–88.

43. "BBC Correspondent Actively Supports Palestinian War against Israel" (accessed December 29, 2008), available from www.camera.org/index.asp?x_context=4&x_outlet=12&x_article=179.

44. Guttman, 212.

45. Hess and Kalb, 187.

46. Eric Westervelt, "Hamas Launches Television Network," NPR transcript, February 3, 2006 (accessed March 25, 2010), available from www.npr.org/templates/story/story.php?storyId=5186883. This station can be seen in much of Europe. See "Hamas TV Banned in France for Inciting Hatred" (accessed May 21, 2011), available from www.google.com/hostednews/afp/article/ALeqM5jFBWq_auf-udWLzDQ_TSUM3H-aKw.

47. Michael Whine, "Islamist Organizations on the Internet," *Terrorism and Political Violence* 11, no. 1 (1999): 128.

48. Yariv Tsfati and Gabriel Weinmann, "WWW.terrorism.com: Terror on the Internet," *Studies in Conflict and Terrorism* 25, no. 5 (2002): 320–25.

49. Palestine Information Center (accessed October 21, 2010), available from www.palestine-info.net/.

50. Islamic Block (accessed March 25, 2010), available from www.islamic-block.net.

51. Al-Qassam (accessed October 21, 2010), available from www.qassam.ps/.

52. *Filasteen Al-Muslima*, A Hamas Journal Published in London and the Palestinian Authority Areas and Worldwide (accessed December 5, 2006), available from www.intelligence.org.il/eng/bu/britain/journal.htm.

53. *Filasteen Al-Muslima* (accessed December 5, 2006), available from www.fm-m.com/2005/Nov2005/issue11-2005.htm.

54. Intelligence and Terrorism Information Center at the Center for Special Studies (C.S.S.) (accessed March 25, 2010), available from www.intelligence.org.il/eng/eng_n/hamas_e.htm.

55. Interview: "Shikaki: Since Israeli Withdrawal from Gaza, Palestinians Now Give Top Priority to Improving Living Standard, Not End to Occupation' (accessed March 25, 2010), available from: www.cfr.org/publication/9055/shikaki.html.

Chapter 11. Israeli Counterinsurgency and Counterterrorism

1. "Gaza Strip" (accessed December 30, 2008), available from www.cia.gov/library/publications/the-world-factbook/geos/gz.html.

2. Interview with Yonatan Fighel, Herzliya, Israel, December 31, 2006.

3. Robert B. Asprey, *War in the Shadows: Guerillas Past and Present* (New York: William Morrow, 1994), 1162.

4. See "Israel/Gaza Operation 'Cast Lead': 22 Days of Death And Destruction," Amnesty International, May 15, 2009; UN General Assembly, *Report of the United Nations Fact-Finding Mission on the Gaza Conflict*, A/HRC/12/48, September 25, 2009.

5. See Enderlin, 8; "Israel's Low Intensity Conflict Doctrine" (accessed December 28, 2008), available from www.janes.com/articles/Janes-Defence-Weekly-2004/ISRAEL-S-LOW-INTENSITY-CONFLICT-DOCTRINE—Inner-conflict.html.

6. UN Secretary General, *Report of the Secretary-General Prepared Pursuant to General Assembly Resolution ES-10/10*, July 30, 2002. See also "Israel and the Occupied Territories: Shielded from Scrutiny: IDF Violations in Jenin and Nablus," Amnesty International, November 4, 2002 (accessed March 31, 2010), available from www.amnesty.org/en/library/asset/MDE15/143/2002/en/c79afe78-d7bc-11dd-b4cd-01eb52042454/mde151432002en.html.

7. "The Phantom Massacre" (accessed December 31, 2008), available from www.freerepublic.com/focus/news/672761/posts.

8. Ibid.

9. Joshua L. Gleis, "Israel's Struggle against Palestinian Terrorist Organizations," in *Countering Terrorism and Insurgency in the Twenty First Century*, vol. 3: *Lessons from the Fight against Terrorism*, ed. James J. F. Forest (Westport, CT: Praeger Security International, 2007), 416.

10. Steven Erlanger, "A Gaza War Full of Traps and Trickery," *New York Times*, January 11, 2009, A1.

11. Joshua L. Gleis, "Lebanese 'Defensive Shield'—No Problem," *Jerusalem Post*, May 27, 2007, 14.

12. Gleis, "A Disproportionate Response? The Case of Israel and Hizballah."

13. For a map highlighting the range of various types of Hamas rockets, see "Terrorism from the Gaza Strip since Operation Cast Lead Data, Type and Trends," Meir Amit Intelligence and Terrorism Information Center, March 3, 2011, 1.

14. "IDF Phones Gaza Residents to Warn Them of Imminent Strikes" (accessed January 4, 2009), available from http://haaretz.com/hasen/spages/1052260.html.

15. *Report of the United Nations Fact-Finding Mission on the Gaza Conflict.*

16. רופא בעזה: חמאס ניפח את מנין ה.הרוגים בלחימה ["Rofeh b'Azah: Hamas Niphakh Eht Minyaan Ha'harugim B'Lekhimah; Gazan Doctor: Hamas Exaggerated Death Toll from Fighting"] (accessed January 22, 2009), available in Hebrew from.nrg .co.il/online/1/ART1/843/877.html.

17. "IDF Releases Cast Lead Casualty Numbers," *Jerusalem Post*, March 26, 2003 (accessed March 31, 2010), available from www.jpost.com/Israel/Article.aspx?id=137286.

18. Interview with Chuck Freilich, Cambridge, MA, November 21, 2006.

19. Doron Almog, "Lessons of the Gaza Security Fence for the West Bank," *Jerusalem Issue Brief* 4, no. 12 (Jerusalem: Jerusalem Center for Public Affairs, December 23, 2004).

20. "Map of Security Fence Project" (accessed December 31, 2008), available from www.securityfence.mod.gov.il/Pages/ENG/seamzone_map_eng.htm.

21. "The Lessons of the West Bank and Lebanon in Gaza" (accessed January 15, 2009), available from www.jinsa.org/node/845.

22. See "The Violence of Construction: Israel's Wall and International Law" (accessed December 31, 2008), available from http://electronicintifada.net/v2/article2133.shtml; Enderlin, 208–9, 216.

23. Enderlin, 217–18.

24. "Israel's Security Fence" (accessed December 31, 2008), available from www.se curityfence.mod.gov.il/Pages/ENG/default.htm.

25. "Exploiting Israel's Humanitarian Policies for Terror Activities" (accessed January 18, 2009), available from http://tinyurl.com/c7wm6m.

26. See Charles Starmer-Smith, "Ring of Steel for Sharm el-Sheikh," *Daily Telegraph*, October 22, 2005, 4; "Saudi Authorities Erect Barriers on Yemeni Border" (accessed December 31, 2008), available from www.yobserver.com/front-page/10013538.html.

27. Ewen MacAskill, "Latest US Solution to Iraq's Civil War: A Three-Mile Wall," *Guardian*, April 21, 2007, 1.

28. Aaron Mannes, "Dangerous Liaisons: Hamas after the Assassination of Yassin," *Middle East Intelligence Bulletin* 6, no. 4 (April 2004), www.meforum.org/meib/articles /0404_pal1.htm.

29. "U.N. Condemns Israel's Assassination of Sheikh Yassin" (accessed August 6, 2008), available from http://findarticles.com/p/articles/mi_moWDQ/is_/ai_114706916.

30. Halevy, 177.

31. "Timeline/Dubai Assassination and Its Aftermath" (accessed March 31, 2010), available from www.haaretz.com/hasen/spages/1152031.html.

32. Ibid.

33. Erlanger.

34. "The IDF Duvdevan Unit" (accessed December 31, 2009), available from www .emergency.com/idfduvan.htm.

35. See "The Shimshon Battalion Celebrates 10 Years of Operations" (accessed December 31, 2008), available from http://dover.idf.il/IDF/English/News/today/2007/09 /1602.htm; Gil Merom, *How Insurgencies Lose Small Wars* (New York: Cambridge University Press, 2003), 41.

36. Interview with Boaz Ganor, Deputy Dean of the Lauder School of Government and Diplomacy at the Interdisciplinary Center and the Executive Director of the International Policy Institute for Counter-Terrorism, Herzliya, Israel, July 5, 2006.

37. For more on Israeli counterinsurgency warfare, see Yaakov Amidror, "Winning Counterinsurgency War: The Israeli Experience," *JCPA Strategic Perspectives* (accessed July 11, 201), available at: www.jcpa.org/text/Amidror-perspectives-2.pdf.

38. Ian O. Lesser [et al.], *Countering the New Terrorism* (Washington, DC: RAND, 1999), 120–22.

Conclusions

1. See, for example, Alagha, 14, 373; Hamzeh, 120.

2. "PLO and Fatah Officials: Hamas Is Responsible for the Deaths of Its People" (accessed December 31, 2008), available from www.memri.org/bin/latestnews.cgi ?ID=SD216408#_ednref3.

3. Avi Kober, "Israel's Wars of Attrition: Operational and Moral Dilemmas," in *Israel's Strategic Agenda*, ed. Efraim Inbar (New York: Routledge, 2007), 188.

4. Dominic Evans, "Hizb Allah Chief Threatens to Seize Control of Galilee," *National Post*, February 17, 2011 (accessed march 30, 2011), available from LexisNexis.

5. " Resistance Setting New Equations to Protect Lebanon," Al-Manar, February 19, 2011 (accessed march 30, 2011), available from LexisNexis.

6. "Speech Delivered by Hezballah Secretary General Sayyed Hassan Nasrallah during a Ceremony Marking the Anniversary of the Martyr Leaders Held in Sayyed Ashuhada Compound on Wednesday February 16, 2011," available from Hezbollah Press Office.

7. " Speech Delivered by Hezbollah Secretary General Sayyed Hassan Nasrallah during the Solidarity Rally with Egypt That Was Held in Ghobairy Municipality Square—Jnah," February 7, 2011, available from Hezbollah Press Office.

8. Ibid.

Glossary

Alawite. An offshoot of Shiite Islam, Alawites (also commonly referred to as Alawis) are predominantly located in Syria, Turkey, and Lebanon, where they are a minority religion in each country. The Alawites enjoyed significant privileges under the Assad dynasty of autocratic rulers who have led Syria for many decades.

Al-Manar. Hezbollah's television "Station of Resistance," it is available throughout the Middle East and much of the world. It serves as the major media and propaganda mouthpiece for Hezbollah and its Iranian backers. It means "The Beacon" in Arabic.

Arab Spring. Social and political grass-roots protest movement that has sought to change the political status quo in many parts of the Middle East. The "Arab Spring" began in Tunisia in December 2010 and then spread to other countries in the region, including Egypt, Libya, Jordan, Bahrain, Yemen, and Syria, also leading to social protests in virtually every country in the Middle East. Its ultimate success in regime change and successfully promoting civil liberties remains to be seen.

Bekaa Valley. An area of southern Lebanon that has been traditionally free of central government control. Dominated by Shiites and Christians, the area was also controlled by the PLO when its forces operated in much of Lebanon during the late 1970s and early 1980s.

Blue Line. The UN-delineated and recognized border between Israel and Lebanon, which was published in the wake of Israel's plan to withdraw from southern Lebanon in 2000.

Camp David Accords. The 1978 peace accords signed by the Egyptians and Israelis under the leadership of U.S. president Jimmy Carter, which led to an end of hostilities between the two states.

Camp David II Peace Negotiations. The Palestinian-Israeli peace talks that took place under the leadership of U.S. president Bill Clinton at Camp David in Maryland. The talks took place in 2000 toward the end of the term of the U.S. presidency and the Israeli prime ministership and failed to reach a final peace agreement.

Druze. A monotheistic, relatively secretive religious offshoot of Islam. Druzes reside primarily in Lebanon, Syria, Israel, and Jordan. With the exception of Druzes of the Golan Heights (who view themselves as Syrian), Druze are generally well integrated in the countries of their birth and usually serve in their respective militaries. Druze are seen as heretics by many Muslim authorities.

Gaza Strip. A small coastal region to Israel's southwest border and north of Egypt's Sinai border, it is recognized as a part of any future Palestinian state and has been a traditionally more Islamist area than its counterpart, the West Bank. The Gaza Strip was occupied by the Egyptians following the 1948 Arab-Israeli War. After the 1967 Six-Day War, the area was occupied by Israel, who withdrew during its unilateral "disengagement" in 2005. Israel and Egypt remain in control of the Gaza Strip's borders, and Hamas is currently the ruling party.

Golan Heights. A strategically significant volcanic and mountainous plateau that oversees Israel, Syria, and parts of Lebanon. The Golan had been part of Syria since its founding in 1946, but was conquered and controlled by Israel since 1967. In 1981 Israel officially incorporated the Golan Heights into Israeli proper, though this was not recognized by the rest of the international community.

Goldstone Report. Officially known as the *Report of the United Nations Fact-Finding Mission on the Gaza Conflict*, it was a UN-led fact-finding mission directed by South African judge Richard Goldstone to investigate potential war crimes committed by the Israelis and Palestinians during the 2006 war in Gaza. The report accused both Israel and the Palestinians of committing war crimes during combat. Richard Goldstone, the lead author of the Goldstone Report, later recanted and claimed he did not have all of the evidence when his report was produced, as Israel did not cooperate with the investigation. The report is still used by human rights organizations and those critical of Israel as evidence of Israeli intransigence.

Greater Syria. A territory centered around Damascus that comprises modern-day Syria and Lebanon, as well as parts of Turkey, Jordan, Israel, and Egypt. The term stems back to pre-Islamic times and was also used during the Ottoman Empire.

guerrilla warfare. A kind of combat that incorporates low-intensity and asymmetrical warfare, sometimes with acts of terrorism as well. Though often confused with *insurgency*, guerrilla warfare is viewed by the authors as more of a tactic.

Hasbara. Roughly translated from Hebrew as "explanation," it is the official public diplomacy effort by the Government of Israel to tell its side of the story in the Arab-Israeli conflict.

hawala. Hawala transactions are transfers of funds between different locations conducted outside the circuits of the conventional banking system. The Hawala system is used throughout the Muslim world to transfer money: it is based on trust, it is anonymous and oral, and it involves little to no physical movement of cash. All these characteristics account for the success of the hawala system and, at the same time, explain why this alternative remittance system also attract illicit and criminal transactions.

insurgency. A style of warfare that incorporates terrorism, guerrilla tactics, social welfare networks, and political pressure, in an effort to "even the playing field" and combat an adversary whose conventional military force is far superior.

Intifada. Roughly translated from Arabic as "uprising" or "to shake off," intifadas have been called by the Arab and Muslim worlds for decades. The word is best known in reference to the two Palestinian uprisings and insurgencies fought against Israel. The first Palestinian Intifada began in 1987 and ended in 1993. The second Intifada, referred by Palestinians as the Al Aqsa Intifada, began around the breakdown of the Camp David peace negotiations in 2000. Its causes and ending are fiercely debated by pro-Israeli and pro-Palestinian sides.

March 8 group. The March 8 coalition refers to a political alliance between the Shiite parties Hezbollah, Amal, and the Christian Free Patriotic Movement. Lebanon's Christian community is split in terms of its support for the March 14 and March 8 parties and therefore has recently determined the final electoral outcome.

March 14 coalition. A Lebanese, "pro-Western" political faction made up of a number of political parties but led by the Sunni Future Movement and to a lesser degree by Christian parties such as the Phalange Party and the Lebanese Forces. The majority of Sunni Muslims in Lebanon align themselves with this coalition party. Lebanon's Christian community is split in terms of its support for the March 14 and March 8 parties, and therefore has recently determined the final electoral outcome.

Maronite. A small sect of (Eastern Catholic) Christianity, Maronites reside almost exclusively in Lebanon, where they make up the majority of the Lebanese Christian population.

Middle East. Also known as the Near East, it is a region of Southwest Asia that includes all North African countries bordering the Mediterranean Sea, Turkey, Israel, the Arab world, and Iran.

Nakba. Arabic for the "catastrophe," the term is used to commemorate the Palestinian loss and Israel's establishment as a result of the 1948 Arab-Israeli War.

Ottoman Empire. A Turkish-based Islamic empire that reigned from 1299 to 1923. At its height, the Ottoman Empire spanned from southeast Europe to southwest Asia and northern Africa.

Quartet. A four-party group encompassing the United States, European Union, United Nations, and Russia that is focused on trying to solve the Arab-Israeli conflict through peace negotiations.

Shiite. Shiite Islam is, after Sunni Islam, the second most practiced form of Islam. It is currently practiced by between 10 and 20 percent of the world's Muslims, with the largest Shiite communities residing in Iran, Iraq, Bahrain, Lebanon, and Azerbaijan. The religious schism between Sunni and Shiite Muslims has led to bloody conflicts throughout much of Islamic history.

Shin Bet / Shabak. Israel's internal domestic security service, it is mandated to operate in Israel, the West Bank, Gaza Strip, and Golan Heights. Israel's Shin Bet is a Hebrew acronym for Sherut ha-Bitachon ha-Klali, which roughly translates to General Security Service (GSS). Often compared to the United States' FBI, the Shin Bet is also responsible for diplomatic security in Israel as well as overseas. It is also known as the Israel Security Agency (ISA).

Sunni. Sunni Islam is the main branch of Islam, practiced by the over-whelming majority of Muslims in the world. The religious schism between Sunni and Shiite Muslims has led to bloody conflicts throughout much of Islamic history.

Taif Accord. Officially known as the Document of National Accord, the Taif Accord shaped Lebanon's transition from the bloody civil war that had raged from 1975 to 1990. The agreement was reached in Taif (Saudi

Arabia) in the fall of 1989 by the surviving members of Parliament who had been elected in 1972 and laid the basis for Lebanon's postwar transition by reforming the electoral system (and equalizing the ratio of seats between Muslims and Christians), and by mandating the dismantling of armed militias. At the same time, the Taif Accord also paved the way for Syria's occupation of Lebanon from 1990 to 2005.

terrorism. According to the U.S. Department of State, terrorism is the "premeditated, politically motivated violence perpetrated against noncombatant targets by subnational groups or clandestine agents."

West Bank. A plateau to the west of the Jordan River, it is widely seen as the basis for a future homeland of the Palestinian people. Jordan occupied the West Bank after the 1948 Arab-Israeli War, and in 1967 Israel wrested control of the area. While occupying the vast majority of the land to this day, Israel ceded large portions of control over the Palestinian population (but over a smaller amount of land) to the Palestinian Authority as part of the 1993 Oslo Accords. Many Jews and others refer to the West Bank by its biblical names of Judea and Samaria, from which the name "Jew" was actually derived.

Zionism. A movement that calls for the Jewish people's right to self-determination and a state of their own in the land of Israel.

For Further Reading

The readings listed represent a wide range of viewpoints.

Hezbollah and Lebanon

Alagha, Joseph Elie. *The Shifts in Hizbullah's Ideology: Religious Ideology, Political Ideology, and Political Program*. ISIM Dissertations. Amsterdam: Amsterdam University Press, 2006.

Azani, Eitan. *Hezbollah: The Story of the Party of God; From Revolution to Institutionalization*. New York: Palgrave Macmillan, 2009.

Cordesman, Anthony. "Iran's Support of the Hezbollah in Lebanon." Center for Strategic and International Studies. Accessed October 12, 2011. Available from http://csis.org /files/media/csis/pubs/060715_hezbollah.pdf.

Cordesman, Anthony, George Sullivan, and William Sullivan. *Lessons of the 2006 Israeli-Hezbollah War*. Washington, DC: Center for Strategic and International Studies, 2007.

Eisenberg, Laurie. "Revisited or Revamped? The Maronite Factors in Israel's 1982 Invasion of Lebanon." *Israel Affairs*, 15, no. 4 (October 2009): 372–96.

Ellis, Kail C., ed. *Lebanon's Second Republic: Prospects for the Twenty-First Century*. Gainesville: University Press of Florida, 2002.

Hamzeh, Ahmad Nizar. *In the Path of Hizbullah*. Syracuse: Syracuse University Press, 2004.

Harb, Mona, and Reinoud Leenders. "Know Thy Enemy: Hizbullah 'Terrorism' and the Polities of Perception." *Third World Quarterly* 6, no. 1 (2005): 173–97.

Harik, Judith Palmer. *Hezbollah: The Changing Face of Terrorism*. London: I. B. Tauris, 2004.

Jaber, Hala. *Hezbollah: Born with a Vengeance*. New York: Columbia University Press, 1997.

Jorisch, Avi. *Beacon of Hatred: Inside Hizballah's Al-Manar Television*. Washington, DC: Washington Institute for Near East Policy, 2004.

Mackey, Sandra. *Lebanon: A House Divided*. New York: W. W. Norton, 2006.

Noe, Nicholas, ed. *Voice of Hezbollah: The Statements of Sayyed Hassan Nasrallah*. London: Verso, 2007.

Norton, Augustus Richard. *Hezbollah*. Princeton: Princeton University Press, 2007.

Qassem, Naim. *Hizbullah: The Story from Within*. London: Saqi, 2005.

Rabil, Robert G., ed. *Embattled Neighbors Syria, Israel, and Lebanon*. Boulder, CO: Lynne Rienner, 2003.

Rubin, Barry, ed. *Lebanon: Liberation, Conflict, and Crisis.* New York: Palgrave Macmillan, 2010.

Saad-Gorayeb, Amal. *Hizbu'llah: Politics and Religion.* London: Pluto Press, 2002.

Young, Michael. *The Ghosts of Martyrs Square: An Eyewitness Account of Lebanon's Life Struggle.* London: Simon & Schuster, 2010.

Hamas and the Palestinians

Alexander, Yonah. *Palestinian Religious Terrorism: Hamas and Islamic Jihad.* New York: Transnational, 2002.

Chehab, Zaki. *Inside Hamas: The Untold Story of the Militant Islamic Movement.* New York: Nation Books, 2007.

Ganim, Asad. *Palestinian Politics after Arafat: A Failed National Movement.* Bloomington: Indiana University Press, 2010.

Gunning, Jeroen. *Hamas in Politics: Democracy, Religion, Violence.* New York: Columbia University Press, 2008.

———. "Peace with Hamas? The Transforming Potential of Political Participation." *International Affairs* 80, no. 2 (2004): 241–55.

Jensen, Michael Irving. *The Political Ideology of Hamas: A Grassroots Perspective.* London: I. B. Tauris, 2009.

Khalidi, Rashid. *Palestinian Identity: The Construction of Modern National Consciousness.* New York: Columbia University Press, 1998.

Kurz, Anat N. *Fatah and the Politics of Violence: The Institutionalization of a Popular Struggle.* Portland, OR: Sussex Academic Press, 2005.

Levitt, Matthew. *Hamas: Politics, Charity, and Terrorism in the Service of Jihad.* New Haven: Yale University Press, 2006.

Lybarger, Loren D. *Identity and Religion in Palestine: The Struggle between Islamism and Secularism in the Occupied Territories.* Princeton: Princeton University Press, 2007.

Milton-Edwards, Beverly. *Islamic Politics in Palestine.* New York: I. B. Tauris, 1999.

Mishal, Shaul, and Avraham Sela. *The Palestinian Hamas: Vision, Violence and Coexistence.* New York: Columbia University Press, 2000.

———. "Participation without Presence: Hamas, the Palestinian Authority and the Politics of Negotiated Coexistence." *Middle Eastern Studies* 38, no. 3 (2002): 1–26.

Robinson, Glenn. "Hamas as Social Movement." In *Islamic Activism*, ed. Quintan Wiktorowicz, 112–39. Indianapolis: Indiana University Press, 2004.

Schanzer, Jonathan. *Hamas vs. Fatah: The Struggle for Palestine.* New York: Palgrave Macmillan, 2008.

Shaery-Eisenlohr, Roschanack. *Shite Lebanon: Transnational Religion and the Making of National Identities.* New York: Columbia University Press, 2008.

Susser, Asher. *The Rise of Hamas in Palestine and the Crisis of Secularism in the Arab World.* Waltham, MA: Brandeis University, Crown Center for Middle East Studies, February 2010.

Tamimi, Azzam. *Hamas: A History from Within.* Northampton, MA: Olive Branch Press, 2007.

The Arab-Israeli Conflict

Bregam, Ahron. *Israel's Wars: A History since 1947.* 2nd ed. London: Routledge, 2002.

Enderlin, Charles. *The Lost Years: Radical Islam, Intifada, and Wars in the Middle East, 2001–2006.* New York: Other Press, 2007.

Karsh, Efraim. *Islamic Imperialism: A History.* New Haven: Yale University Press, 2007.

———. *The Arab-Israeli Conflict: The Palestine War of 1948.* Oxford: Osprey, 2002.

Kurtzer, Daniel, and Scott B. Lasensky. *Negotiating Arab-Israeli Peace: American Leadership in the Middle East.* Washington, DC: United States Institute of Peace Press, 2008.

Lozowick, Yaacov. *Right to Exist: A Moral Defense of Israel's Wars.* New York: Doubleday, 2003.

Maoz, Zeev. *Defending the Holy Land: A Critical Analysis of Israel's Security and Foreign Policy.* Ann Arbor: University of Michigan Press, 2006.

Morris, Benny. *1948: A History of the First Arab-Israeli War.* New Haven: Yale University Press, 2008.

Oren, Michael. *Six Days of War: June 1967 and the Making of the Modern Middle East.* Oxford: Oxford University Press, 2002.

Rabinovich, Itamar. *Waging Peace: Israel and the Arabs, 1948–2003.* Princeton: Princeton University Press, 2004.

Rosenthal, Donna. *The Israelis: Ordinary People in an Extraordinary Land.* New York: Free Press, 2003.

Ross, Dennis. *The Missing Peace: The Inside Story of the Fight for Middle East Peace.* New York: Farrar, Straus and Giroux, 2005.

Said, Edward W. *The Question of Palestine.* New York: Vintage Books, 1992.

Van Kreveld, Martin. *The Sword and the Olive.* New York: Public Affairs, 2002.

Israeli Counterinsurgency and Counterterrorism

Black, Ian, and Benny Morris. *Israel's Secret Wars: A History of Israel's Intelligence Services.* New York: Grove Weidenfeld, 1991.

Byman, Daniel. *A High Price: The Triumphs and Failures of Israeli Counterterrorism.* New York: Oxford University Press, 2011.

Catignani, Sergio. *Israeli Counter-insurgency and the Intifadas: Dilemmas of a Conventional Army.* London: Routledge, 2008.

Cordesman, Anthony. *Arab-Israeli Military Forces in an Era of Asymmetric Wars.* Stanford: Stanford University Press, 2008.

Halevy, Efraim. *Man in the Shadows: Inside the Middle East Crisis with the Man Who Led the Mossad.* New York: St. Martin's Press, 2006.

Gleis, Joshua. *Withdrawing under Fire: Lessons Learned from Islamist Insurgencies.* Washington, DC: Potomac Books, 2011.

Guttman, Stephanie. *The Other War: Israelis, Palestinians and the Struggle for Media Supremacy.* San Francisco: Encounter Books, 2005.

Harel, Amos, and Avi Issacharoff. *34 Days: Israel, Hezbollah, and the War in Lebanon.* New York: Palgrave Macmillan, 2008.

Muravchik, Joshua. *Covering the Intifada: How the Media Reported the Palestinian Uprising.* Washington, DC: Washington Institute for Near East Policy, 2003.

Pedahzur, Ami. *The Israeli Secret Services and the Struggle against Terrorism*. New York: Columbia University Press, 2009.

Sobelman, Daniel. "New Rules of the Game: Israel and Hizbollah after the Withdrawal from Lebanon." Memorandum no. 59. Tel-Aviv: Jaffee Center for Strategic Studies, 2004.

Index